Zarathustra's Moral Tyranny

Every smallest step in the field of free thought, of a life shaped personally, has always had to be fought for with spiritual and bodily tortures ... there is in fact no more important subject than the age-old tragedy of the martyrs *who wanted to stir up the swamp.* Nothing has been more dearly bought than that little bit of human reason and the feeling of freedom which now constitutes our pride.

Friedrich Nietzsche, *Daybreak*, §18

Zarathustra's Moral Tyranny

Spectres of Kant, Hegel and Feuerbach

Francesca Cauchi

EDINBURGH
University Press

Edinburgh University Press is one of the leading university presses in the UK. We publish academic books and journals in our selected subject areas across the humanities and social sciences, combining cutting-edge scholarship with high editorial and production values to produce academic works of lasting importance. For more information visit our website: edinburghuniversitypress.com

© Francesca Cauchi, 2022, 2024

Edinburgh University Press Ltd
The Tun – Holyrood Road
12(2f) Jackson's Entry
Edinburgh EH8 8PJ

First published in hardback by Edinburgh University Press 2022

Typeset in 11/13 Foundry Sans and Foundry Old Style
IDSUK (DataConnection) Ltd

A CIP record for this book is available from the British Library

ISBN 978 1 3995 0431 7 (hardback)
ISBN 978 1 3995 0432 4 (paperback)
ISBN 978 1 3995 0433 1 (webready PDF)
ISBN 978 1 3995 0434 8 (epub)

The right of Francesca Cauchi to be identified as the author of this work has been asserted in accordance with the Copyright, Designs and Patents Act 1988, and the Copyright and Related Rights Regulations 2003
(SI No. 2498).

Contents

Acknowledgments ix
Abbreviations and Translations x

Introduction 1
   The naturalist-normative problem 2
   The morality problem 9
   Max Stirner and the 'tyranny of mind' 15
   Kant, Hegel and Feuerbach 18

1 Nietzsche's Ascetic Morality 29
   Pitting a 'morality of reason' against the Christian
     morality of feeling 31
   Nietzsche's self-eviscerating 'morality of sacrifice' 38
   Do 'free-spirited moralists' have the right to
     inflict their cruelty on others? 41
   Austerity and artifice 47

2 The Kantian Rational Will and the Tyranny of
   Self-Overcoming 63
   Autonomy and universality 65
   Creator-destroyers and hammer-wielding
     legislators 70
   Shattering the Christian table of values 76
   Erkenntniss and the hard labour of reorienting
     the affects 81
   Reverence and martyrdom: willing the *Übermensch* 88

3 Hegel's 'Labour of the Negative' and the Lacerations
of Self-Negation   101
   Affirmative negation and Deleuzian derision   102
   Spirit's 'labour of the negative'   107
   Practical freedom and the planting of thought
      into the passions   114
   Spirit's vicious cycle of bitter deaths and
      interminable resurrections   119

4 The Bitter Cup of Pure Love: Feuerbach and Zarathustra 137
   Reclaiming the 'divine' powers of human greatness 138
   Love as a human absolute   143
   Christ's Passion and Zarathustra's sacrificial love   148
   An excursus on self-love and the I and thou of
      compassion   152

Conclusion   171
   Zarathustra's violent rhetoric of truth incorporation 172
   Zarathustra's moral tyranny   175

Bibliography   181
Index   193

Acknowledgments

I would first like to thank my brother, Anthony Cauchi, for meticulously proofreading the manuscript and Trevor Hope for his invaluable feedback at the critical book proposal stage. I would also like to thank Claus-Artur Scheier, Stephen Houlgate, Tom Bailey and Dan Conway for giving so generously of their to time to read and comment on earlier drafts of either one or several of the chapters contained in this book. I would further like to thank Nisreen Salti for securing scanned copies of vital secondary sources that I was unable to source elsewhere and Philip Koh for bringing to my attention a number of scholarly works on theology that would otherwise have remained unknown to me. I am also indebted to the two anonymous readers who provided detailed and constructive comments on early drafts of Chapters 2 and 3. Last, but not least, I would like to thank Alper Alp for attending to all my grocery needs during the pandemic so that I could focus on the task in hand – not, I hasten to add, the task of self-overcoming.

Abbreviations and Translations

Nietzsche's Works

A	*The Antichrist: A Curse on Christianity*
AOM	*Assorted Opinions and Maxims* (*Human All Too Human* Volume II)
AS	'Attempt at a Self-Criticism' (1886 preface to *The Birth of Tragedy*)
BGE	*Beyond Good and Evil: Prelude to a Philosophy of the Future*
BT	*The Birth of Tragedy out of the Spirit of Music*
CW	*The Case of Wagner: A Musician's Problem*
D	*Daybreak: Thoughts on the Prejudices of Morality*
EH	*Ecce Homo: How to Become What You Are*
GM	*On the Genealogy of Morals* (also translated as *On the Genealogy of Morality*)
GS	*The Gay Science*
HH	*Human, All Too Human: A Book for Free Spirits* Volume I
HH I P	Spring 1886 Preface to Volume I of *Human All Too Human*
HH II P	Autumn 1886 Preface to Volume II of *Human All Too Human*
KSA	*Sämtliche Werke: Kritische Studienausgabe*, 15 vols, ed. G. Colli and M. Montinari (de Gruyter)
KSB	*Sämtliche Briefe: Kritische Studienausgabe*, 8 vols, ed. G. Colli and M. Montinari (de Gruyter)

NCW	*Nietzsche Contra Wagner: From the Files of a Psychologist*
TI	*Twilight of the Idols: or How to Philosophize with a Hammer*
UM	*Untimely Meditations* (also translated as *Unfashionable Observations*)
WLN	*Writings from the Late Notebooks*
WP	*The Will to Power*
WS	*The Wanderer and His Shadow* (*Human All Too Human* Volume II)
Z	*Thus Spoke Zarathustra: A Book for Everyone and No-One*
ZP	'Zarathustra's Prologue'
Z1	*Thus Spoke Zarathustra*: Part 1
Z2	*Thus Spoke Zarathustra*: Part 2
Z3	*Thus Spoke Zarathustra*: Part 3
Z4	*Thus Spoke Zarathustra*: Part 4

Kant's Works

AA	*Akademieausgabe von Immanuel Kants Gesammelten Werken* (23 vols)
	Groundwork of the Metaphysic of Morals / Grundlegung zur Metaphysik der Sitten (AA 4)
	Critique of Practical Reason / Kritik der praktischen Vernunft (AA 5)
	The Metaphysics of Morals / Die Metaphysik der Sitten (AA 6)
	'An answer to the question: What is enlightenment?' / 'Beantwortung der Frage: Was ist Aufklärung?' (AA 8)

Hegel's Works

EL	*Encyclopedia of the Philosophical Sciences in Basic Outline. Part I: Science of Logic) / Enzyklopädie der philosophischen Wissenschaften im Grundrisse. Erster Teil. Die Wissenschaft der Logik* (W 8)
LPH	*Lectures on the Philosophy of History / Vorlesungen über die Philosophie der Geschichte* (W 12) See RH

LPR	*Lectures on the Philosophy of Religion Vol. 1 / Vorlesungen über die Philosophie der Religion I* (W 16)
PhS	*Phenomenology of Spirit / Phänomenologie des Geistes* (W 3)
PR	*Elements of the Philosophy of Right or Natural Law and Political Science in Outline / Grundlinien der Philosophie des Rechts oder Naturrecht und Staatswissenschaft im Grundrisse* (W 7)
RH	*Reason in History: A General Introduction to the Philosophy of History / Die Vernunft in der Geschichte: Einleitung in die Philosophie der Weltgeschichte*
SL	*Science of Logic / Wissenschaft der Logik I* (W 5)
W	G. W. F. Hegel: *Werke 1832–1845* (Suhrkamp, 20 vols)

Feuerbach's Works

GW	*Ludwig Feuerbach Gesammelte Werke* (Akademie Verlag, Berlin 2006)
EC	*The Essence of Christianity / Das Wesen des Christentums* (GW 5)

References and Translations

References to Nietzsche's works follow the standard English abbreviations listed above, followed by section/aphorism number (e.g. GS 338, BGE 45) or chapter title followed by numbered subsection (e.g. Z3 'On Old and New Tables' 22 = *Thus Spoke Zarathustra*, Part 3, 'On Old and New Tables' subsection 22; EH 'Why I am a destiny' 3). After the English reference, volume and page number of the German source text is given (e.g. D 215, KSA 3:192 = *Daybreak* section 215; *Kritische Studienausgabe*, volume 3, page 192).

All references to Nietzsche's *Nachlass* are to Rüdiger Bittner's edited volume *Writings from the Late Notebooks* followed by volume and page number from the German source text (e.g. WLN 9[97]:157, KSA 12:389).

With the sole exception of Bittner's edited selection of Nietzsche's *Writings from the Late Notebooks*, translated by Kate Sturge, all Nietzsche translations are my own. These have benefited greatly, however, from the guidance afforded by the Cambridge University Press editions of Nietzsche's works.

References to the English translations of Kant's *Grundlegung zur Metaphysik der Sitten* and *Was ist Aufklärung?* (cited in Chapter 2) and to Feuerbach's *Das Wesen des Christentums* (cited in Chapter 4) follow the English abbreviations listed above followed by page number. References to the German source text follow the German source text abbreviation listed above followed by corresponding page number.

References to the six Hegel works cited in Chapter 3 are as follows:

Phänomenologie des Geistes (PhS) and *Enzyklopädie der philosophischen Wissenschaften* (EL)
    Abbreviation followed by section number
    German source text abbreviation followed by volume number and page number (e.g. PhS §19, W 3:24)

Grundlinien der Philosophie des Rechts (PR)
    Abbreviation followed by section number and page number
    German source text abbreviation followed by volume number and page number (e.g. PR §4, 36; W 7:47)

Vorlesungen über die Philosophie der Geschichte (LPH); *Vorlesungen über die Philosophie der Religion I* (LPR); and *Wissenschaft der Logik* (SL)
    Abbreviation followed by page number
    German source text abbreviation followed by volume number and page number (e.g. LPH 23, W 12:31)

Translations of Kant, Hegel and Feuerbach citations are those of the English-language editions listed in the bibliography. I have, however, heavily redacted George Eliot's translation of the second edition of Feuerbach's *The Essence of Christianity* and reinstated all of Feuerbach's original emphases, most of which Eliot elected not to reproduce.

All italicised words, phrases and clauses appearing in the citations are faithfully reproduced from the source German text. In rare instances where I have sought to emphasise a word or phrase within a citation, this has been parenthetically indicated.

Introduction

Towards the end of the last millennium, when the postmodernist trend in Nietzsche reception was slowly abating,[1] the 'immoralist' philosopher of 'will to power', but also of 'will to truth', quietly entered the lists of moral philosophy under the banner of normative ethics. Of particular interest to contemporary Anglo-American moral philosophers is Nietzsche's theory of value, the specific type of ethical theory that might be attributed to him and his views on normativity. While the former theoretical concerns lie outside the scope of this study,[2] the normative dimension of Nietzsche's work lies at the very heart of my critique and is writ large in the text with which I am principally concerned, namely *Thus Spoke Zarathustra*. My primary objective is to interrogate the normative injunction that dominates the first half of *Zarathustra* and lay bare the means of its execution as set down by Zarathustra. The said injunction is the self-overcoming of the lingering but ingrained residues of Christian morality in the human breast. And the means by which this overcoming is to be put into practice is through an ascetic discipline of self-legislation, self-negation and self-sacrifice. It is my contention that these three practices as delineated by Zarathustra can be respectively and fruitfully compared to the Kantian rational will, the Hegelian 'labour of the negative' and Feuerbach's indivisible trinity of love, sacrifice and suffering. These concepts, I submit, resurface in Nietzsche's *Zarathustra* as the joint agents of a ferocious, self-eviscerating doctrine of self-overcoming that bears all the marks of a moral tyranny.

Another formula for self-overcoming is what Nietzsche in *The Gay Science* refers to as '*incorporating knowledge* and making it instinctive' (GS 11, KSA 3:383). 'To what extent can truth endure incorporation?' he asks later in the same work; 'that is the question; that is the experiment' (GS 110, KSA 3:471). In *Zarathustra*, 'that' experiment is figuratively rendered as the planting of one's highest aim into the heart of the passions and is enjoined by *Zarathustra* through a profusion of violent rhetorical tropes. It is an experiment, moreover, which Zarathustra himself is in the midst of conducting but with self-shattering results. One of the metaphors he uses to describe this *in vivo* implantation of knowledge is vivisection, or spirit cutting into itself and through its own torment increasing its knowledge (Z2 'On the Famous Wise Men', KSA 4:134), and the person tasked with performing this surgical operation is 'the knower' (*der Erkennende*) (Z1 'On the Hinterlanders', KSA 4:37 and *passim*). Imbued with the knowledge that Christian morality has depleted and/or vitiated the human passions and instincts, the knower is required to employ his rational will, or will to truth, as a scalpel with which to vivisect the allegedly compromised affects. This reading of Zarathustra's doctrine of self-overcoming as a form of rational self-mastery over the affective manifold brings my study into the thick(et) of the naturalist-normative debate which in recent years has galvanised anglophone Nietzsche scholarship. It is to this debate that I shall now briefly turn.

The Naturalist-Normative Problem

Sitting on a similar fault line to that of free will and determinism,[3] the naturalist-normative problem can be briefly articulated as follows: if our thoughts and actions are causally determined by our physiology ('ontological naturalism'), we do not have free will, autonomy or a transcendental 'I' since the first necessarily precludes, or is incompatible with, the second. And if we have neither rational autonomy nor the transcendental 'I' of a unitary self-consciousness, we lack the wherewithal to respond to any normative ethical demands that may be made upon us. Herein lies what many consider to be an irresolvable problem in Nietzsche's philosophy. As most commentators would agree, Nietzsche both subscribes to a naturalist view of man and launches volley after volley of normative ethical pronouncements in his published works. The latter is egregiously the case in *Zarathustra*, a text constructed around a series of sermon-like speeches delivered by a prophet-like protagonist promulgating the ethical goal of self-overcoming – a goal that, semantically at least, presupposes a dual notion of self and autonomy. In the following study, the normative dimension of these discourses will be made to bear the evidential burden of my claim that Zarathustra is not only advancing a new morality, but one that is paradoxically more tyrannical and ascetic than the Christian morality to which it is ostensibly opposed.

It is worth pausing here to consider to whom Zarathustra's normative injunctions are in fact addressed. The full title of the work is *Thus Spoke Zarathustra: A Book For All and None*, the subtitle of which can be read in a number of ways. Adrian Del Caro holds that 'we readers are the "disciples" or "children" of Zarathustra, and we are not supposed to follow him so much as we are supposed to use him to find ourselves'.[4] Alexander Nehamas reaches the same conclusion, asserting that *Zarathustra* is a book for all and none in that 'all can read it, but it is written for no one's sake. We learn no lesson from it. Better, we learn that its lesson cannot be taught.'[5] Paul Loeb, on the other hand, argues that Nietzsche is 'challenging his readers to find themselves . . . so that eventually they will be in a better position to understand and follow Zarathustra and his teachings'.[6] I agree with Loeb but am inclined to go further and assert that Zarathustra's envisaged 'children', the putative goal of his teaching (to be discussed in Chapter 3), were viewed by both Zarathustra and his author as no more than an artistic creation, an impossible ideal. 'From this point on [i.e., post-*Zarathustra*]', writes Nietzsche in *Ecce Homo*, 'all my writings have been fish hooks . . . If nothing was *caught*, it wasn't my fault. *There weren't any fish . . .*' (EH 'BGE' 1, KSA 6:350 – ellipses in the original). And in Part 3 of *Zarathustra*, having cut short for a second time his homiletic teaching, it suddenly dawns on Zarathustra that the reason why he has been unable to find 'companions . . . and children of his hope' is because he has yet to create them. He further realises that this creation will not be possible until he has completed his own work of self-re-creation qua knowledge incorporation: 'I am in the middle of my work, to my children going and coming: for the sake of his children must Zarathustra perfect himself.' But however much 'misery' he voluntarily subjects himself to 'for *my* final test and realisation' (Z3 'On Involuntary Bliss', KSA 4:203-4), we find him at the close of *Zarathustra* still striving after his work and his ever-elusive children (Z4 'The Sign', KSA 4:408).

To return to the naturalist-normative debate, If the normative dimension of Nietzsche's work is now generally accepted among anglophone moral philosophers,[7] the naturalist position continues to elicit discrete and often conflicting views. This is largely due to the fact that Nietzsche is an unsystematic thinker whose preferred form of argumentation is the aphorism and whose preferred form of rhetoric is the barbed and ironic. As Sebastian Gardner observes, there is a distinctly '*centrifugal* character' to Nietzsche's philosophy: its component parts seem 'to want to fly apart in opposite directions'. Thus, while 'a unified Nietzschean theory of the self is a possibility ... it is not, in fact, what Nietzsche aims to provide'.[8] Consequently, the secondary literature is filled with multiple accounts of Nietzsche's naturalism, ranging from the broad to the specific. These accounts either propose various strategies for accommodating Nietzsche's notions of freedom, autonomy and self-determination within a naturalist framework (compatibilism), or deny that any such accommodation or reconciliation is logically possible (incompatibilism).

A leading proponent of the broad compatibilist reading of Nietzsche's naturalism is Christopher Janaway.[9] Janaway asserts that Nietzsche's naturalism is on the one hand a rejection of transcendent metaphysics (whether Christian or Platonic) and of notions such as the immaterial soul, the pure intellect and an absolutely free will; on the other, it is an attempt 'to explain numerous phenomena by invoking drives, instincts, and affects which [Nietzsche] locates in our physical, bodily existence'.[10] Against this type of 'Laundry List Naturalism'[11] and at the narrower, incompatibilist end of the spectrum, Brian Leiter characterises

Nietzsche as both a 'Speculative Methodological-Naturalist' in the Humean mould and a materialist-naturalist in the German Materialist tradition of Ludwig Feuerbach and Friedrich Lange.[12] A speculative methodological naturalist, according to Leiter, is necessarily speculative due to the lack of systematic data in what was then the nascent science of psychology, but who nevertheless seeks to 'construct theories that are "modelled" on the sciences . . . in that they take over from science the idea that natural phenomena have deterministic causes'. Similarly, the German Materialists of the 1850s viewed man as a product of nature rather than of God and accordingly predicated their materialist view of man on the burgeoning natural sciences of chemistry and physiology.[13]

Contra Leiter's construal of Nietzsche's naturalism as fundamentally methodological and grounded in empirical, scientific facts, Richard Schacht points to *Gay Science* 373 (KSA 3:624–6), in which Nietzsche ridicules 'a "scientific" world-interpretation' as being as interpretatively impoverished as a scientific interpretation of 'what is actually *music* in a piece of music'. Schacht attributes to Nietzsche an 'extended' form of naturalism, one that is 'historical-developmental' rather than 'scientistically reductionist'. This type of naturalism, argues Schacht, takes into account not just the biological and psycho-physiological aspects of the human animal, but also the social, political and historical phenomena which have arguably played a role in shaping humankind.[14] Peter Sedgwick endorses Schacht's reading but enlarges upon the socio-political aspect by drawing out the far-reaching biopolitical implications of Nietzsche's 'disruptive and exaggerated' form of naturalism which, like the violent biopolitical colonisation it imagistically exposes and rhetorically re-enacts, invites 'a radical rethinking of the legitimacy of the liberal state in modern social orders'. On the subject of Nietzsche's so-called scientific method, Sedgwick builds on Eugen Fink's observation regarding the 'intentionally coarse hyperbole' of Nietzsche's naturalistic discourse to argue that 'rather than conforming to the conventional demands of systematic argument and consistency', its figurative and hyperbolic style 'does not even pretend to emulate the good manners of "scientific," value-free description. It is not "method." It is lived.'[15]

Endorsing either a broad or narrow interpretation of Nietzsche's naturalist stance will depend, at least in part, on how much weight one chooses to give to Nietzsche's *Nachlass*. A preponderant emphasis on the late notebooks will doubtless yield a more coherent, deterministic and scientifically grounded naturalist theory than the less limiting, more fluid accounts of naturalism contained in Nietzsche's published works. A further consideration when evaluating the different types of naturalism attributed to Nietzsche is the extent to which the performative (in the sense of self-dramatisation) and polemical aspects of Nietzsche's published work are taken into account. Unlike the relatively unself-conscious transparency of his notebook fragments, Nietzsche's published texts present the reader with manifold interpretative hurdles. The performative hurdle requires the reader to be ever alert to Nietzsche's carefully crafted self-projection, often signalled by the 'we' pronoun, but rarely as floodlit as *Ecce Homo's* chapter titles such as 'Why I am so wise' and 'Why I am a destiny'. The rhetorical hurdle includes Nietzsche's taste for parody, provocation, mischief, irony (often self-directed), hyperbole and masks. Not only must the reader be alive to these rhetorical tics, but also to the normative and didactic ends to which these rhetorical strategies are deployed.

In order to illustrate the textual and textured dissonance between Nietzsche's notebooks and his published works, I have selected a few examples from each. The first set of examples, culled from Nietzsche's late notebooks, evinces his theoretical naturalist stance, while the second, extracted from *Zarathustra*, exemplifies his normative stance. Here is the first set:

> The assumption of the *single subject* is perhaps unnecessary; perhaps it is just as permissible to assume a multiplicity of subjects on whose interplay and struggle our thinking and our consciousness in general is based? A kind of *aristocracy* of 'cells' in which mastery resides? ... *My hypotheses*: the subject as multiplicity ... the constant transience and volatility of the subject, 'mortal soul'[,] *number* as perspectival form. (WLN 40[42]:46, KSA 11:650)

this whole phenomenon 'body' is as superior to our consciousness, our 'mind', our conscious thinking, feeling, willing, as algebra is superior to the times tables. (WLN 37[4]:29, KSA 11:577)

I don't concede that the 'I' is what thinks. Instead, I take the *I itself to be a construction of thinking*, of the same rank as 'matter', 'thing', 'substance', 'individual', 'purpose', number': in other words to be only a *regulative fiction* with the help of which a kind of constancy and thus 'knowability' is inserted into, *invented into*, a world of becoming. (WLN 35[35]:20–1, KSA 11:526)

The 'I' (which is *not* the same thing as the unitary government of our being!) is, after all, only a conceptual synthesis. (WLN 1[87]:61, KSA 12:32)

The first of the four citations articulates what Leiter refers to as Nietzsche's 'speculative methodological-naturalism'. Indeed, its speculative nature is heavily marked here. While the sequential references to 'a kind of *aristocracy* of "cells"', to 'the subject as multiplicity' and to the oxymoronic 'mortal soul' as 'perspectival form' collectively suggest the primacy of biology over consciousness, the conditional 'perhaps', the flagged 'hypotheses' and the scare-quoted 'cells' leave open the question of whether the cells and the mortal soul might not equally be considered as instances of 'perspectival form'.[16] In stark contrast to this, the second citation is an unambiguous statement on the primacy of body to consciousness and, by implication, on the causal relationship between the two; it can also be read as a clear precursor to Feud's id-ego formulation.[17] The third and fourth citations respectively reduce the notional, unitary 'I' to a 'regulative fiction' or a 'conceptual synthesis', but if the marked similarity between these two epithets and the earlier 'perspectival form' underscores the speculative nature of all three collocations, they are arguably no more nor less speculative than Nietzsche's hypotheses regarding the subject as multiplicity.

In the second set of examples, the 'regulative fiction' of the 'I' is not immediately apparent, despite Zarathustra's explicit reference to such a fiction early in Part 1: 'You say "I" and are proud of this word. But what is greater is that in which you do not want to believe – your body and its great reason: it does not say I but does I' (Z1 'On the Despisers of the Body', KSA 4:39). Nevertheless, to whatever extent the 'I' is shaped and driven by the affective 'self', it is an 'I' which, according to Sebastian Gardner, 'plays for Nietzsche a fundamental, pervasive, and ineliminable role'.[18] This is certainly the case, I would argue, in the following citations from *Zarathustra*:

> All beings hitherto have created something beyond themselves and you want to be the ebb of this great flood and prefer to go back to animals than overcome man? (ZP 3, KSA 4:14)

> You planted your highest aim into the heart of these passions: there they became your virtues and joys. (Z1 'On the Joyful and Painful Passions', KSA 4:43)

> You call yourself free? Your ruling thought I want to hear and not that you escaped from a yoke. (Z1 'On the Way of the Creator', KSA 4:81)

> Spirit is life which itself cuts into life; by its own torment it increases its own knowledge. (Z2 'On the Famous Wise Men', KSA 4:134)

The first of these citations immediately raises the question of who or what is doing the overcoming and implies that the object of this overcoming is the animal in man. The remaining three citations, in their respective and successive appeals to a 'highest aim', a 'ruling thought' and a scalpel-like spirit that 'cuts into life', appear to reverse the primacy of affect over conscious thought as declared in the second of the *Nachlass* citations listed above. Suffice to say that while the naturalist-normative problem is not one with which my study is directly concerned, I proceed on the assumption that Zarathustra's doctrine of self-overcoming presupposes a concept or a 'regulative fiction' of self that includes a form of rational agency that not only stands apart from the passions but exerts its authority over them.

The Morality Problem

Is Nietzsche advancing a morality of his own? This is the question that Peter Railton asks in his 2012 essay on Nietzsche's normative 'theory'. Acknowledging that Nietzsche's critique of morality is not merely critical, but appears to be 'a wholesale revision of what to think about how to live',[19] Railton asks whether Nietzsche's normative view constitutes 'a higher morality' rather than a 'transcending' of morality.[20] Certainly, Nietzsche's claim (cited by Railton) that there is 'a *distinction of rank* between man and man and consequently between morality and morality' (BGE 228, KSA 5:165) does not rule out such a question. Nor, I would add, does Nietzsche's assertion that '*Morality in Europe today is herd animal morality* . . . beside, before and after which many other, above all *higher* moralities are or should be possible' (BGE 202, KSA 5:124). Towards the end of Railton's essay – a highly technical discussion of Nietzsche's normative stance viewed through the dual lens of 'normative concepts proper' and 'evaluative concepts' – Railton concludes that 'Nietzsche is not holding out to us the prospect of a new *morality*. The notion of value involved is relational, not absolute or impersonal, and it makes no claim of universality.'[21] Contra Railton, if it is the case that Nietzsche *is* advancing a higher type of morality than the 'herd animal morality' to which he refers in BGE 202 above, then might not the values of this higher type of morality be deemed to be higher by virtue of their being relational rather than absolute, exceptional rather than universal?

An alternative approach to the question of whether Nietzsche is advancing his own morality is to use his own definition(s) of morality as our primary evaluative tool, notwithstanding the centrifugal and rhetorical difficulties noted above. I have selected four broadly naturalistic definitions which I shall deal with first, followed by two very differently weighted definitions. The first of the naturalistic definitions is fairly self-explanatory: 'Moralities are ... merely a *sign language of the affects*' (BGE 187, KSA 5:107), which simply means that all moralities express the affective needs of the person or group espousing that morality. The second definition fleshes out the BGE 228 'distinction of rank' assertion by ranking two different types of morality and expressing, albeit indirectly, a preference for one over the other:

> Every naturalism in morality, which is to say every *healthy* morality, is governed by an instinct of life ... But *anti-natural* (*widernatürlich*) morality, which is to say almost every morality that has hitherto been taught, venerated and preached, turns precisely *against* the instincts of life ... it *condemns* these instincts. (TI 'Morality as Anti-Nature' 4, KSA 6:85)[22]

By 'an instinct of life', Nietzsche means 'an instinct for growth, for duration, for accumulation of force, for *power*' (A 6, KSA 6:172). Take, for example, the Christian virtues of humility, meekness and brotherly love. Nietzsche sees these 'virtues' as symptomatic of a herd-like need for commonality, communality and security, in contrast to the ancient warrior virtues of pride, courage, fortitude and audacity which to Nietzsche evince an instinctual need for feats of strength and daring. In terms of force, the first set of virtues denotes contraction or stasis; the second, potency and accumulation. Accordingly, when measured by an evaluative standard of an instinct for growth, endurance and power, the first set is deemed by Nietzsche to be 'unnatural'; the second, 'healthy'. What we notice, however, is that the Christian moral binary of good and evil has simply been supplanted by the alternative (moral?) binaries of 'healthy' and 'unhealthy', 'natural' and unnatural', while the evaluative virtue/vice binary remains intact.[23]

The third definition is taken from Nietzsche's *Nachlass*: 'By morality, I understand a system of valuations which is contiguous with a being's conditions of life' (WLN 34[264]:16).[24]

Unlike the first and second definitions, both of which are unambiguously naturalistic, the third leaves open the question of whether a being's 'conditions of life' reside exclusively in the affective manifold or include other conditions such as self-restraint, self-mastery or self-determination. This brings us to the fourth definition which, while not a definition per se, pertains to the question of whether Nietzsche's corpus can be said to propose a new morality:

> Gradually it became clear to me what all great philosophy hitherto has been: the self-confession of its author and a kind of inadvertent and unconscious memoir; likewise, that the moral (or immoral) intentions in every philosophy constitute the real living seed from which the whole plant has always grown. (BGE 6, KSA 5:19–20)

Regarding this citation, if we grant that Nietzsche is not exempting his own philosophy from what he asserts is true of all previously great philosophies, and if we further grant that Nietzsche viewed his own philosophical project as having 'immoral' intentions, then what remains to be ascertained is the precise meaning of 'immoral'.

The explanatory weight of the fourth definition of morality hinges on its antonym 'immorality'. At the risk of sounding banal, it is worth bearing in mind that Nietzsche described himself as an 'immoralist' not an 'amoralist'. The negating prefix of the former indicates an opposition, and the morality to which Nietzsche is chiefly opposed is Christian morality, as attested by the following statement of allegiance: 'We immoralists and anti-Christians' (TI 'Morality as Anti-Nature' 3, KSA 6:84). Nietzsche gives a fuller account of the anti-Christian negation implicit in 'immoralist' in the following passage from *Ecce Homo*:

> Basically, my word *immoralist* comprises two negations. On the one hand, I am negating a type of man who up to now was regarded as the highest, the *good*, the *benevolent*, the *charitable*; on the other, I am negating a type of morality

that has attained dominance and validity as morality per se – decadence morality or, to speak plainly, *Christian* morality. It would be permissible to regard the second opposition as decisive, since on the whole I see the overestimation of goodness and benevolence as a consequence of decadence, as a symptom of weakness, as incompatible with an ascending and yes-saying life: negation and *destruction* is a precondition of yes-saying. (EH 'Why I am a destiny' 4, KSA 6:367–8)

The key words here are 'type' and 'decadence'. Nietzsche is not negating morality *tout court*. Rather, he is negating a decadent type of morality that purports to be 'morality per se' but is in Nietzsche's view a symptom of weakness and decline.[25] What is 'decisive' here is Nietzsche's valorisation not only of 'an ascending and yes-saying life', but, more importantly, of the negation and destruction intrinsic to such an ascent/assent. In Chapters 2 and 3, I shall argue that this negation and destruction is presented in *Zarathustra* as the necessary precondition of yes-saying and is, moreover, a role assigned not to the non-rational will to power, but to the rational will in its ferocious battle against 'moral prejudices' and other vestiges of Christian morality that have become 'our flesh and blood' (GS 380, KSA 3:632–3).

In marked contrast to the broadly naturalistic accounts of morality furnished above is the following passage from *Beyond Good and Evil*:

In contrast to *laisser aller*, every morality is a piece of tyranny against 'nature', also against 'reason'. But this in itself is no objection ... What is essential and invaluable in every morality is that it is a protracted constraint (*ein lange Zwang*) ... that there be *obedience* for a long time and in one direction: out of which came and has always come something for the sake of which it is worth living on earth, such as virtue, art, music, dance, reason, intellect – something transfiguring, refined, great and divine. The protracted bondage (*die lange Unfreiheit*) of the spirit, the sceptical constraint (*Zwang*), ... the protracted spiritual will (*der lange geistige Wille*) ... instilled in the European spirit its strength, ruthless curiosity and subtle agility. (BGE 188, KSA 5:108–9)[26]

This passage, with its repeated emphasis on a sustained constraint, is pivotal to the core argument of my study, namely that the principal agent of Zarathustra's doctrine of self-overcoming is a tyrannical rational will: a spiritual constraint that 'unreasonably' seeks to counter the ontological will to power of human nature. Of particular interest to me in the above quotation are the phrases 'protracted constraint', 'protracted bondage of the spirit' and 'protracted spiritual will', all of which emphasise the time needed to tyrannise successfully over nature and are closely related to the rational will qua engine of self-overcoming.

The first thing to note regarding Zarathustra's concept of self-overcoming (*Selbst-Überwindung*) is the semantic freight of the word 'overcoming'. The literary meaning of the German verb *überwinden* is 'to vanquish', which is synonymous with *besiegen* and *bezwingen*, both of which mean 'to defeat' or 'to conquer'. The verb *bezwingen*, however, carries the additional meaning of 'to master' or 'to control' and the usage example given by Langenscheidt is '*seine Wünsche bezwingen*', meaning to suppress one's desires. This latter meaning of mastery or *bezwingen* is central to Kant's moral philosophy. In his late work *The Metaphysics of Morals* (to be discussed in Chapter 2), Kant defines virtue as 'a self-constraint (*Selbstzwang*) in accordance with a principle of inner freedom' (AA 6:394). And in the same work, he repeatedly uses the word 'constraint' (*Zwang*) to denote 'the concept of a *necessitation* (constraint) of free choice through the law' (AA 6:379). It is this type of necessitation, I contend, that impels Zarathustra's doctrine of self-overcoming.

'Obedience' is another significant word in the BGE 188 passage cited above and is a key virtue in what I take to be Zarathustra's morality: 'Let obedience be your distinction! Let your commanding be itself an obeying!' urges Zarathustra (Z1 'Of War and Warriors', KSA 4:59). This obedience to one's own command is implicitly juxtaposed by Zarathustra to the obeying of Christian obeisance. In both cases, obedience is linked to commanding. But whereas the Christian is required to obey the commands of a putatively transcendent God, the practitioner of self-overcoming is required to obey the commands of his own ruling thought, namely the *Übermensch*, which on my reading symbolises the goal of knowledge incorporation. This ruling thought, incidentally, is the joint product of three items in Nietzsche's list of what makes life 'on earth' worth living: 'reason, intellect' and the 'transfiguring' art of invention (see BGE 188 passage above). 'Those who cannot obey themselves will be commanded', declares Zarathustra in his key discourse entitled 'On Self-Overcoming' (KSA 4:147), and the ones who will command them are 'the knowers' (*der Erkennenden*). They alone are capable of obeying their own commands through the exercise of a Kantian rational will.

The final definition of morality that I have selected is taken from *The Wanderer and His Shadow*, which Nietzsche wrote in 1880, two years after completing *Human, All Too Human*:

> All those who do not have enough control of themselves and do not know morality as a continual self-mastery and self-overcoming practised in the great and in the smallest of things, involuntarily become glorifiers of the good, compassionate, benevolent impulses (*Regungen*), of that instinctive morality which has no head but seems to consist solely of heart and helping hands. It is indeed in their interest to cast suspicion on a morality of reason and to make of that other morality the only one. (WS 45, KSA 2:573-4)

As this passage is dealt with in Chapter 1 of my study, I shall not dwell on it here. Suffice to say that its definition of morality likewise contains a distinction of rank between two moralities. But whereas the distinction in the *Twilight of the Idols* passage (the second naturalistic definition cited above) ranks a naturalist morality higher than an 'unnatural' (*widernatürlich*) morality that turns against the instincts, here in *The Wanderer and His Shadow* passage and implicit in the BGE 188 passage cited above, the unnatural 'morality of reason' is ranked above the natural 'instinctive morality' of 'benevolent impulses'. A further thing to note is that this rational morality, here characterised as 'a continual self-mastery and self-overcoming' and favourably contrasted with a morality that is all heart and no head, presents the reader with a normative ethic seemingly at odds with an incompatibilist naturalism. To reiterate, it is precisely this rational morality of self-mastery, together with the negation and destruction it entails, that I am designating a moral tyranny and attributing to Zarathustra's doctrine of self-overcoming.[27]

Max Stirner and the 'Tyranny of Mind'

In his notorious 1844 masterpiece, *The Ego and His Own* (*Der Einzige und sein Eigentum*, hereafter '*Ego*'),[28] Stirner charts the irresistible rise of 'spirit' or mind and what he perceives to be its concomitant tyranny over the body. This tyranny, according to Stirner, has its source in the Sophists and the Sceptics and reaches its apotheosis, via Christianity, in the works of Luther and Descartes: 'I myself am nothing else than mind, thinking mind (according to Descartes), believing mind (according to Luther). My body I am not' (*Ego* 109). A similar, if radically abbreviated history of the mind's tyranny over the body is set down by Nietzsche in his celebrated one-page chapter in *Twilight of the Idols*, 'How the "true world" finally became a fable: The history of an error' (KSA 6:80-1). The latter history also begins with the Greeks. Starting with Plato's Forms, Nietzsche charts the passage of the notional 'true world' via Christianity's eternal paradise to the Kantian *Ding an sich*. And just as Stirner had observed that when spirit becomes 'your *ideal*, the unattained (*unerreichte*), the otherworldly (*Jenseitige*) ... you [start to] play the zealot against *yourself*' (*Ego* 39), so too Nietzsche: 'The true world - unattainable (*unerreichbar*), indemonstrable, unpromisable; but the very thought of it - a consolation, an obligation, an imperative.'[29] As indicated in the previous section, a similar 'tyranny of mind' (*Ego* 81), which for Stirner represents the defining and debilitating mark of modernity, is also at work in Nietzsche's *Zarathustra*. More specifically, Stirner's bruising critique of Hegel and Feuerbach serves to crystallise the continuity between their ideas and those presented in *Zarathustra*.

In Stirner's *Ego*, Hegel stands accused of hypostatising thought and bringing it to 'its highest pitch of despotism and sole dominion' (*Ego* 95), while Feuerbach is charged with 'restoring' to man the divine essence that Christianity attributes to God but which on Feuerbach's showing is intrinsic to man.[30] Paraphrasing the core argument of Feuerbach's *The Essence of Christianity*, Stirner writes:

> The essence of man is man's supreme being; now by religion, to be sure, the *supreme being* is called *God* and regarded as an *objective* essence, but in truth it is only man's own essence; and therefore the turning point of the world's history is that henceforth no longer *God*, but man, is to appear to man as God. (*Ego* 41)

Stirner's rebuttal is that man's purportedly 'supreme being' [*höchste Wesen*] or highest essence, whether objectified in God or internalised in a divinised concept of man, is an idea to which man qua human animal is oppressively subjugated. In other words, the notion of an essence or immanent Being is superimposed; it is an idea against which man is measured, judged and condemned. As Stirner argues, precisely because man's so-called supreme being is said to be

> his *essence* and not he himself, it remains quite immaterial whether we see it outside him and view it as 'God', or find it in him and call it 'Essence of Man' or 'Man'. *I* am neither *God* nor *Man*, neither the supreme essence nor my essence, and therefore it is all one in the main whether I think of the essence as in me or outside me. (Ibid.)

It is self-alienating concepts such as these, concepts to which man subjects himself to the detriment of his inalienable or unique self (*Einzige*), that Stirner denounces as *idées fixes* or 'wheels in the head' (*Ego* 54).

The *idée fixe* and 'self-rolling wheel' (Z1 'On the Three Metamorphoses', KSA 4:31) in Nietzsche's head at the time of his writing *Zarathustra* is the *Übermensch*. Neither divine essence nor *Ding an sich*, the *Übermensch* is the singular 'ruling thought' or visionary ideal to which man is exhorted by Zarathustra not only to aspire but to sacrifice himself. 'The *Übermensch* is the meaning of the earth', proclaims Zarathustra in his prologue. 'Let your will (*Wille*) say: the *Übermensch shall be* the meaning of the earth!' (ZP 3, KSA 4:14). Man is to be re-created, not in God's image but in the image of an ideal man of the future – or, to use Stirner's expression, of an *idée fixe*. It is to this *übermenschlich* type of man, who will justify rather than vilify earthly existence, that man is to sacrifice himself. In doing so, he must submit to the higher human powers of reason, will and love, which Feuerbach designates as the divine, if demythologised, trinity within man and which collectively underpin Zarathustra's doctrine of self-overcoming. To these three human powers must man submit if he is to aspire towards a higher, but paradoxically more earthly, ideal:

> I love the one who lives in order to know, and who wants to know so that the *Übermensch* may one day live. Thus he seeks his own destruction (*Untergang*).
>
> I love the one who loves his virtue: because virtue is the will to perish (*Wille zum Untergang*) and an arrow of longing [for the *Übermensch*].
>
> I love the one who holds back not a single drop of spirit for himself, but rather wills to be wholly the spirit of his virtue: thus he walks as spirit over the bridge [to the *Übermensch*]. . . .
>
> I love the one who justifies the future ones and redeems the past ones: for he is willing to perish (*zu Grunde gehen*) through the present ones.
>
> I love the one who castigates his god, because he loves his god: for he must perish (*zu Grunde gehen*) through the wrath of his god. . . .
>
> I love the one who is of a free spirit and a free heart: thus is his head only the bowels of his heart, but his heart drives him to his destruction (*Untergang*). (ZP 4, KSA 4:17-18)

In the above paean to self-destruction lies the type of 'tyranny of mind' reviled by Stirner and implicit in my titular charge of moral tyranny. Here is the higher ideal on the altar of which man is to sacrifice ('*unterzugehen*' and '*zu Grunde gehen*') all his former beliefs, opinions and metaphysical comforts, not to mention his natural proclivities. Only by implanting the idea of the *Übermensch* ('head' being an obvious metonymy for thought or idea) into 'the bowels of his heart', we are told, can man justify earthly existence. Only by assimilating and aspiring towards this ideal of a higher human being can man walk 'as spirit' over the bridge to the *Übermensch*. But if this higher ideal or ruling thought is to become one's god, one's goal, one's heart's desire, in what meaningful way can the heart be said to be free? Is it not compelled by an idea, 'a spook' (*Ego* 44 and *passim*), a word, a redemptive ideal, or in the Kantian idiom, a categorical imperative?[31] Has the Word not become flesh? (Ibid.) Or, to borrow Zarathustra's trope, has the idea not become a knife that cuts into the flesh and, on the evidence of Zarathustra's shadow in *Zarathustra* Part 4 ('The Shadow', KSA 4: 338–41), bleeds the heart to death on the altar of such an ideal?

Kant, Hegel and Feuerbach

In his outstanding 1995 monograph *Nietzsche: The Ethics of an Immoralist*, Peter Berkowitz argues that when Nietzsche attacks morality or seeks to determine the value of morality, 'he speaks in the name of a higher morality or ethic'. He goes on to argue that Zarathustra's ethics is enmeshed in the moral and philosophical tradition it sets out to overcome.[32] In the following chapters, I aim to keep Berkowitz's interpretative torch burning by tracing the three cardinal virtues in Zarathustra's doctrine of self-overcoming – self-mastery, self-denial and self-sacrifice – back to works by Kant, Hegel and Feuerbach, respectively. This comparative exercise is not intended to be an argument for direct influence, but rather for a constellation of ideas and ethical ideals that recall their original formulations in Kantian philosophy and its German Idealist outgrowth. In Chapter 1, the sovereignty of reason over the passions is shown to be a dominant ideal advocated by Nietzsche in his three pre-*Zarathustra* works: *Human, All Too Human*, *Daybreak* and *The Gay Science*. In Chapter 2, the self-legislating rational will that is pivotal to Kant's normative moral theory is echoed in Zarathustra's vision of a leonine will that tears into life. In Chapter 3, the dialectical transformation of spirit from camel to lion to child is read as a striking recapitulation of Hegel's 'labour of the negative'. And in Chapter 4, sacrificial love as an ideal of human perfection – a cherished ideal in Feuerbach's *The Essence of Christianity* – is shown to be a foundational tenet of Zarathustra's teaching and one that is enjoined on those brave enough to labour towards his vision of a higher, *übermenschlich* type of human being.

Chapter 1 shores up the book's titular claim by tracing its declared moral tyranny back to the ascetic virtues espoused by Nietzsche in the three works that immediately precede *Zarathustra*. In *Human, All Too Human* and *Daybreak*, in particular, Nietzsche juxtaposes his own morality, which he explicitly designates as such, to Christian morality. What is most striking about this juxtaposition is that Nietzsche's morality features the same virtues as the Christian morality he is opposing. Moreover, the Christian virtues that he appropriates and repurposes are those principally noted for their severity, such as obedience, self-restraint, self-denial and sacrifice. For example, Nietzsche opposes his own morality of 'real sacrifice and devotion' to what in his view is the 'intoxication and excess' that passes for sacrifice and devotion in Christian morality (D 215, KSA 3:192). He further ponders the right of such self-sacrificing 'free-spirited moralists' (D 209, KSA 3:189) to inflict on others the severity of their own self-sacrifice. Chapter 1 closes with a detailed account of Nietzsche's own pre-*Human All Too Human* self-sacrifice, which entailed a complete abstinence from what he considered to be the emotional excesses of Romantic music, especially Wagner's, and the suppression of an equally debilitating form of Romanticism, namely Schopenhauer's nihilistic-quietistic philosophy.

In Chapter 2, parallels are drawn between the autonomous, self-legislating, rational will of Kantian ethics and Zarathustra's concept of a destructive-generative rational will that has sufficient intellectual rigour to interrogate entrenched moral dogmas and the requisite strength to overcome these dogmas through the incorporation of a new law: the law of perpetual becoming. Driving this rational will, I submit, is a relentless will to truth that in its resolute opposition to inclination and self-interest is a spiritual transposition of the ontological law of becoming into the normative doctrine of self-overcoming. In the rational will's tyranny over the will to power of the affects can be seen distinct traces of Kant's concept of the 'good will' that 'does not serve my inclination, but outweighs it' (AA 4:400). In a similar vein, Zarathustra's radical re-evaluation of the three Christian 'evils' of voluptuousness, lust for power and selfishness presents the genuinely free man as one who is able to hold tyrannical sway over the affects and compel the affective will towards an uncompromising ethical goal. This tyranny of a scrupulously fastidious reason, reasons Zarathustra, is the most effective counter-force to the tyranny of assimilated Christian values.

In Chapter 3, Zarathustra's ethical goal of self-overcoming is shown to be predicated on spirit's progress towards self-realisation. Like the *Bildung* or transformation of *Geist* in Hegel's *Phenomenology of Spirit*, spirit's transformation in *Zarathustra* entails a violent confrontation with itself. What is envisaged here is an intellectual as opposed to mystical *via negativa*: a purging not of the body but of a mind which in Nietzsche's view has been vitiated by Christian precepts that demonise the body. This cognitive stripping away of allegedly erroneous moral and philosophical assumptions in order to lay bare a less tendentious, less compromised form of knowledge is what Hegel terms the 'labour of the negative' and Zarathustra a threefold metamorphosis of spirit from camel to lion to child. In both formulations, a dialectical discipline of thought will purportedly enable spirit to liberate and substantiate itself in a life lived in accordance with a higher ideal. The second half of the chapter addresses the near impossibility of spirit's third and final metamorphosis, the prerequisite for which is the forcible planting of the 'ruling idea' or 'abstract universal' into the soil of the passions.

In Chapter 4, love is revealed as foundational to Zarathustra's moral project. Without steadfast love for the *übermenschlich* ideal, the rational will lacks the necessary courage for the negative labour of purging, pruning and propelling the once guilt-ridden affects towards self-affirmation. Such love, however, demands the suffering of self-sacrifice, which for Feuerbach is most potently rendered in the Passion of Christ. This supreme form of love, asserts Feuerbach, 'impels the sacrifice of self to another' (EC 53–5, GW 5:108–11). It is the same type of love, I contend, that impels Zarathustra to sacrifice his former youthful loves to an ideal of human perfectibility and his contemplative solitude to the rigours of peripatetic proselytisation. But if the rhetoric of Zarathustra's sermons demands self-immolation on the altar of a higher ideal, at the sub-textual level a compassionate love speaks to the common suffering of mankind.

Notes

1. In line with a growing number of Nietzsche scholars who over the past thirty years have challenged the postmodernists' reading of the philosopher whom they hailed as their progenitor, Ken Gemes records how 'Nietzsche's perspectivism, his suspicion of metaphysics (ultimate ontology), his radical scepticism and interrogation of conventional notions of truth, have been taken to mark him as an agent of dissolution, of polyphony, a practitioner of the hermeneutics of suspicion.' Ken Gemes, 'Postmodernism's Use and Abuse of Nietzsche', *Philosophy and Phenomenological Research*, 62:2 (2001), p. 338. See also *Nietzsche as Postmodernist: Essays Pro and Contra*, ed. Clayton Koelb (Albany, NY: SUNY Press, 1990).
2. The range of ethical theories considered are virtue ethics, ethical egoism, consequentialism, perfectionism, proto-existentialism and 'quasi-aesthetic individualist perfectionism'. The last is put forward by Simon Robertson in 'The Scope Problem – Nietzsche, the Moral, Ethical, and Quasi-Aesthetic', in *Nietzsche, Naturalism, and Normativity*, eds. Christopher Janaway and Simon Robertson (Oxford: Oxford University Press, 2012), p. 108. For a detailed account of the theoretical issues at stake see Simon Robertson, 'Nietzsche's Ethical Revaluation', *Journal of Nietzsche Studies*, 37 (Spring 2009), pp. 66–90. I endorse Brian Leiter's view that Nietzsche's primary interest was not in philosophical theories of morality but in '*morality* as a real cultural phenomenon' and in the insidious effects of that phenomenon. Brian Leiter, 'Nietzsche and the Morality Critics', *Ethics*, 107:2 (1997), p. 252.

3. Distinguishing between 'deserts free will', which is concerned with the ascription of punishment and reward, and 'agency free will', which is concerned with the question of agency and autonomy, Ken Gemes asserts that Nietzsche affirms agency free will. In support of his claim, Gemes cites Nietzsche's idea of a 'sovereign individual' – 'this master of a *free* will' who is in possession of 'his own independent, protracted will' (GM II 2, KSA 5:293) – and concludes that Nietzsche 'is a compatibilist in the sense that he does not take determinism to be incompatible with free will'. Ken Gemes, 'Nietzsche on Free Will, Autonomy, and the Sovereign Individual', in *Nietzsche on Freedom and Autonomy*, ed. Ken Gemes and Simon May (Oxford: Oxford University Press, 2009), pp. 33–9.
4. Adrian Del Caro, '"Zarathustra Is Dead, Long Live Zarathustra!"', *Journal of Nietzsche Studies*, 41:1 (2011), p. 89.
5. Alexander Nehamas, 'For whom the Sun shines. A Reading of *Also sprach Zarathustra*', in *Friedrich Nietzsche: Also Sprach Zarathustra*, ed. Volker Gerhardt (Berlin: Academie Verlag, 2012), p. 141.
6. Paul S. Loeb, 'Zarathustra Hermeneutics', *Journal of Nietzsche Studies*, 41:1 (2011), p. 107.
7. To cite a recent article on Nietzsche's normative ethics, Jonathan Mitchell argues that Nietzsche's concept of self-overcoming is 'a distinctive kind of first-personal, and ethical, re-evaluative activity' – a reading that is entirely consonant with the one I am advancing in this book. In contrast to other recent commentaries that view self-overcoming exclusively through the lens of a will-to-power psychology, Mitchell maintains that self-overcoming as conceived by Nietzsche involves the overcoming of a 'self-evaluative framework' pursuant upon a personal re-appraisal of the normative standards through which one has previously defined one's 'practical identity' or has formed one's self-conception. In common with my reading of self-overcoming, Mitchell's is informed by Zarathustra's assertion that the greatest thing an individual can experience is 'the hour of the great contempt' (ZP 3, KSA 4:15). Jonathan Mitchell, 'Nietzschean Self-Overcoming', *Journal of Nietzsche Studies*, 47:3 (2016), pp. 323–31.
8. Sebastian Gardner, 'Nietzsche, the Self, and the Disunity of Philosophical Reason', in Gemes and May, pp. 13–14.
9. Peter Poellner also offers a compatibilist reading of Nietzsche, construing the latter's conception of free agency as the congruence of one's desires and values. Peter Poellner, 'Nietzschean Freedom', in Gemes and May, pp. 151–79.

10. Christopher Janaway, *Beyond Selflessness: Reading Nietzsche's 'Genealogy'* (Oxford: Oxford University Press, 2007), p. 34.
11. Brian Leiter, 'Nietzsche's Naturalism Reconsidered', in *The Oxford Handbook of Nietzsche*, ed. Ken Gemes and John Richardson (Oxford: Oxford University Press, 2013), p. 577.
12. Nietzsche read Friedrich Albert Lange's *History of Materialism and Critique of Its Meaning in the Present* in August 1866, the year in which it was published. Thomas H. Brobjer, *Nietzsche's Philosophical Context: An Intellectual Biography* (Urbana and Chicago: University of Illinois Press, 2008), pp. 32–3.
13. Brian Leiter, 'Nietzsche's Naturalism Reconsidered', pp. 576–80. Leiter's essay is in large part a recapitulation of the arguments contained in his 2002 monograph, *Nietzsche on Morality* (London: Routledge).
14. Nietzsche's naturalism, avers Schacht, 'is *not* wedded to the view that everything that happens in human life and in the development and unfolding of human reality and experience can be adequately explained and fully comprehended in terms of natural-scientific or natural-scientifically-modelled concepts and processes, "causality" first and foremost among them'. On the contrary, argues Schacht, in GS 373 Nietzsche is actively opposed to such a view. Richard Schacht, 'Nietzsche's Naturalism and Normativity', in Janaway and Robertson, pp. 240–2.
15. Peter R. Sedgwick, 'Hyperbolic Naturalism: Nietzsche, Ethics, and Sovereign Power, *Journal of Nietzsche Studies*, 47:1 (2016), pp. 141–66.
16. These notebook musings on 'the subject as multiplicity' and the concept of a 'mortal soul' re-emerge in BGE 12 in which Nietzsche entertains a type of naturalism that is not so narrow or so 'clumsy' as to exclude a refashioned concept of 'soul': 'the belief which regards the soul as something indestructible, eternal, indivisible, as a monad, as an atom: *this* belief ought to be evicted from science! Between ourselves, it is not at all necessary to get rid of "the soul" itself and to renounce one of the oldest and most venerable hypotheses – as is customarily the case with the clumsy naturalists who no sooner touch "the soul" than they lose it. But the way is open for new versions and refinements of the soul-hypothesis; and concepts such as "mortal soul", and "soul as subjective multiplicity", and "soul as social structure of the drives and affects", want henceforth to have civil rights in science' (KSA 5:27). As R. Lanier Anderson points out, this passage, while routinely cited in

support of naturalist readings of Nietzsche aimed at reducing the Nietzschean self to a Humean-like bundle of drives, appears to reject any such reductionism insofar as the new 'soul-hypotheses' of soul as *subjective* multiplicity' and as *social structure* of the drives and affects' suggests something more than a mere hodgepodge of drives. This 'something more than' a chaotic bundle of drives forms the basis of Anderson's own interpretation of the Nietzschean self. Steering a course between the reductionist-naturalist and the transcendentalist readings of Nietzsche, Anderson argues for a 'minimalist' Nietzschean self: a self, that is to say, 'not as identical to the strongest drive, nor as a bundle of drives, but as an ordered structure of drives *and affects*'. R. Lanier Anderson, 'What is a Nietzschean Self?', in Janaway and Robertson, pp. 211-16. Anderson's emphases.
17. Leiter remarks that Nietzsche's self-designation as 'the first psychologist' was in fact borne out by his anticipation of results that took psychologists another century to discover. Brian Leiter, 'Nietzsche's Theory of the Will', in Gemes and May, p. 107. Others have argued, however, that the 'first' position rightfully belongs to Schopenhauer. For two persuasive accounts of the extent to which Schopenhauer anticipated Freud beyond the long-established will-id parallel see R. K. Gupta, 'Freud and Schopenhauer', *Journal of the History of Ideas*, 36:4 (1975), pp. 721-8, and Christopher Young and Andrew Brook, 'Schopenhauer and Freud', *The International Journal of Psycho-Analysis*, 75:1 (1994), pp. 101-18. Both articles hold that Freud's theories of repression, neurosis and sexuality were first articulated by Schopenhauer. A reprint of Young and Brook's article appears in *The Oxford Handbook of Philosophy and Psychoanalysis*, ed. Richard G. T. Gipps and Michael Lacewing (Oxford: Oxford University Press, 2019), pp. 63-82.
18. Sebastian Gardner, 'Nietzsche, the Self, and the Disunity of Philosophical Reason', in Gemes and May, p. 8. R. Lanier Anderson, however, rejects Gardner's attribution of 'a buried transcendental dimension' to Nietzsche's thought on the grounds that Gardner's argument rests on what appear to be 'alleged presuppositions of Nietzschean positions' – presuppositions, moreover, that reflect Gardner's own 'post-Kantian commitments' – rather than on any text-based evidence. 'What is a Nietzschean Self?', in Janaway and Robertson, p. 206.

19. One might be forgiven for construing the rather awkward phrasing of 'a wholesale revision of what to think about how to live' as a 'normative-lite' circumlocution of 'a wholesale revision of how one ought to live'.
20. Peter Railton, 'Nietzsche's Normative Theory? The Art and Skill of Living Well', in Janaway and Robertson, p. 21.
21. Ibid. p. 48.
22. Cf. 'With the word "vice" I fight against every type of anti-nature or, if you love pretty words, idealism' (EH 'Why I write such good books' 5, KSA 6:307).
23. In his exceptionally astute reading of *Zarathustra*, Peter Berkowitz notes how 'Zarathustra permits himself to invoke traditional categories of praise and blame while repudiating the traditional support of such moral judgements.' Peter Berkowitz, *Nietzsche: The Ethics of an Immoralist* (Cambridge, MA: Harvard University Press, 1995), p. 144.
24. This citation appears neither in the Colli and Montinari *Kritische Studienausgabe*, nor in the digital online source eKGWB. It does, however, appear in *The Will to Power* where it is numbered 256 (1887–8). Friedrich Nietzsche, *The Will to Power*, ed. Walter Kaufmann (New York: Vintage, 1968), p. 148. German original: *Nietzsche's Werke*, vol. 15, *Nachgelassene Werke: Ecce homo; Der Wille zur Macht* (first and second books), (Leipzig: Alfred Kröner Verlag, 1922), p. 334.
25. Leiter, whose categorisation of Nietzsche as an incompatibilist naturalist has already been discussed, refers to Nietzsche's backward inference from a type of morality to the 'psycho-physical constitution' of the type of person espousing it as the 'Doctrine of Types' and cites a number of passages throughout Nietzsche's corpus in which this doctrine is articulated. The clearest and most succinct articulation is the one already cited from BGE 187: 'Moralities are ... merely a sign language of the affects.' Brian Leiter, 'Nietzsche's Theory of the Will', in Gemes and May, pp. 115–16.
26. Cf. 'And so perhaps the most beautiful still appears only in the dark and sinks, scarcely born, into eternal night – namely the spectacle of that strength, which employs genius *not on works* but *on himself as a work*; in other words, on his own mastery, on the purification of his imagination, on the imposition of order and choice upon the influx of tasks and ideas' (D 548, KSA 3:319).

27. In his brilliantly illuminating work on *Zarathustra*, T. K. Seung also views mastery of the passions as a necessary prerequisite to becoming an *Übermensch*. T. K. Seung, *Nietzsche's Epic of the Soul: 'Thus Spoke Zarathustra'* (Oxford: Lexington Books, 2005), pp. 25–34.
28. The publisher of the first English language edition of Stirner's *Der Einzige und sein Eigen* favoured the looser but more euphonic title *The Ego and His Own* to the clumsier, more literal *The Unique One and His Property*. Benjamin Tucker, 'Publisher's Preface', in Max Stirner, *The Ego and His Own*, trans. Steven T. Byington (New York: Benj. R. Tucker, 1907), pp. ix–x. A new English translation by Wolfi Landstreicher, entitled *The Unique and Its Property*, appeared in May 2017 (Baltimore: Underworld Amusements).
29. The question of Max Stirner's possible influence over Nietzsche dates back to the turn of the last century, shortly after Nietzsche's death in 1900. Among the most notable figures in the anti-influence camp are: Albert Lévy, *Stirner et Nietzsche* (Paris: 1904); Georg Simmel, *Schopenhauer and Nietzsche: Ein Vortragszyklus* (Leipzig: 1915); and Rudolph Steiner, *Friedrich Nietzsche, Fighter for Freedom* (New York: 1960). Among those in the pro-influence camp are Gilles Deleuze, *Nietzsche et la philosophie* (Paris: 1962) and Paul Carus, *Nietzsche and other Exponents of Individualism* (Chicago and London: 1914). Referenced in Thomas H. Brobjer, 'A possible solution to the Stirner-Nietzsche question', *The Journal of Nietzsche Studies*, 25 (2003), pp. 109–114. But if the question of influence is one that can never be definitively answered, it is impossible to deny that many of Stirner's ideas uncannily anticipate the critical insights commonly associated with Nietzsche. Here is a list of some of the more striking correspondences of thought: (1) Stirner's depiction of man as (a) an abyss of chaotic impulses: '"What am I?" each of you asks himself. An abyss of lawless and unregulated impulses, desires, wishes, passions, a chaos without light or guiding star [*Leitstern*]!' (*Ego* 212), cf. Zarathustra's: 'Man is a rope stretched between beast and *Übermensch* – a rope over an abyss' (ZP 4, KSA 4:16) and 'I tell you: one must still have chaos in one if one is to give birth to a dancing star [*tanzenden Stern*]' (ZP 5, KSA 4:19); and (b) a 'creative nothing . . . out of which I myself as creator create everything' (*Ego*, 6), cf. Zarathustra: 'Let the value of everything be newly ordained by you! Therefore shall you be fighters! Therefore shall you be creators!' (Z1 'On the Bestowing Virtue' 2, KSA 4:100). (2) Stirner's depiction of the individual as something

'unique' (*einzige*), cf. Nietzsche's dismissal of reciprocity as 'a great piece of vulgarity . . . except in the *choicest sphere* of "my equals", inter pares; . . . because one is *something unique* and only does unique things' (WLN 11[127]:226, KSA 13:61). (3) Stirner's exposure of the affective self-interest that drives the pious no less than the impious, cf. Nietzsche's *On the Genealogy of Morals*, especially the third essay. (4) Stirner's dismissal of essence, spirit or *Ding an sich* as fabrications that reduce the body to a vassal of the mind and the phenomenal world to a mere shadow-play, cf. Nietzsche's 'How the "true world" finally became a fable: The history of an error' in *Twilight of the Idols* (KSA 6:80–1) and Zarathustra: 'Once the soul looked contemptuously on the body . . . the soul wished the body meagre, ghastly and famished' (ZP 3, KSA 4:15). And (5) Stirner's assertion that 'Our atheists are pious people' (*Ego* 241), cf. Nietzsche's claim that 'all these pale atheists . . . these ultimate idealists of knowledge' are merely the latest incarnation of the ascetic ideal (GM III 24, KSA 5:398–9). The number of *Zarathustra* citations in the examples given above lends support to John Glassford's argument for a similarity in style. But whereas Glassford judges Nietzsche's use of metaphor to be more successful than Stirner's, J. L. Walker, in his Introduction to the 1907 translation of *Der Einzige*, holds that 'In style Stirner's work offers the greatest possible contrast to the puerile, padded phraseology of Nietzsche's *Zarathustra* and its false imagery' (p. xiv) – a view with which I am largely in sympathy. John Glassford, 'Did Friedrich Nietzsche (1844–1900) Plagiarise from Max Stirner (1806–56)?', *The Journal of Nietzsche Studies*, 18 (Fall 1999), pp. 73–9; J. L. Walker, *Ego* (1907), p. xvi.

30. In his 1977 landmark study, *God as the Mystery of the World*, Eberhard Jüngel argues that 'Feuerbach is always presupposing that God is that "than which nothing greater can be conceived." Only on the basis of that presupposition is it sensible to assert that "God is the reason expressing, affirming itself as the highest existence." / Hence the critical derivation of theology from anthropology moves in a circle, in that the concept of the highest being, the highest *object* of thought, is understood precisely as "the *highest degree* of the thinking power" [cited from St. Anselm's *Proslogium*] – a post-Hegelian variation of *noēseōs noēsis* ('thinking thought'). The concept of the highest being is used not only for God but also for reason, because reason attains its very essence only in the thought of the highest being.' Eberhard Jüngel, *God as the Mystery of the World: On the Foundation of the Theology of the*

Crucified One in the Dispute between Theism and Atheism, trans. Darrell L. Guder (Grand Rapids, MI: Wm. B. Eerdmans Publishing, 1983), pp. 145-6.

31. Paul Loeb points out that the penultimate section of the second essay of Nietzsche's *Genealogy* (GM II 24, KSA 5:335-6) contains four references to the *redemptive* role of a putative 'man of the future, who will redeem us not only from the hitherto reigning ideal' and the nihilism to which it has given rise, but will be the 'bell-stroke of noon . . . that makes the will free again, that gives back to earth its goal and to humankind its hope'; and that in the closing section of the same essay (GM II 25, KSA 5:337), Nietzsche identifies Zarathustra as that 'godless' man of the future. But as I shall argue in the following chapters, the redemption that Zarathustra offers 'from the hitherto reigning ideal' is through an alternative ideal 'that makes the will free again', but only by means of a tyrannical reorientation of the will towards an *übermenschlich* goal. Loeb's reading of *Zarathustra* is also heavily influenced by Nietzsche's retrospective and largely revisionist account of the work in *Ecce Homo*. Thus it is that Loeb is able to characterise *Zarathustra* as Nietzsche's 'attempt to envision a philosopher stronger than himself . . . [who] will be able to do what he, Nietzsche, knows he can never do himself: reverse the bad conscience, overturn the hitherto reigning ideal, conquer God, and liberate the will'. Paul S. Loeb, *The Death of Nietzsche's Zarathustra* (Cambridge: Cambridge University Press, 2010), pp. 208-13. But as Zarathustra himself confesses in his 'stillest hour', he is 'ashamed' at not being strong enough to be that man and, more culpably, at not even wanting to be that man (Z2 'The Stillest Hour', KSA 4:187-90). In short, Zarathustra's will is far from free and the Zarathustra who appears in the work which bears his name has a very different character to Nietzsche's hyperbolic representation of Zarathustra in *Ecce Homo*. Thus, when Nietzsche asserts in *Ecce Homo* that wisdom and 'the art of speaking' never existed before Zarathustra, or that Zarathustra's imagery stratospherically surpasses even the greatest of all previous metaphors, or that at every moment in *Zarathustra* 'man has been overcome, the idea of the *Übermensch* has become the highest reality' (EH, 'Z' 6, KSA 6:343-5), Nietzsche is either revelling in poetic licence or suffering from a spell of selective amnesia.

32. Berkowitz, *Nietzsche*, pp. 48 and 131.

1
Nietzsche's Ascetic Morality

> In themselves, ascetic habits and exercises are still far from indicating an anti-natural attitude, a hostility to existence, or degeneration and sickness
>   self-overcoming, with harsh and dreadful inventions: a means of having and demanding respect for oneself: ascesis as a means of *power*
>   (WLN 7[5]:131, KSA 12:271)

Few commentators would dispute the claim that Nietzsche's works are principally concerned with the question of morality. But within that scholarly consensus there is a tendency to overlook the fact that Nietzsche's sustained critique of morality is itself an extension or a refinement of the morality under scrutiny. As Nietzsche succinctly puts it in one of his late notebook entries: '*Morality itself*, as honesty, *compels* us to negate morality' (WLN 5[58]:113, KSA 12:206),[1] or in a more effusive entry written slightly earlier: 'that one must subject moral valuations themselves to a critique . . . is *itself our present form of morality*, as a sublime sense of honesty . . . as the most sublime kind of probity' (WLN 2[191]:96, KSA 12:161–2). We hear the same refrain (but see Introduction, n31) in his retrospective work, *Ecce Homo*: 'Zarathustra is more truthful than any other thinker. His teaching, and his alone, posits truthfulness as the highest virtue' (EH 'Why I am a Destiny' 3, KSA 6:367). Thus, notwithstanding the scorn habitually heaped by Nietzsche on the 'will to truth' as a tenacious moral residue in the fields of science and philosophy (see GS 357, KSA 3:600), it is with this will that Nietzsche flushes out what in his view is 'the most malicious form of the will to lie', namely Christian morality. 'Have I made myself understood?' he bristles in *Ecce Homo*; 'What defines me, what sets me apart from the rest of mankind is that I have *unmasked* Christian morality' (EH 'Why I am a Destiny' 7, KSA 6:371-2). But if truth is 'the highest virtue' in Nietzsche's system of values, it is but one of a number of Christian virtues which he appropriates and repurposes in a critical onslaught that consumed the greater part of his productive life.

This chapter will focus on the three major works that Nietzsche wrote immediately prior to *Zarathustra*: *Human, All Too Human: A Book for Free Spirits* (together with its two supplementary works, *Assorted Opinions and Maxims* and *The Wanderer and His Shadow*),[2] *Daybreak: Thoughts on the Prejudices of Morality* and *The Gay Science*. I shall refer to these works as his 'middle works' rather than his 'middle period works' since the latter designation suggests a fixed start and end point, thereby obscuring or discounting the persistence of ideas and attitudes throughout the Nietzsche corpus.[3] In focusing on these middle works, my aim is to foreground Nietzsche's juxtaposition of his own morality – which he specifies as such and does so, moreover, without the use of scare-quotes – to Christian morality. More importantly, we shall see how these juxtapositions often feature not only the same virtue as the one being countered, but a virtue which is particularly noted for its severity.[4] Self-restraint, self-denial, sacrifice and obedience, for example, are contradistinguished from their Christian counterparts on the grounds that, within the context of Nietzsche's morality, these acts are informed by greater knowledge, a sharper eye for truth, a more fastidious intellectual conscience,[5] and are oriented towards a radically different goal. This goal, we shall discover, is the planting of truth in the soil of the passions or, as Nietzsche phrases it in *The Gay Science*, of '*incorporating knowledge* and making it instinctive' (GS 11, KSA 3:383).[6] It is the same goal, I shall argue, that lies at the heart of *Zarathustra*.

Pitting a 'Morality of Reason' against the Christian Morality of Feeling

I shall begin with the long aphorism that closes out the first chapter of Volume I of the two-volume *Human, All Too Human*. In this aphorism, Nietzsche refers to the man who, like himself, has liberated himself from the fetters of conventional norms and values and lives only to 'discern (*erkennen*) better'. Such a man must be able 'to forgo (*verzichten*) without envy and irritation' all the myriad 'untruths' enshrined in custom, law and tradition under which mankind habitually lives (HH 34, KSA 2:55). The severity of this self-denial is illustrated a few pages later, in the second chapter, in a passage on the ascetic rigours of the Jesuit priests. Opening with the astute observation that 'No power can maintain itself if its representatives are patent hypocrites', followed by the more contentious assertion that the Catholic Church, material wealth notwithstanding, derives its strength from the Jesuits' harsh but earnest discipline of 'self-overcoming', Nietzsche goes on to affirm that the only thing distinguishing these priestly natures from the more contemplative natures is a difference in insight. He ends the aphorism by asking whether 'we enlightened ones would be . . . equally admirable in self-conquest (*Selbstbesiegung*), tirelessness or devotion' (HH 55, KSA 2:74–5) – a question that is neither rhetorical nor ironic. On the contrary, it lauds a particular set of qualities traditionally associated with the Jesuit priest and which, as the subsequent chapters of this monograph will detail, constitute a necessary prerequisite for anyone seeking to impose upon themselves Zarathustra's draconian doctrine of self-overcoming.

Also in the second chapter of *Human, All Too Human*, Nietzsche counterposes the 'morality of the mature individual' to what he refers to as the 'impersonal' morality of custom and tradition (HH 95, KSA 2:91–2). The latter, he asserts, will apply the term 'good' to any act that conforms to a long-established law or tradition, which law or tradition is ultimately and primarily concerned with the preservation of the community (HH 96, KSA 2:92–3).[7] Such an act has the added advantage of being accompanied by a pleasurable sensation on account of its having been sanctioned by custom, having proved itself to be useful and, in the fullness of time, having acquired both moral stature and the unthinking ease of habit (HH 97, KSA 2:94). The 'morality of the mature individual', on the other hand, will determine the goodness of an act not in accordance with what has long been deemed to be in the interests of the community, nor indeed by any attendant sensation of pleasure, but by the individual's mature and discriminating judgement as to whether the act in question will be in his *own* best interest. This interest (to be further discussed in Chapter 3), avers Nietzsche, will be understood by the mature individual solely in terms of wholeness or self-completion: 'to make of oneself a complete *person* and in all that one does to keep in view the *highest good* of this person' (HH 95, KSA 2:92).

Nietzsche's emphasis on the 'highest good' of the individual, rather than on the overall good of the community, reads like an ironic inversion of Jeremy Bentham's utilitarian maxim of 'the greatest good for the greatest number'. But if Nietzsche prioritises the highest good of the one over that of the many – a core premise of his counter-Christian morality – he is far from advocating rampant individualism.[8] Indeed, in an 1885 notebook fragment, he dismisses as 'utterly nonsensical' Bentham's attempt to prove that 'it is moral to do what satisfies our interest . . . and [that] that alone is supposed to be morality' (KSA 11:34[239]:500). To the contrary, Nietzsche believes that we ought to work for our fellow men (a belief to which I shall return later in this chapter), but not at the expense of sacrificing the individual to either the state or to the needs of others. Rather than succumb to 'those compassionate impulses (*Regungen*)[9] and actions for the benefit of others', he argues, we should first ascertain our own 'highest advantage' and only then seek to realise it in working towards the greater good. How one perceives that advantage, however, will all depend on whether one is a mature, rational individual or an 'immature, undeveloped, coarse individual' (HH 95, KSA 2:92). As he points out in a contiguous aphorism, what appears to a particular individual to be good or useful for him will be relative to 'the degree of his intellect, the measure of his rationality at any given time' (HH 102, KSA 2:99). It will also depend on the degree of his self-knowledge, the universal paucity of which, according to Nietzsche, renders the words 'Know thyself', 'when addressed by a god to a human being, well-nigh malicious' (GS 335, KSA 3:560).

The unit of measurement with which Nietzsche gauges the level of a person's intellect and, by extension, their maturity is the degree to which the intellect of that person is able to assert its authority over the affects. This degree, he asserts, can be inferred from an individual's propensity to yield to the aforesaid 'compassionate impulses':

> *Morality of compassion in the mouth of the immoderate.* – All those who do not have enough control of themselves and do not know morality as a continual self-restraint (*Selbstbeherrschung*) and self-overcoming (*Selbstüberwindung*) practised in the great and in the smallest of things, involuntarily become glorifiers of the good, compassionate, benevolent impulses (*Regungen*), of that instinctive morality (*instinktiven Moralität*) which has no head but seems to consist solely of heart and helping hands. It is indeed in their interest to cast aspersions on a morality of reason and to make of that other morality the only one. (WS 45, KSA 2:573-4)

Once again, Nietzsche relegates the New Testament virtue of compassion to a commonplace human impulse and sets above it the faculty of reason.[10] But whereas in the earlier-cited aphorisms (HH 95-7), the emphasis had been on reason's independence (beyond the confines of custom and tradition) in its assessment of the merits or demerits of acceding to the 'compassionate impulses', in the indented citation above it is the rational levers of 'self-restraint' and 'self-overcoming' that are set against these impulses. What Nietzsche characterises here as an 'instinctive morality' of compassion[11] is repudiated as both immoderate and self-serving in contrast to 'a morality of reason' that seeks to curb the affects.[12]

A 'morality of reason' reads like a succinct definition of Kantian morality, the chief virtue of which is self-restraint. In the second part of his late work *The Metaphysics of Morals* (1797), under the subheading 'On the Doctrine of Virtue in Accordance with the Principle of Inner Freedom', Kant states that the two requirements for 'inner freedom' are to be master (*Meister*) of oneself (*animus sui compos*) and to have command (*Herr*) over oneself (*imperium in semetipsum*). Expressing it more narrowly, he specifies that one needs to tame (*zähmen*) the affects and to govern (*beherrschen*) the passions. Implicit here is a subtle distinction between an affect and a passion, which Kant fleshes out in the next section, entitled 'Virtue Requires, in the First Place, Governing (*Herrschaft*) Oneself'. In this section, Kant defines an affect as a (pre-reflexive) 'feeling', and a passion as 'a sensible *desire* that has become a lasting inclination', which suggests that while a blind instinct-driven affect can only ever be subdued, an object-driven passion is susceptible to discipline and direction. The example given by Kant is anger (affect) and hatred (passion), the first being an involuntary burst, while the second bears the mark of something festering and entrenched. 'Since virtue is based on inner freedom', concludes Kant, 'it contains a positive command to a man, namely to bring all his capacities and inclinations [passions] under his (reason's) control and so to rule over himself' (AA 6:407–8).[13] It is this type of inner freedom, by means of which one rules over oneself, that is enjoined by Zarathustra and constitutes the critical focus of Chapter 2.

In *Zarathustra*, the person who has the capacity not only to bring his passions under rational control, but to channel them towards a self-determining goal, is 'the discerning one (*der Erkennende*)' (Z1 'On the Hinterlanders', KSA 4:37 and *passim*). These 'awakened' and 'knowing ones (*Wissende*)' (Z1 'On the Despisers of the Body', KSA 4:39) will possess the requisite intellectual maturity to calibrate the claims of head and heart, together with the equally necessary powers of discernment to discriminate between hot-headed acts and cool-headed acts, between 'hot toads' and 'cold frogs' (Z1 'On the Three Metamorphoses', KSA 4:29) and between a summery heart and a sultry, clammy heart (Z2 'On the Rabble', KSA 4:124–6). Most importantly of all, such maturity is shown to be the hard-won privilege of those rare individuals who have subjected their own head and heart to a dual baptism of fire and ice. As we shall see in the next section, not until thought and feeling, in the mind's pursuit of truth and self-knowledge, have been subjected to the metaphorical extremes of desert heat and mountain frost can one presume to know.

A couple of brief examples will afford a preliminary glimpse into Zarathustra's method of adjudicating between the competing claims of head and heart. The first example is taken from Zarathustra's discourse 'On the Compassionate (*Mitleidigen*)' – an abiding concern in Nietzsche's work, not least because he knew compassion to be his Achilles heel. As he freely admits in *The Gay Science*, were he to expose himself to the sight of dire distress, he too would be lost (GS 338, KSA 3:567).[14] In Zarathustra's discourse 'On the Compassionate' (KSA 4:113–16), Nietzsche reprises the attack he had launched in *Human, All Too Human* on the benevolent impulses of the heart and censures those who yield to them for thoughtless self-indulgence. Such 'merciful' ones, he observes, are too 'blissful in their compassion; they are too much lacking in shame'. Enveloped in the heart-warming glow of their benevolence and 'blissfully' unaware of the shame it may cause, they are swept away by their heart. 'Hold fast to your heart', counsels Zarathustra, 'for if one lets it go, how quickly one then loses one's head!' And as we have already seen, the ones most likely to lose their head the fastest are in Nietzsche's view those immature, immoderate types who are least able to conquer their compassion.[15]

The second example also relates to the benevolent impulse, but a benevolent impulse of a very different kind to the one cited above. Far from being an emotional reflex, this particular type of benevolent impulse is the product of both head and heart. Zarathustra calls it 'the bestowing virtue' or a 'bestowing love' and it is this impulse 'to bestow and distribute' (ZP 1, KSA 4:11) that prompts him to leave the rarefied air of Alpine contemplation to impart his wisdom to the inhabitants of the figurative lowlands. Unlike the Christian virtue of compassion, the bestowing virtue takes cognisance of the fact that overtly compassionate acts induce not only greater suffering in the pitied object, but also ill will: 'Great obligations do not make people grateful, but vengeful' (Z2 'On the Compassionate', KSA 4:114). Imbued with the knowledge that its bestowal of wisdom is aimed at minimising shame, a bestowing love is a deliberative act rather than a blind, thoughtless impulse. Accordingly, while both the Christian and non-Christian types of benevolence emanate from the heart, only one takes counsel from the head.

Returning to Nietzsche's middle works, one can trace in them a clear line of argumentation setting the forces of reason against those of unbridled emotion. In *Daybreak*, for example, Nietzsche denounces Christianity for branding doubt, reflection and rationality as sinful activities and for promoting in their stead 'blindness and frenzy and an eternal song over the waves in which reason has drowned!' (D 89, KSA 3:83). He also charges Christianity with supplanting the ancient philosophical concept of virtue qua 'victory of reason over affect' with the 'virtue' of affective indulgence. This latter, he argues, is nurtured and sanctified by Christianity as '*love* of God, *fear* of God, as fanatical *belief* in God, as the blindest *hope* in God' (D 58, KSA 3:59). Nietzsche's concern is not, however, for the 'infatuated' Christian. Rather, it is for the integrity of philosophy and for the rich legacy of rational enquiry that was bequeathed to man by the Enlightenment and that in Nietzsche's view continues to be compromised by the residual effects of Christianity's cultivation of feeling. However, as Nietzsche was to observe six years later in his newly added Book V of *The Gay Science*, the scientific rigour of Enlightenment thought was itself a late blossom of Christian moral truthfulness: 'One can see what has actually triumphed over the Christian God: Christian morality itself, the concept of truthfulness taken ever more strictly, the Father-Confessor's refinement of the Christian conscience, translated and sublimated into a scientific conscience, into intellectual cleanliness at any price' (GS 357, KSA 3:600, also cited by Nietzsche in GM III 27, KSA 5:409–10).

A notable example for Nietzsche of the triumph of Christian morality over Enlightenment thought is Arthur Schopenhauer, whose atheistic philosophy had 'killed off' God many years prior to Nietzsche's parabolic madman distractedly seeking the moribund God in *Gay Science* 125 (KSA 3:480-2). What Nietzsche discerned in the work of his earliest and greatest 'educator'[16] was not just the rigour of Enlightenment reason, but the aforesaid traces of Christianity's cultivation of feeling. On the one hand, Nietzsche admired Schopenhauer's preference for hard facts and rational clarity; 'the strength of his intellectual conscience', evidence of which Nietzsche found in what he judged to be the many contradictions in Schopenhauer's work; and his utter fastidiousness in all matters pertaining to the Christian God and its church, 'for in this he was cleaner than all previous German philosophers, such that he lived and died "a Voltairean"'.[17] On the other hand, Nietzsche deplored Schopenhauer's positing of compassion as the source of all morality[18] and such 'mystical embarrassments' (GS 99, KSA 3: 453-4) as his belief in the Buddhistic dissolution of the many into the One[19] and the Kantian-inspired notion of a pure (disinterested) will-less contemplation of a work of art through which the contemplator intuits 'the eternal Ideas' and thereby communes with or dissolves into the noumenal realm.[20]

Nietzsche had his own share of mystical embarrassments, including the following unabashedly Schopenhauerian passage from his first published work, *The Birth of Tragedy*:

> in the blissful ecstasy which rises from the innermost ground of man, indeed of nature itself, whenever the shattering of the *principium individuationis* occurs, we catch a glimpse of the essence of the *Dionysian*, which is best conveyed by the analogy of *intoxication*. (BT 1, KSA 1:28)

But if Nietzsche was soon to distance himself from these mystical-Romantic effusions, we should not on that account presume to dismiss his post-*Birth of Tragedy* enthusiasm for the Age of Reason as a temporary corrective measure, a brief 'positivist' interlude between the Romanticism of his first work and the anti-Romanticism of his later works.[21] On the contrary, the argument I am advancing in this monograph is that the weight given by Nietzsche to reason over passion in the three published works that immediately preceded *Zarathustra* is equally pronounced in the latter text.

Nietzsche's Self-Eviscerating 'Morality of Sacrifice'

In his middle works, Nietzsche not only pits a 'morality of reason' against the Christian morality of feeling, but tasks his own reason with the identification and dissection of 'those heavy and pregnant errors contained in moral, religious and metaphysical concepts' (WS 350, KSA 2:702) – a dissection which fills the pages of both his published and unpublished work. Among the aforesaid errors, one to which he repeatedly returns is the Christian virtue of so-called selflessness or self-sacrifice. Be it love of one's neighbour, benevolent acts, or absolute devotion to God, Nietzsche detects behind each of these ostensibly unegoistic or self-effacing gestures an egoistic need for gratification. Of neighbourly love, Nietzsche simply has this to say:

> The most senile thing ever thought about man is contained in the famous phrase 'the ego is always hateful'; the most childish, in the even more famous 'love thy neighbour as thyself'. – In the former, knowledge of human nature has ceased; in the latter, it has not even begun. (AOM 385, KSA 2:528)

He uses a much finer brush in his depiction of benevolence. Distinguishing between 'gushing sentimentalism (*Gefühlsschwärmerei*)' and a genuine desire to help, Nietzsche links the latter to 'purity (*Reinlichkeit*) of thought' and self-restraint, and the former to muddy thinking and 'a reckless will' (AOM 196, KSA: 2:464). As for the giving of oneself to God, Nietzsche dismisses this as no more than a surrender of oneself to oneself insofar as the source of the ecstasy accompanying such surrender is the 'intoxicating thought of now being at one with the Mighty Being' (D 215, KSA 3:192). In other words, what one believes to be self-sacrifice is nothing more than the ecstatic feeling of power and self-aggrandisement as one basks in the reflected glory of the object of devotion.

In *Daybreak* 215 (KSA 3:192), Nietzsche contradistinguishes this morality of 'intoxication and excess' from a 'sober morality, which demands self-restraint, severity, obedience' and 'duty' – a morality which bears all the hallmarks of the Jesuitical asceticism he had admired in Volume I of *Human, All Too Human*. It also bears distinct traces of the 'ascetic cruelty' that in *Daybreak* 339 (KSA 3:236) Nietzsche reads in Kant's demand that duty must always be felt as a burden and never become a matter of habit and custom. In place of the ecstasies of sacrifice and devotion, Nietzsche proposes a rational morality of 'real sacrifice and devotion' (ibid.), the nature of which is set out in *Daybreak* 221:

> The morality which measures itself according to sacrifice is at the semi-savage stage. Here reason has secured only a hard and bloody victory within the soul, where powerful counter-drives have to be overthrown; without this kind of cruelty, as with the sacrifices demanded by cannibal gods, there will be no victory. (D 221, KSA 3:195)

Nietzsche speaks from personal experience. In his retrospective 1886 preface to Volume II of *Human, All Too Human*,[22] he recounts his own savage suppression of the affects. Casting his mind back to the years between the publication of *The Birth of Tragedy* in 1872 and the first volume of *Human, All Too Human* published in 1878, he characterises this period as one of 'moral scepticism and anatomisation' (HH II P1, KSA 2:370). The purpose of this dissection was not, however, primarily speculative. Rather, it was intended to be a personal exercise in the kind of self-evisceration that Nietzsche euphemistically but emphatically terms '*overcomings* (*Überwindungen*)' (ibid.): 'I took sides *against* myself and *for* everything that hurts me and is particularly hard on *me*' (HH II P4, KSA 2:373).

In *Daybreak* 18, this morality of 'real sacrifice and devotion' is again shown to be *qualitatively* akin to its Christianised version. Under the heading 'The morality of voluntary suffering', Nietzsche offers a highly idiosyncratic account of the genealogical roots of the moral valorisation of voluntary suffering.

He argues that since 'cruelty belongs to the oldest festive joys of mankind . . . one thinks that even the gods are refreshed and festive when offered the sight of cruelty'. To this non-sequitur he attributes the value and meaning traditionally accorded to 'self-chosen torture (*Marter*)' and, by extension, man's subsequent suspicion that suffering is more beloved of the gods than excessive well-being. What is interesting here is not the uncharacteristic looseness of Nietzsche's deductive reasoning, but that instead of repudiating this 'morality of voluntary suffering' as an egregious form of self-harm, he endorses it as a salutary exercise in self-discipline:

> the virtue of the most frequent suffering, of privation, of the hard way of life, of cruel mortification – *not*, to repeat it again and again, as a means of discipline, of self-restraint, of satisfying the desire for individual happiness – but as a virtue which will put the community in good odour with the evil gods and which steams up to them like a perennial propitiatory sacrifice on the altar. (D 18, KSA 3:30–2)[23]

What is viscerally depicted here is not only the suffering and privation to which Nietzsche voluntarily subjected himself in his post-*Birth of Tragedy* interregnum, but its 'frequent' returns, as satirised in Part 4 of *Zarathustra* and to be discussed in the final section of this chapter.[24] Once again, the above passage marks the difference between the 'cruel mortification' practised by the Christian ascetic and the same mortification inflicted by Nietzsche on himself as one of orientation. Whereas the pagan's sacrifice is an act of appeasement performed in the interests of the community, Nietzsche's self-dissection and self-abnegation is performed in the disciplined 'self-interest' and 'self-restraint' of the mature individual.

Equally striking is the parallel Nietzsche goes on to draw between those intrepid spiritual leaders whose opposition to established practices gave rise to pangs of compunction followed by penitential self-flagellation and the free-spirited progenitors of new ideas whose 'heroic souls' also suffer in their kindred opposition to a regnant moral paradigm:

Every smallest step in the field of free thought, of a life shaped personally, has always had to be fought for with spiritual and bodily tortures: not only the step forward, no! the step itself, movement, change has needed its countless martyrs throughout all the long path-seeking and ground-laying millennia ... and within this so-called world-history ... there is in fact no more important subject than the age-old tragedy of the martyrs *who wanted to stir up the swamp.* (D 18, KSA 3:31)

Nietzsche's rationale for linking these two vastly different mindsets is what he describes as their shared 'logic of feeling' consequent upon such swamp stirring. What Nietzsche means by this oxymoronic expression is not entirely clear, but one interpretation might be that pain axiomatically follows 'every smallest step in the field of free thought'. However, whereas the feeling that attends the torments of the groundbreaking spiritual leader is remorse for having defied the moral paradigm, that of the secular martyr is a mixture of 'awe and dread' (D 14, KSA 3:27). A striking example of this is Nietzsche's 'madman', already alluded to in the previous section. A not entirely ironic epithet for 'all those superior men who were irresistibly drawn to throw off the yoke of any kind of morality and to enact new laws' (ibid.), Nietzsche's madman asks how we, the murderers of God, can possibly atone for having killed 'the holiest and mightiest' of beings. 'Who will wipe this blood from us? With what water are we to cleanse ourselves? ... Must we not have to become gods ourselves just to appear worthy of it?' (GS 125, KSA 3:481). In *Zarathustra*, we learn that this godly role entails the creation of new laws and, most importantly, the willingness to submit oneself to these self-imposed laws (to be discussed in the next chapter). In the earlier *Daybreak*, however, Nietzsche asks whether these new laws ought to be imposed on others.

Do 'Free-Spirited Moralists' have the Right to Inflict their Cruelty on Others?

While the epithet 'free-spirited moralists' is taken from *Daybreak* 209 (KSA 3: 189),[25] the above question is the subject of *Daybreak*

436 (KSA 3:267–8) in which this 'agonising' dilemma is presented in the form of Plato's ship of fools allegory.[26] In this aphorism, Nietzsche compares the man of insight and superior intelligence to that of a passenger on a ship who realises that the captain and helmsman are nautically incompetent. The said passenger also realises, however, that if he incites a mutiny there is a very real danger of the entire ship going down. The question that 'always' remains, concludes Nietzsche, is 'what guarantees us our superiority, our belief in ourselves?' He confronts the same dilemma in *Daybreak* 108. But in this aphorism, instead of focusing on the conflict between responsibility and self-doubt in the mind of the man of superior intelligence – the type of man whom Zarathustra refers to as 'the discerning one' (Z1 'On the Hinterlanders', KSA 4:37 and *passim*), Nietzsche questions both the wisdom and practicability of trying to impose a moral law on mankind in the absence of a 'universally recognised goal':

> Only if mankind possessed a universally recognised *goal* would it be possible to propose 'such and such should be done': at present there is no such goal. It is thus unreasonable and foolish to impose the demands of morality upon mankind. – To *commend* a goal to mankind is something completely different: the goal is then thought of as something which *lies in our own discretion*; supposing that mankind favoured the commendation, it could thereupon also *impose* upon itself a moral law, likewise out of its own choice. (D 108, KSA 3:96)

The protagonist-prophet of *Zarathustra* has no such qualms. He neither proposes nor commends his far from universally recognised goal to mankind. On the contrary, he tries to impose it first on the public, then on a handful of acolytes or pupils – a pedagogic shift precipitated by his early realisation that the most rudimentary of rhetorical weapons such as blandishments and sophistry are not in his demagogic arsenal. Even among his followers he is wont to adopt a tone as imperative as it is hortatory. And whereas the Nietzsche of *Daybreak* believes that no universally recognised goal currently exists, Zarathustra is actively engaged in the promulgation of what he declares to be a universally applicable end, namely the goal of humanity:

> A thousand goals have there been until now, for there have been a thousand peoples. Only the fetter for the thousand necks is still lacking, the one goal is lacking. Humanity still has no goal. (Z1 'On the Thousand and One Goals', KSA 4:76)

As Zarathustra reminds us in the summative chapter entitled 'On Old and New Law Tables', not only is humanity in need of a goal; it is a goal that can only be bestowed by 'the creator!' Only the creator 'creates a goal for man' and thereby 'gives the earth its meaning and its future' (Z3 'On Old and New Tablets' 2, KSA 4:247). The creator of this goal and this meaning is none other than Zarathustra himself: 'Behold, I teach you the *Übermensch*!' he proclaims in his inaugural speech before a scoffing market-square crowd; 'The *Übermensch* is the meaning of the earth' (ZP 3, KSA 4:14).

In another *Daybreak* passage on the question of a universal goal, Nietzsche writes of the necessity for any such goal to be clearly defined. Under the heading 'Against the definitions of the goal of morality', Nietzsche dismisses the stock definition of the day, namely that the goal of morality is 'the preservation and advancement of mankind', as an empty formula. What needs to be clarified, he insists, is the 'preservation *of what?*' the 'advancement *to what?*' For in the absence of this information 'our duty' necessarily lacks a moral compass. What precisely are we to keep in view, he asks. Is it 'the longest possible existence of mankind? Or the greatest possible de-animalisation of mankind?' To which he then adds:

> How different the means, that is to say the practical morality, would have to be in the two cases! Suppose one wanted to bestow on mankind the highest possible rationality: this would certainly not guarantee it the longest possible duration! (D 106, KSA 3:93–4)

If, as seems to be the case here, Nietzsche is saying that the practical morality most conducive to the greatest possible de-animalisation of mankind is one that prescribes the highest possible rationality, then he is arguably, if unwittingly, endorsing Kant's position in his famous essay on enlightenment.

Responding to the question 'What is enlightenment?' Kant defines enlightenment as man's emergence from his voluntary, infantile dependence on others in the matter of knowledge. '*Sapere aude*! [Dare to know]', he exhorts; 'Have courage to make use of your *own* understanding!' (AA 8:35).[27] What is most striking here in terms of a consonance of ideas between the two thinkers is not Kant's insistence on independent thought but his appeal to courage – a virtue which Nietzsche unequivocally extols throughout his work and which, like Kant, he values most in the realm of rational inquiry. In *Daybreak* 551, under the heading 'Of future virtues', Nietzsche imagines a time when 'courage in thinking will have grown so great that . . . the sage, as the most courageous, will see himself and existence farthest beneath him' (KSA 3:321). Reflecting on his own feats of courageous thinking prior to writing *Human, All Too Human* and on the protracted illness that followed in its wake, Nietzsche lauds men who possess the necessary courage to overcome the age ('*Zeit-Überwinder*') in which they live: 'you rare, most imperilled, most intellectual (*geistig*), most courageous men, who have to be the *conscience* of the modern soul and as such must have *knowledge*'. In men such as these, among whom he indubitably counts himself, 'all that exists today of sickness, poison and danger comes together' (HH II P6, KSA 2:376).

Returning to Kant's 'What is Enlightenment?', while 'laziness and cowardice (*Faulheit und Feigheit*)' (AA 8:35) are the reasons Kant gives for man's adult infancy and lack of courage, he reserves his sharpest criticism for society's self-appointed guardians. It is these purported custodians of knowledge whom he holds responsible for having promoted and perpetuated, largely through religious means, this dual state of passivity and timidity. Their dictums and nostrums, he argues, 'make their domestic animals dumb and carefully prevented these placid creatures from daring to take a single step without the walking cart in which they have confined them' (ibid.). Compare this statement with the following broadside delivered by Zarathustra:

> At bottom, these simple ones simply want one thing most: that no one should harm them. So they pre-empt everyone by doing a good deed.
>
> But this is *cowardice*, even if it is called 'virtue' . . .
>
> To them virtue is whatever makes humble and docile: with it they made the wolf into a dog and man himself into man's best domestic animal. (Z3 'Of the Virtue that Makes Small' 2, KSA 4:214)

Kant, Nietzsche and Zarathustra all agree that it is from the precepts and proscriptions of guardians such as these that domesticated man must now break free. And the person whose duty it is to coax man out of this timidity, asserts Kant, is the rare individual who has successfully cast off the yoke of tutelage. Having done so, he ought 'to make *public use* of [his] reason in all matters' by submitting his enlightened ideas to the reading public. To which assertion he categorically adds: 'The *public* use of one's own reason must always be free, and it alone can bring about enlightenment among human beings' (AA 8:36-7).[28]

Nietzsche's works, I would argue, bespeak above all else a Kantian duty to enlighten man[29] – a duty, moreover, that Nietzsche felt compelled to perform and for which he suffered not only on his own account, but on account of those who were about to taste the bitter fruits of his superior understanding:

> *Twofold patience* – 'You will cause thereby pain to many people'. I know; and I also know that I shall have to suffer twice for it: once through compassion for their suffering and then through the revenge they will take on me. Nevertheless, it is no less necessary to do as I do. (D 467, KSA 3:280)

Nietzsche confesses to the same deeply felt yet inwardly contained compassion in *Gay Science* 311, but also to sporadic doubt over the necessity of inflicting such pain on others: 'One is not always brave; and when one gets tired, one of us is also likely to lament: "It is so hard to hurt people – oh, why is it necessary!"' (KSA 3:547). Despite this inner conflict and the occasional pang of compunction (the 'logic of feeling', perhaps, adverted to above), Nietzsche deemed the infliction of suffering on others to be an unavoidable consequence of carrying the Enlightenment torch forward (WS 221, KSA 2:654). With his own reluctant and vulnerable benefactors in mind, he cautions the wise man 'not to resemble a steamroller which advances like a fatality'.[30] Rather, he must temper the severity of his teaching by openly admitting to his own faults and foibles (D 469, KSA 3:281), as Nietzsche himself does: 'Here are my shortcomings and mistakes, here is my delusion, my bad taste, my confusion, my tears, my vanity, my owlish seclusion, my contradictions!' (GS 311, KSA 3:547).

It is a piece of advice which Zarathustra signally fails to heed. Steamrolling into the market square at the start of *Zarathustra*, the protagonist-prophet taunts and insults the bemused crowd in his eagerness to impart his new goal for mankind, namely the *Übermensch*. 'It is time for man to fix his goal' (ZP 5, KSA 4:19), he declaims,

> Man is something that is to be overcome. What have you done to overcome him?
>
> All beings hitherto have created something beyond themselves: and you want to be the ebb of this great flood and would rather go back to the animal than overcome man? . . .
>
> You have made your way from worm to human, and much of you is still worm. Once you were apes, and even now man is more ape than any ape. (ZP 3, KSA 4:14)

The immediate goal of Zarathustra's project of de-animalising man is to forestall any further atavistic decline. For what Zarathustra fears is an accelerated diminution of mankind to the debased level of 'the last man' – the type of man, already thick on the ground, who lives in warm, bovine happiness; who derives comfort from the homogeneity of the herd; and 'who can no longer despise himself' (ZP 5, KSA 4:19). If mankind is to entertain any hope of overcoming its gradual domestication, this herd-like spirit must be crushed.[31]

One of the first steps towards vanquishing the herd spirit is the renunciation of what Nietzsche refers to as the 'bourgeois morality' of preserving the well-being of our neighbour at all costs. As he wryly observes, if we are to treat our neighbour as we do ourselves, then the free-spirited moralist should require his neighbour to undergo the same rigours of self-sacrifice that he himself has done:

> Why should a few individuals of the present generation not be sacrificed to coming generations? so that their grief, their unease, their despair, their mistakes and fearful steps would be found necessary, because a new ploughshare is to break up the ground and make it fruitful for all? (D 146, KSA 3:138)

'Fruitful for all' brings us back to Kant's 'What is Enlightenment?' and to that 'world society of citizens' to which the rare, enlightened individual is duty-bound to impart the fruits of his reason. However bitter the fruits, however keen the edge of the ploughshare's blade and however tenacious the blighted harvest of Christian morality, the enlightened individual must steel himself against compassion: 'not to perish from inner distress and uncertainty when one inflicts great suffering and hears the cry of this suffering' is for Nietzsche the true mark of greatness (GS 325, KSA 3:553; see also D 467 cited above).

Austerity and Artifice

If Nietzsche had occasional misgivings over the shattering and irreversible effects that his violation of moral 'pieties' (GS 4, KSA 3:376) would have on those courageous enough to attempt a self-evisceration of their Christian heritage – the ropedancer plunging to his death in 'Zarathustra's Prologue' is an obvious case in point – he was utterly ruthless when it came to his own soul. In the second of his late prefaces to *Human, All Too Human*, Nietzsche recalls the severity of his earlier overcomings. The principal target of these was emotional excess: not of Christian piety, which he had shed somewhere between Schulpforta and the University of Bonn,[32] but of Romanticism.

> I was sick, more than sick ... nauseated by the femininity and rapturous indulgence of this Romanticism, by the whole idealist pack of lies and effeminacy of conscience ... I began to *forbid* myself, totally and on principle, all Romantic music, that ambiguous, meretricious, oppressive art that deprives the spirit of its severity and cheerfulness and allows every kind of vague longing and spongy desire to run riot. (HH II P3, KSA 2:372–3)

The foremost purveyors of this 'most dangerous form of Romanticism' (ibid.), avers Nietzsche, were Schopenhauer and Richard Wagner. As early as 1874, Nietzsche was writing disapprovingly of what he saw as an egregious lack of restraint and moderation in Wagner[33] – two virtues which, as we have already seen, lie at the moral heart of *Human, All Too Human*.[34] It was not until 1888, however, shortly before insanity engulfed him, that Nietzsche unleashed *The Case of Wagner: A Musician's Problem*, swiftly followed by *Nietzsche Contra Wagner*. While the latter provides a retrospective account of its titular antithesis, the former mounts a full-scale attack on the man who had been the greatest living influence on the young classical philologist and to whose innovative form of epic music drama Nietzsche's *Birth of Tragedy* stands as a near-hagiographic tribute.

In the first of these two texts on Wagner, Nietzsche admits to having been 'one of the most corrupted Wagnerians' (CW 3, KSA 6:16). The source of this corruption, he tells us, is the insidiously seductive effect of Wagner's music on the emotions:

> There never was a greater master in stupefying hieratic perfumes – never lived such a connoisseur of *trifling*

infinities, of everything tremulous and rapturous, of all femininities from the idioticon of happiness! ... Ah, this old sorcerer! This Klingsor of Klingsors! How he wages war against *us* with [his art]! Against us, the free spirits! How he appeals to every faintheartedness of the modern soul with the feminine tones of his sorcery! There has never been such a *deadly hatred* of knowledge. One must be a cynic not to be seduced. (CW First Postscript, KSA 6:43-4)

Nietzsche was no cynic, of course. But if he believed in the innocence of the affects,[35] he was also acutely aware of the dangers of unbridled emotion and the even greater danger of trying to overcome them. Suffice to say that his '*anti-Romantic* self-treatment' (HH II P2, KSA 2:371) came at considerable personal cost. As he confides in one of his late prefaces, such a prolonged Jesuit-like asceticism necessitated an equally prolonged period of convalescence. Without it, he would not have been able to gain the requisite distance between himself and his former '*disciplina voluntatis*' to be able to record, 'for the sake of knowledge', the results of his self-dissection. But even at this distance, he confesses, it is not to be wondered at if 'some blood occasionally flows' (HH II P1-2, KSA 2:369-71). Nor, one might add, is it to be wondered at if the ghosts of these anti-Romantic overcomings come back to haunt him, as they do in Part 4 of *Zarathustra* (to be discussed below).

Zarathustra contains numerous allusions to the bloody business of self-overcoming and its aftermath. Indeed, Zarathustra's inaugural address to his followers principally pertains to the rigours of self-overcoming. In this key speech, which opens Part 1 of *Zarathustra*, the self-inflicted pain of loneliness and self-denial are figuratively and respectively represented by 'the desert' and 'the lion'. The former represents the battleground of self-conquest and is redolent of the Judean desert of the gospel narrative where Christ is said to have battled for forty days and forty nights against the temptations of Satan (Mark 1:12-13; Luke 4:1). In the *Zarathustra* narrative, the desert of self-overcoming is referred to as 'the loneliest desert', the adjectival superlative a recurring epithet for those brave enough to disembowel their internalised cultural heritage. The correlative lion connotes the ferocity of the nay-saying spirit, its savagery necessitated by the tenacity of entrenched values and Romantic enticements, and by a reason intent on eviscerating them. A fuller depiction of the lion spirit is given in Part 2 of *Zarathustra* in a discourse on the 'Famous Wise Men' (KSA 4:132–5). Unlike the self-deluded 'wise men', whose so-called wisdom is mired in mistaken truths, the genuine 'truthful ones' are those rare 'free spirits' who possess a lion spirit, or a 'lion-will', and dwell in scorching deserts. 'Hungry, violent, lonely, [and] godless', these truthful ones are willing to sacrifice themselves (not unlike the sacrificial beasts of the earlier-mentioned cannibal gods) on the altar of knowledge. 'Spirit is life that itself cuts into life', proclaims Zarathustra; 'by its own torment it increases its own knowledge' (Z2 'On the Famous Wise Men', KSA 4:134).

We encounter a similar metaphorical desert in Zarathustra's speech 'On the Way of the Creator'. The titular 'way' is the path to oneself and to the overcoming of oneself and is to be undertaken within the 'desolate (*öde*) space and icy breath of aloneness (*Alleinsein*)'. It is here that one must wage war on one's inner demons and be prepared for the inevitable day when the loneliness of the 'lonely one (*Einsamen*)' will fell both pride and courage and fill one with dread (*Furcht*) and despair. Feelings such as these, warns Zarathustra, 'want to kill the lonely one' (Z1 'On the Way of the Creator', KSA 4:80–3), just as they had wanted to kill Nietzsche in the years prior to the publication of *Human, All Too Human*. Once again, Nietzsche uses his retrospective prefaces to the latter work to reflect upon these 'desert' years of 'morbid isolation' and self-experimentation. He marks this period as one of an 'ever more threatening, choking, heart-constricting' solitude, beyond which lay the long road to 'that *mature* freedom of spirit which is equally self-restraint and discipline of the heart' (HH I P3–4, KSA 2:17–18). But as Zarathustra discovers in Part 4 of *Zarathustra*, such disciplined self-control is not a definitive goal but something one has to master again and again.

The fourth and final part of *Zarathustra* opens with the erstwhile prophet comfortably ensconced in his mountain refuge and about to be ambushed in quick succession by each of his former demons.[36] The most tenacious of these, we are told, are his compassion and Romantic pessimism. The latter is allegorically represented as both 'the soothsayer' and 'the sorcerer', who in turn respectively represent the Romantic enticements of Schopenhauer and Wagner. It was through the works of these two giants that Nietzsche succumbed to the most seductive and, for him personally, most treacherous forms of Romantic pessimism. The seductions of Wagner's art and the mystical effusions of Schopenhauer's philosophy have already been alluded to above. For the dangers of Schopenhauerian pessimism, one need look no further than Part 4 of *Zarathustra*. In a chapter entitled 'The Cry of Distress', a happily sequestered Zarathustra is intruded upon by the sudden appearance of 'the soothsayer' – that 'prophet of great weariness' whom Zarathustra had, figuratively speaking, 'once wined and dined at his table'. It is the same soothsayer whose pessimistic doctrine 'Everything is empty, everything is the same, everything has been' had afflicted Zarathustra so grievously towards the end of Part 2 that he could neither eat, drink, speak nor sleep for three days (Z2, 'The Soothsayer', KSA 4:172). Catching sight of the soothsayer, Zarathustra immediately recalls and rehearses the pessimistic mantra that had felled him in Part 2: 'Everything is the same, nothing is worthwhile, the world is meaningless, knowledge chokes' (Z4 'The Cry of Distress', KSA 4:300), a mantra which encapsulates Schopenhauer's grim pronouncements on the value of earthly existence and which Zarathustra (and Nietzsche too, of course) had imbibed in his formative years.[37]

Romantic pessimism is not, however, the only danger stalking Zarathustra in his mountain sanctuary. A far more treacherous inner demon, we are told, is Zarathustra's compassion (*Mitleid*), which in Part 3 of *Zarathustra* he had referred to as 'the deepest abyss' (Z3 'On the Vision and Riddle' 1, KSA 4:199). Here in his Part 4 encounter with the soothsayer, it is Zarathustra's compassion for the 'higher men' which takes centre stage. These 'higher men' are the ones who had the courage to plunge themselves into the icy waters of knowledge, as Nietzsche and Zarathustra have done, but who never fully recovered from their hypothermic recoil (Z2 'On the Exalted Ones', KSA 4:150-2). It is to this 'final sin' of compassion that the soothsayer has come to seduce Zarathustra. Alerting him to the higher men's cry of distress and standing calmly by to watch Zarathustra teeter on the brink of abyssal compassion, the soothsayer gently taunts: '"Oh Zarathustra", he began with a sad voice; "you stand not like one whose happiness makes him giddy: you will have to dance if you don't want to keel over!"' Whereupon Zarathustra pulls himself together and beats a hasty retreat, the words of his (inner) tormentor ringing sharply in his ears:

> 'I know you want to be rid of me! You would rather run into the woods and stalk evil animals!
> 'But how will that help you? In the evening you will have me back again, sitting there in your own cave, patient and heavy like a log – and waiting for you!' (Z4 'The Cry of Distress', KSA 4:303)

With these words in mind, it is hard to view Zarathustra's 'rosy crown of laughter', a ubiquitous stage prop throughout Part 4, with anything but suspicion.[38]

And yet, it is to laughter, however confected, that Nietzsche turns for '*this-worldly* comfort' (AS 7, KSA 1:22), when the ferocity of sacrifice and self-overcoming threatens to vanquish his lion spirit. In answer to his own question, 'To what extent can truth stand to be incorporated?' (GS 110, KSA 3:471), he writes: to the extent that truth can be converted into untruth. Only 'as an aesthetic phenomenon is existence still *endurable* for us', for without art:

> *Honesty* would result in disgust and suicide . . . we need all exuberant, floating, dancing, mocking, childish and blissful art in order not to lose that *freedom over things* which our ideal demands of us. It would be a *relapse* for us, especially with our irritable honesty, to get completely caught up in morality and for the sake of the overly severe demands we duly make on ourselves to become virtuous monsters and

scarecrows. We should *be able* to stand *above* morality: and not only stand with the anxious rigidity of someone who is afraid of slipping and falling at any moment, but also hover and play above it! How then could we dispense with art and the fool? (GS 107, KSA 3:464-5)[39]

These are weighty admissions that ought to give every reader of Nietzsche serious pause. On the one hand, we have Nietzsche's moral 'ideal' – an ideal that makes such 'overly severe demands' on the advocate and initiate of that ideal that he either becomes a 'virtuous monster' or is driven to 'suicide'. On the other, we have the jester's stock-in-trade – Nietzsche's preferred and life-preserving diversion from the 'irritable honesty' that drives him to ever more heroic feats of self-destruction.

The art of playing the fool, not in motley but in self-parody, is on full display in Part 4 of *Zarathustra*.[40] Indeed, the whole of Part 4 can be read as an elaborately staged exercise in self-parody qua 'aesthetic phenomenon'. We have already seen how the soothsayer, the first of Zarathustra's spectres of past overcomings, mocks the erstwhile prophet for having mislaid his cap and bells and exhibited what is described in the indented citation above as 'the anxious rigidity' of someone who is afraid of succumbing to his inner demons. Another Part 4 self-parody is the conscientious man of the spirit: a black-comedic caricature of Nietzsche's intellectual honesty, the cardinal virtue in his ascetic morality:

> I am *the conscientious of spirit* . . . and in matters of the spirit one can hardly be stricter, narrower and harder than I, except the one from whom I learned it, Zarathustra himself.

> Better to know nothing than to half-know a lot! Better to be a fool on one's own account than a wise man according to a stranger's judgment. I – get to the bottom of things . . .

> Where my honesty ends, I am blind and also want to be blind. But where I want to know, I also want to be honest, namely hard, strict, narrow, cruel and inexorable.

What *you* once said, O Zarathustra: 'Spirit is life which itself cuts into life', is what led and seduced me to your teaching. And, truly, with my own blood I increased my own knowledge!' (Z4 'The Leech', KSA 4:311-12)

We meet another allegorised self-projection in Part 1 of *Zarathustra*, namely Zarathustra's despair and self-doubt, presented to us in the guise of a young man:

> I no longer trust myself since I sought out the heights . . . the frost of loneliness makes me shiver . . .
>
> How ashamed I am of my climbing and stumbling! How I jeer at my heavy breathing! How I hate the one who flies! How weary I am on the heights! (Z1 'On the Tree on the Mountain', KSA 4:52)

Once again, the ironic stance of self-parody is laced with self-mockery, but whereas in Part 4 the jeers are muted by comic caricature, here they simply add to the pathos of loneliness and failure.

It is illuminating to read the above-cited lines alongside *Daybreak* 14. In this aphorism, bearing the heading 'The morality of voluntary suffering', Nietzsche ridicules the Indian medicine-man, the medieval Christian saint, the angekok of Greenland and the Brazilian pajee for their extreme ascetic abstinence. Behind the mockery, however, can be discerned the compassion of a fellow-sufferer:

> Who dares to take a look into the wilderness of bitterest and most superfluous agonies of soul in which probably the most fruitful men of all times have languished! To hear the sighs of these lonely and stricken ones: 'Ah give me madness, you heavenly powers . . . terrify me with frost and fire such as no mortal has ever felt . . . so that I may come to believe in myself! I am consumed by doubt, I have killed the law. (KSA 3:26-8)

As I have intimated above via other Nietzsche passages, it is the same frost and fire, the same icy breath of aloneness, that the creator must suffer if he is to break the chains of the old moral law and frame the new. In the following chapters, the (superfluous?) agonies of suffering, sacrifice, self-negation and devotion, all vigorously advocated by Nietzsche in his middle works, will be shown to be conditional upon a Kantian rational will, a Hegelian 'labour of the negative' and the kind of sacrificial suffering that Feuerbach deifies as the highest form of human love.

Notes

1. Cf. 'Blindness in the presence of Christianity is the *crime* par excellence – the crime against life' (EH 'Why I am a Destiny' 7, KSA 6:371).
2. *Assorted Opinions and Maxims* and *The Wanderer and His Shadow* were first published in 1879 and 1880, respectively, as a continuation and addendum to Volume I of *Human, All Too Human*. It was not until 1886, when Volume I of the latter was re-released, that Nietzsche combined these two formerly independent texts to form Volume II of *Human, All Too Human* and published both volumes under the same title.
3. Horst Hutter likewise eschews the scholarly convention of dividing Nietzsche's corpus into early, middle and late periods and of privileging the later at the expense of the earlier. While acknowledging a developmental aspect to Nietzsche's thought, Hutter points out that this development has 'the structure of a living entelechy, in which later stages recuperate earlier ones and earlier ones hold in themselves all grounds of future unfolding.' Horst Hutter, *Shaping the Future: Nietzsche's New Regime of the Soul and Its Ascetic Practices* (Lanham, MD: Lexington Books, 2006), p. 4. Paul Franco also argues for a more fluid, more porous approach to the relationship between Nietzsche's middle and late works. Paul Franco, *Nietzsche's Enlightenment: The Free-Spirit Trilogy of the Middle Period* (Chicago and London: The University of Chicago Press, 2011).
4. As Keith Ansell-Pearson notes in the preamble to his study on Nietzsche's three middle works, 'it is something of a myth to contrast the middle and late periods [of Nietzsche's thought] in

terms of "soft" and "hard" Nietzsches'. Keith Ansell-Pearson, *Nietzsche's Search for Philosophy: On the Middle Writings* (London: Bloomsbury, 2018), p. 1. It is indeed a myth. And it is precisely the 'hard' rather than the 'soft' Nietzsche of the middle works that I shall be focusing on in this chapter.

5. '[G]iven the current state of knowledge, one can no longer have any truck with [Christianity] without utterly defiling one's intellectual conscience' (HH 109, KSA 2:108–9).

6. This citation from *The Gay Science*, together with the following line from *Zarathustra*, 'You planted your highest aim into the heart of these passions: there they became your virtues and joys' ('On the Joyful and Painful Passions'), militates against John Richardson's assertion that 'Nietzsche rejects agency's picture of itself as properly independent of the drives. He preaches to agents – his readers – to give credit to their drives, and to learn to dovetail their agency to them . . . We need to watch for what distinguishes us in our drives and passions, and learn to subordinate our agency . . . to this.' John Richardson, 'Nietzsche's Freedoms', in Gemes and May, p. 143. On my reading, however, Nietzsche and Zarathustra both call upon a rational will to impose order and hierarchy on the affects, not vice versa.

7. In *Daybreak* Nietzsche deals at length with the hegemony of tradition and the 'morality of custom' (see D 9, KSA 3:21–4; D 14, KSA 3:26–8, and D 18, KSA 3:30–2).

8. As Paul Katsafanas notes, Nietzsche is not 'a radical subjectivist who argues that there are no constraints on our values and norms'. Paul Katsafanas, 'The Problem of Normative Authority in Kant, Hegel and Nietzsche', in *Nietzsche and Kantian Ethics*, eds. João Constâncio and Tom Bailey in vol 2 of *Nietzsche's Engagements with Kant and the Kantian Legacy*, 3 vols, eds. Marco Brusotti, Herman Siemens, João Constâncio and Tom Bailey (London: Bloomsbury, 2017), p. 28.

9. In another notebook fragment, written shortly before the Bentham-related fragment already cited, Nietzsche refers to the scare-quoted 'instinct of compassion (*Instinkt des Mitleidens*)', which he attributes to the philosophy of Kant and Schopenhauer (KSA 11:34[39]:432).

10. Taking the default naturalist line and leaning heavily on *The Will to Power*, Michael Green argues that reason for Nietzsche 'is merely desire that is ordered and structured in a certain fashion, "a system of relations between various passions and desires"' (WP 387, KSA 13:11[310]:131). The latter citation is dated 1887–8, as

are all but one of Green's other *Will to Power* references on the subject of Nietzsche's naturalism, and does not therefore reflect Nietzsche's very different stance towards reason and the affects in his middle works. Michael Steven Green, *Nietzsche and the Transcendental Tradition* (Urbana and Chicago: University of Illinois Press, 2002), p. 55.
11. See note 9 above. See also the closing section of Chapter 4 for an extended discussion on Zarathustra's 'suffering with' (*mit-leiden*) of compassion (*Mitleid*).
12. On the subject of what Nietzsche denounces as the self-interested, self-gratifying nature of compassion, Michael Ure asserts that in the middle works Nietzsche sees *pitié/Mitleid* as one more 'pathology of narcissism. Boldly stated, [Nietzsche] argues that as a psychological transaction *Mitleid* satisfies the ego's desire to assuage its loss of narcissistic plenitude.' Michael Ure, *Nietzsche's Therapy: Self-Cultivation in the Middle Works* (Plymouth: Lexington Books, 2008), p. 185.
13. Immanuel Kant, *The Metaphysics of Morals*, trans. Mary Gregor (Cambridge: Cambridge University Press, 1991).
14. I fully concur with Ruth Abbey that Nietzsche's middle period works present 'a far more subtle and nuanced attitude toward pity' than is commonly attributed to Nietzsche. Ruth Abbey, *Nietzsche's Middle Period* (New York: Oxford University Press, 2000), p. 53.
15. Cf. '[T]he "religion of compassion" (or "the heart") commands one to help, and one believes that one has helped best when one has helped the fastest!' (GS 338, KSA 3:566).
16. 'Schopenhauer as Educator' is the title of the third of four essays that Nietzsche published under the title *Untimely Meditations* or *Unfashionable Observations*. The other three essays, in order of chronology, are 'David Strauss, the Confessor and the Writer', 'On the Uses and Abuses of History for Life' and 'Richard Wagner in Bayreuth'.
17. Remarking on Nietzsche's growing ambivalence towards Schopenhauer in the mid-1870s, Paul Franco observes, correctly in my view, that in the 1874 essay 'Schopenhauer as Educator' Nietzsche is clearly 'more interested in Schopenhauer as a heroic example of radical honesty and truthfulness than in his metaphysical doctrines of the will and resignation'. Paul Franco, *Nietzsche's Enlightenment*, p. 7.
18. Arthur Schopenhauer, *On the Basis of Morality*, trans. A. B. Bullock (London: George Allen & Unwin, 1915).

19. In Schopenhauer's epistemology, 'the many' equates to the plurality of appearance conditioned by time and space to which the *principium individuationis* belongs, while 'the One' signifies the unconditioned thing-in-itself that lies beyond the phenomenal world. Arthur Schopenhauer, *The World as Will and Representation*, trans. E. F. J. Payne (New York: Dover, 1969), vol. 1, §23 and *passim*.
20. Ibid. §36. Cf. 'We somewhat mistrust all those enraptured and extreme states in which one fancies one "grasps the truth in one's hands"' (WLN 15[70]:269, KSA 13:452).
21. Jonathan Cohen's essay 'Nietzsche's Fling with Positivism' is representative of this reading. See Babette E. Babich, ed., *Nietzsche, Epistemology, and Philosophy of Science: Nietzsche and the Sciences II* (Dordrecht: Springer Science, 1999), pp. 101-7. Paul Franco, on the other hand, considers the 'positivist' tag that is often applied to Nietzsche's middle works to be 'misleading'. In harmony with the central claim of my study, Franco does not view Nietzsche's rationalistic stance in his middle works as 'either inconsistent or anomalous with respect to his later outlook. The commitment to reason, intellectual honesty, and science – in a word, freedom of spirit – remains absolutely vital to Nietzsche's mature philosophy.' Paul Franco, *Nietzsche's Enlightenment*, pp. x–xii.
22. In 1886, Nietzsche wrote four prefaces for the re-release of the following four texts: *The Birth of Tragedy, Human, All Too Human* Volumes I and II (he wrote a preface for each volume), and *Daybreak*.
23. In translating this passage I leaned heavily on R. J. Hollingdale's 1982 translation of the same, which perfectly captures Nietzsche's derisory tone.
24. As Kathleen-Marie Higgins persuasively argues, Part 4 of *Zarathustra* can be profitably read as a form of Menippean satire. Kathleen-Marie-Higgins, *Nietzsche's Zarathustra* (Philadelphia: Temple University Press, 1987).
25. In *Daybreak* 209, Nietzsche reflects upon the way in which prejudiced, partisan (i.e., unfree-spirited) moralists are willing to overlook the weakness of members in their own camp while at the same time utilising the weaknesses of those in the opposing camp for *ad hominem* attacks: 'the lives of free-spirited moralists have always been put under the microscope: the rationale being that an indiscretion in life is the surest argument against an unwelcome insight' (KSA 3:189).

26. Plato's ship of fools allegory appears in Book 6 of *The Republic* (488a–489d). And just as in Plato's allegory the crew mocks the true pilot of the ship as 'a star-gazer, an idle babbler', so too is Zarathustra mocked by the market-square mob for his talk of 'last men' and 'dancing stars' (ZP 5, KSA 4:19).
27. 'An answer to the question: What is enlightenment?' in Immanuel Kant, *Practical Philosophy*, trans. and ed. Mary J. Gregor (Cambridge: Cambridge University Press 1999).
28. Ibid. pp. 17–18.
29. Beatrix Himmelmann makes a similar point, noting that Nietzsche styled himself as a radical enlightener. Likewise citing from Kant's essay 'What is Enlightenment?', Himmelmann reminds us that for Kant, as for Nietzsche, it was 'especially in religious matters' that man needs to be liberated from his prejudices. Beatrix Himmelmann, 'Kant, Nietzsche und die Aufklärung', in *Kant und Nietzsche im Widerstreit* (Berlin: de Gruyter, 2005), pp. 32–3.
30. Once again, I am indebted to R. J. Hollingdale for this felicitous turn of phrase.
31. Regarding the happiness of the last man, T. K. Seung astutely observes that 'There appears to be nothing wrong with them until they are subjected to [Zarathustra's] superhuman ideal ... only by taking Feuerbach's stand that the superhuman aspiration is the essence of humanity' can Zarathustra's debasing view of humanity be justified. Seung notes a number of similarities between Feuerbach and Nietzsche, the most palpably evident being their 'secular superhumanism', by which he means their joint advocacy of an *übermenschlich* ideal of human perfection. He calls the Zarathustra of the prologue 'a Young Hegelian, for whom the death of God transforms the ideal of divine perfection to the ideal of human perfection', and further points out that 'The notion of superhuman (*übermenschlich*), which was chiefly adjectival in Feuerbach's use, becomes a noun, the superman (*Übermensch*), for Zarathustra.' T. K. Seung, *Nietzsche's Epic of the Soul* (2005), pp. 10–19.
32. After finishing his high-school education at Schulpforta in 1864, Nietzsche went on to study theology and classical theology at the University of Bonn.
33. Paul Franco, *Nietzsche's Enlightenment*, p. 6.
34. It is worth noting that the German word *Strenge* (meaning severity, austerity, strictness), together with its adjectival and superlative forms, appears no less than forty-five times in the two volumes of *Human, All Too Human*.

35. 'Now one finally discovers that this nature cannot be accountable inasmuch as it is an altogether necessary consequence and assembled out of the elements and influence of things past and present' (HH 39, KSA 2:63).
36. For an extended reading of Zarathustra's inner demons see my 1998 monograph, *Zarathustra contra Zarathustra: The Tragic Buffoon* (Aldershot: Ashgate, 1998; repr. Routledge, 2018).
37. Schopenhauer's pessimistic *Weltanschauung* was shaped by his reading of the Upanishads and the Hindu concept of Maya at their core. For a recent study on Schopenhauer's encounter with Indian philosophy and, in particular, on the extent to which Schopenhauer's understanding of the ancient Hindu concept of Maya informed his epistemological, metaphysical and ethical theories, see Douglas L. Berger, *The Veil of Maya: Schopenhauer's System and Early Indian Thought* (New York: Global Academic Publishing, 2004). For parallels between Nietzsche's thought and Asian thought, see Graham Parkes, *Nietzsche and Asian Thought* (London and Chicago: University of Chicago Press, 1991).
38. Thomas Mann astutely remarked of Nietzsche's Zarathustra that 'This faceless, formless, monstrous *Flugelmann* with the rosy crown of laughter on his unrecognisable head, his "be hard!" and his dancer's legs is not an artistic creation but something rhetorical, an excited play with words, a tortured voice and a despairing prophecy, a spectre of helpless *grandezza*, something touching, but most of all embarrassing, a spectre tottering on the edge of the risible.' Thomas Mann, 'Nietzsche's Philosophy in the Light of our Experience', in Thomas Mann, *Last Essays*, trans. Tania and James Stern (New York: Knopf, 1959), pp. 141–77. David Aiken, in his exploration of nineteenth-century literary heroic models that might have informed Nietzsche's 'derivative epic hero [Zarathustra], a deliberately fashioned literary composite', draws our attention to Arthur Symons's preface to *The Collected Drawings of Audrey Beardsley*. In his preface, Symons describes Verlaine's *fin de siècle* Pierrot gamin as 'one of the types of our century': 'He feels himself to be sickening with a fever, or else perilously convalescent ... it is hard to distinguish, under the chalk, if the grimace which twists his mouth awry is more laughter or mockery. He knows that he is condemned to be always in public, that emotion would be supremely out of keeping with his costume, that he must remember to be fantastic if he would not be merely ridiculous. And so be becomes exquisitely false, dreading above

all things that "one touch of nature" which would ruffle his disguise, and leave him defenceless.' Cited in David Wyatt Aiken, 'Nietzsche's Zarathustra: The Misreading of a Hero', *Nietzsche-Studien*, 35:1 (2006), pp. 76 and 99.

39. Cf. 'from [the tyranny of the true], one must now and then be able to *find relief* in the untrue' (D 507; KSA 3:297). In his immensely illuminating essay on the relationship between laughter and the negation of limits, Lawrence Hatab observes that Nietzsche's recommended response of laughter to 'an existential confrontation with the terror of existence (the priority of becoming and a continual negation of "being")' is for Nietzsche 'the only alternative to a pessimistic denial of existence, or to an optimistic fantasy that negation and limits can somehow be resolved'. Hatab proceeds to link this tragicomic nexus back to (1) Nietzsche's interpretation of Attic tragedy as the *affirmative* interplay between Dionysian destruction and Apollonian form and beauty, and (2) to the sombre and hedonistic elements of Dionysian rites. As Hatab notes, both the frenzied re-enactments of Dionysus's dismemberment/death and the joyfully erotic feasts were believed to be cathartic. Lawrence J. Hatab, 'Laughter in Nietzsche's Thought: A Philosophical Tragicomedy', *International Studies in Philosophy*, 20:2 (1988), pp. 68–70.

40. The self-parody contained in Part 4 is a precursor to Nietzsche's 1886 'Attempt at a Self-Criticism' which he appended as a preface to the second edition of *The Birth of Tragedy*. The self-critique, argues Daniel Conway, is employed by Nietzsche as an exercise in 'strategic self-parody', the dual aim of which is to exercise 'the art of *this-worldly* comfort' (AS 7, KSA 1:22), but also 'to mitigate the effects of his own decadence, by undermining his various claims to philosophical authority'. In the context of *Zarathustra*, opines Conway, 'the laughter Zarathustra pronounces holy is best understood as a self-referential, self-consuming laughter', a view with which I am in full agreement. Daniel W. Conway, 'Nietzsche's Art of This-Worldy Comfort: Self-Reference and Strategic Self-Parody', *History of Philosophy Quarterly*, 9:3 (1992), p. 347.

2
The Kantian Rational Will and the Tyranny of Self-Overcoming

> Those law-giving and tyrannical spirits capable of *tying fast* the meaning of a concept, *holding fast* to it, men with that spiritual force of will . . . commanding men in the highest sense.
>
> (WLN 34[88]:6, KSA 11:449)

The first anglophone book-length study on Kant and Nietzsche appeared in 2005, opening a rich vein of inquiry into the theoretical intersections between the two philosophers.[1] Entitled *Nietzsche's Critiques: The Kantian Foundations of His Thought* – the word 'critiques' a punning reference to Kant's foundational three *Critiques* – R. Kevin Hill's landmark text mounts a compelling defence of its sub-titular claim. 'For Nietzsche, as for Hegel', asserts Hill, 'Kant is *the* philosopher with whom one must come to terms. One must either become a Kantian, or, starting from a Kantian foundation, think one's way out of Kantianism.'[2] He further claims that Nietzsche's knowledge of Kant was not confined to the critical works of Schopenhauer, Lange and Kuno Fischer, whom Hill collectively designates as 'early Neo-Kantians', but was informed and augmented by his own reading of Kant. Library records, together with statements made by Nietzsche in his letters and notebooks, strongly suggest a first-hand acquaintance with Kant's second and third *Critiques*; far less evidence exists of his ever having read the first *Critique*. What *is* certain, contends Hill, is Nietzsche's intellectual debt to Kant: not only to Kant's epistemology and critique of metaphysics, but also to Kant's rejection of consequentialism and his substitution of intention for consequence in determining the moral status of a given act. That Kant's critique of metaphysics effectively laid the groundwork for Nietzsche's own robust critique of a purported metaphysical beyond is surely beyond doubt. Similarly, few would contest Hill's claim that Kant's epistemology was the source of Nietzsche's settled conviction concerning the limited, 'perspectival' scope of human cognition. Whether, on the other hand, Kant's substitution of intention for consequence in the field of ethics was the inspiration behind Nietzsche's genealogical method, a method whereby the value of a purportedly ethical act is traced back to the undisclosed values that underlie (and often belie) the moral system prescribing that act, is a moot point.[3]

The critical focus of this chapter also relates to Kantian ethics. Indeed, it lies at the epicentre of Kantian ethics, namely the rational will. Autonomous and self-legislating,[4] which for Kant are synonymous metaphysical terms ('metaphysical' in the sense of being *purely* rational principles and pure in the sense of independent of feeling), the rational will resists and conquers the natural impulses (AA 6:380-1). It is my contention that a similarly autonomous 'lawgiving reason' (ibid.) drives Zarathustra's doctrine of self-overcoming – a doctrine that is encapsulated in the following fragment from Nietzsche's *Nachlass*: '*Summa*: to master the passions, *not* to weaken or exterminate them! the greater the mastering force of the will, the more freedom may be given to the passions' (WLN 9[139]:163, KSA 12:414). Two aspects of the Kantian rational will are of particular interest to me here. The first is what Kant in *The Metaphysics of Morals* refers to as the '*autocracy* of practical reason', which is autocratic in the sense that it 'involves consciousness of the *capacity* to master (*Meister*) one's inclinations' (AA 6:383).[5] The second, which elucidates the mastery of the first, is the Kantian notion of 'free self-constraint' (AA 6:383). As I shall argue in this chapter, both of these aspects are intrinsic to Zarathustra's doctrine of self-overcoming.

Autonomy and Universality

R. Lanier Anderson opens his 2012 essay 'What is a Nietzschean Self?' by acknowledging, like Hill, the ineluctable challenge posed by Kant to the philosophers immediately succeeding him: 'I am among those who see the history of nineteenth-century philosophy largely as a story about Kantianism. German thought of the period was dominated by strands occupied with working out the challenges Kant posed and exploring the resources of his system.'[6] One such strand is the value, the *non plus ultra* of value, that Kantian ethics places on autonomous agency. This value, I submit, is one that is shared by Nietzsche. Witness his idealised 'free spirits' (already discussed in Chapter 1) who have liberated themselves from custom and tradition, or his equally idealised 'sovereign individual' who has likewise liberated himself from the 'morality of custom' and is now a 'master of *free* will' (GM II 2, KSA 5:293). Where Kant and Nietzsche part company, according to Anderson, is on the locus and scope of that autonomy. Anderson's argument runs as follows: Whereas Kant's moral theory rests on the dual assumption that reason and inclination are fundamentally distinct and that autonomy depends on reason's capacity to 'stand back' from the drives and affects and to impose its rational laws over them, Nietzsche rejects this Kantian notion of a 'pure' practical reason, just as he rejects the idea of 'a simple, essentially unified and conscious, transcendental ego, which is fundamentally different in kind from the attitudes that compose it'.[7] The only kind of autonomous, normative self that Nietzsche recognises, holds Anderson, is a 'minimal self' that 'is not merely a Humean "bundle" of intrinsically unrelated "distinct existences"', but 'a diachronic, structured whole within which enduring drives and affects stand in causal and functional relations with identifiable patterns'.[8]

Pace Anderson, I endeavoured to show in Chapter 1 that passages in both *Human, All Too Human* and *Daybreak* appear to endorse a Platonic and Kantian dualism of reason and passion. This dualism, I argued, can be seen in Nietzsche's championing of a 'morality of reason' (WS 45, KSA 2:574) and in his positing of an ascetic 'sober morality which demands self-control, severity, obedience' as a necessary antidote to what he decries as the Christian morality of 'intoxication and excess' (D 215, KSA 3.192). The same set of stringent rational demands resurfaces in the metaphor-laden rhetoric of Zarathustra, again bringing into view the naturalist-normative tension in Nietzsche's work. Thus, while Nietzsche faults 'The mistaking of passion and *reason*, as if the latter were an entity of its own rather than a state of relations between different passions and desires' (WLN 11[310]:236, KSA 13:131) – a passage routinely cited in naturalist readings of Nietzsche, he also enjoins us to '*restrict* ourselves to the purification (*die Reinigung*) of our opinions and valuations and to the *creation of our own new tables of good*' (GS 335, KSA 3:563). Read from a naturalist-normative perspective, the latter injunction raises the question of the precise agent of purification or what Nietzsche more often refers to as a revaluation of values. Is it that 'sublime sense of honesty' (WLN 2[191]:96, KSA 12:161) with which Nietzsche exposes the affective needs and proclivities underlying the old values of good and evil, that 'intellectual cleanliness' (GM III 24, KSA 5:398) which might be said to be clean or pure in the Kantian sense of resisting the peremptory promptings of inclination? Or is it simply reason doing the bidding of our passions and desires? If the latter, then in what sense and by what method are our opinions and valuations to be purified?

Another descriptor of autonomy in Nietzsche's work is 'constraint' (see my reading of BGE 188 in 'The morality problem' section of my Introduction). In *The Gay Science*, Nietzsche commends those 'strong, commanding natures who enjoy their most exquisite pleasure in such constraint (*Zwang*), such bondage and perfection under their own law ... even when they have palaces to build and gardens to lay out, they resist giving nature free rein' (GS 290, KSA 3:530). This kind of pleasure, it needs to be said, is almost entirely absent from *Zarathustra*. Within the profit-loss economy of Zarathustra's doctrine of self-overcoming, constraint is presented as the most tyrannical form of self-deprivation. It is compared to 'a star [being] hurled out into desolate space and into the icy breath of aloneness' (Z1 'On the Way of the Creator', KSA

4:80–2), a form of self-denial so extreme that it requires the figurative images of murder, strangulation, vivisection and blood sacrifice to convey the magnitude of its violence. Most importantly, this constraint is to be freely undertaken – free in the sense of self-legislated; only in this way can bondage be felt as perfection. This type of freedom is what Kant oxymoronically designates as 'free self-constraint (*freien Selbstzwange*)' and identifies with the concept of duty (AA 6:383). In the 'Introduction to the Doctrine of Virtue' (AA 6:379–413), which opens the second part of *The Metaphysics of Morals*,[9] Kant uses the word 'constraint' (*Zwang*) – reiterated more than a dozen times – to denote 'the concept of a *necessitation* (constraint) of free choice through the law' (AA 6:379). It is this concept, I contend, that appears to be operating in Zarathustra's doctrine of self-overcoming.

Nietzsche's 'mistaking of passion and *reason*' statement quoted above is also cited by Simon Robertson in his contribution to the second of a recent three-volume anthology entitled *Nietzsche's Engagements with Kant and the Kantian Legacy*.[10] Despite devoting two out of the three sections of his essay to Nietzsche's normativity and his concept of legislation, Robertson concludes his critique with an endorsement of the broad, naturalist reading of Nietzsche. Thus, having noted (1) that Nietzsche repeatedly makes normative claims, sometimes in the explicit form of 'oughts' and 'shoulds'; (2) that he 'connects his normative claims to laws quite explicitly'; and (3) that independent thought, an 'uncompromisingly honest self-scrutiny', the imposition of laws on oneself and 'an independent self-determining will' are all hallmarks of Nietzsche's free-spirited, higher type of individual,[11] Robertson nevertheless maintains, admittedly with the support of multiple textual citations, that Nietzsche denies Kant's concept of autonomy because 'Nietzsche denies that practical deliberation can be *pure* (which Kant thinks it must be if a person is to govern himself autonomously)'. Normative judgements, concludes Robertson, even those of Nietzsche's free-spirited higher types, 'are necessarily shaped and constrained by one's motives' and therefore not pure in the Kantian sense of being uncontaminated by subjective motives.[12] It is this naturalist reading of Nietzsche, for which there is indeed ample textual evidence, that I sought to challenge in Chapter 1 in the context of Nietzsche's 'morality of reason' that demands reason's mastery over the affects. In this chapter, I shall invite the reader to reflect upon a number of passages from *Zarathustra* which in my view bear comparison with Kant's concept of autonomy as a will that is uncontaminated by subjective motives.

A further reason why Nietzschean autonomy is generally deemed to be distinct from Kantian autonomy is the issue of universality. As commentators have been quick to point out, while the Kantian concept of an autonomous will is implicit in Nietzsche's concept of the 'sovereign individual' whose iron will affords him the freedom and power to determine his own destiny, the rarity and exceptionality of such an individual is incompatible with the universalisability criterion of Kant's categorical imperative ('act only on that maxim that you will to become a universal law'). Tom Bailey, for example, observes that while the Kantian notion of an autonomous will is central to Nietzsche's account of moral agency, the requirements of equality and universality entailed in Kant's categorical imperative are clearly incompatible with Nietzsche's view of the 'sovereign individual' – an individual who, being in possession of his *own* measure of value, would balk at the 'doctrine of equality' and demand 'Equal for equals, unequal for unequals' (TI 'Raids of an Untimely Man' 48, KSA 6:150).[13] Garrath Williams likewise contrasts Kant's ethical universalism with Nietzsche's elitism, arguing that while Kantian morality is one to which all humans have access through the exercise of their reason, Nietzsche restricts his idea of a higher, autonomous morality to 'the very few'.[14] Setting the universality question aside for a moment, it is my contention that Nietzsche's idea of a higher, autonomous morality, which Bailey and Williams both take to be implicit in Nietzsche's account of the sovereign individual, is also implicit in Zarathustra's doctrine of self-overcoming. This 'master of *free* will ... with this mastery (*Herrschaft*) over himself', which in the second essay of his *Genealogy of Morals* Nietzsche presents as the epitome of autonomy (GM II 2, KSA 5:293-4), is the same kind of idealised individual[15] that in *Zarathustra* is said to have the capacity not only to plant his highest aim or ruling thought into the heart of his warring passions, but to transform the latter 'wild dogs' into songbirds (Z1 'On the Joyful and Painful Passions', KSA 4:43).

The same universalisability objection is raised by R. Kevin Hill, who argues that 'in appropriating Kant's notion of autonomy while rejecting its link to the categorical imperative and the "formal constraints" interpretation of morality, Nietzsche creates his own ideal of the autonomous individual, an individual who in self-legislating *transcends moral constraints altogether*' (my emphasis).[16] However, if we take a closer look at the autonomous, self-legislating individual whom Zarathustra invokes, exemplifies and addresses as 'the knower', we shall see how such an individual voluntarily subjects himself to the same three formal constraints as those given in Kant's universalisation formulations of the categorical imperative, namely the 'law-like character of moral reasons' (first constraint), the 'supremacy of moral reasons' (second constraint) and 'proper object of respect' (third constraint).[17] If, as I aim to show in this chapter, Zarathustra's knower is someone who transposes the universal law of becoming into the supreme unconditional practical law of self-overcoming and freely submits to this practical law out of respect for the universal law. And if this practical law can be construed as a *moral* law insofar as the normative injunction to self-overcome – a doctrine figuratively represented in *Zarathustra* by the *Untergang* trope – accords with Nietzsche's definition of morality as 'a continual self-mastery and self-overcoming practised in the great and in the smallest of things' (WS 45, KSA 2:573-4), 'a piece of tyranny against "nature" ... a protracted constraint' against the natural impulses (BGE 188, KSA 5:108-9). Then the tyranny of Zarathustra's doctrine of self-overcoming, a tyranny inscribed in the self-inflicted act of *Untergang*, can arguably be said to conform to Kant's three formal constraints.

My twofold argument in this chapter is (1) that the act of self-overcoming as articulated by Zarathustra presupposes *a form of rational agency* that in certain particulars bears a striking resemblance to the autonomous, self-legislating, rational will of Kantian ethics, and (2) that the blood sacrifice and martyrdom demanded by Zarathustra's doctrine of self-overcoming is an unwitting transformation of the Kantian rational will into a tyrannical overlord. The aforesaid particulars of Kantian rational agency fall under the following four heads, each of which is respectively addressed in the four remaining sections of this chapter:

- the first is what Kant refers to as 'the principle of freedom of internal lawgiving' (AA 6:378);
- the second is the mind's 'capacity and considered resolve' to resist and conquer the natural impulses (AA 6:380);
- the third is Kant's concept of the 'good will' which acts exclusively in accordance with what reasoned judgement decrees to be the 'highest good', but which can only so act after reason's 'interference with the purposes of inclination' (AA 4:396); and
- the fourth is the Kantian precept 'that reverence for a mere Idea – should function as an inflexible precept for the will' (AA 4:439).

Creator-Destroyers and Hammer-Wielding Legislators

In aphorism 36 of *Beyond Good and Evil*, Nietzsche 'hypothetically posit[s] the causality of the will as the only causality'.[18] On the basis of this hypothesis, to which he adds the correlative assumption that '"will" can naturally only act (*werken*) on "will"', he goes on to claim 'the right to define *all* active force (*wirkende Kraft*) unequivocally as *will to power*' (KSA 5.55).[19] The inference to be drawn from the stressed 'all' and the collocation 'active force' is that 'will to power' denotes a universal force qua causal principle, or what Nietzsche in a *Nachlass* fragment refers to as a 'quantum of power . . . characterised by the effect it exerts and the effect it resists' (WLN 14[79]:246, KSA 13:258). This universal will is akin to Schopenhauer's concept of the noumenal will. But whereas the latter is fundamentally a 'will to life' (*Wille zum Leben*), Nietzsche's 'will to power' is emphatically not a will to life – 'Not self-preservation', adds Nietzsche in the same *Nachlass* fragment. As Zarathustra confides, quoting an allegorised Life who once imparted her 'secret' to him, the will's surge towards power entails a wanton squandering of life:

> Where there is destruction (*Untergang*) and the falling of leaves, behold, there life sacrifices itself – for power! ...
>
> the one who shot at truth with the words 'will to existence (*Dasein*)' did not hit it: this will – does not exist! ...
>
> Only where there is life, is there also will; not will to life (*Leben*), but rather – thus I teach you – will to power! (Z2 'On Self-Overcoming', KSA 4:148–9)

Succinctly articulated in these lines and figured in the autumnal shedding of leaves is the destructive-generative dynamic between sacrifice and power. It is the same dynamic, outlined at the end of the previous section on autonomy and to be discussed in detail below, that obtains between the autonomous power of the rational will and the sacrifice demanded by it in the *Untergang* of self-overcoming. In the same *Zarathustra* chapter as the one cited above, we find seven out of the book's eight iterations of the phrase 'will to power', together with a clear indication of its meaning. After figuratively rendering the concept as a 'river of becoming', Zarathustra identifies this river as 'the will to power – the inexhaustible generative life-will (*der unerschöpfte zeugende Lebens-Wille*)'. The direct correlation here between becoming and generative fecundity is reinforced a little later in the chapter where the same two attributes of will to power are subsumed under the destructive-generative concept of 'overcoming':

> 'Behold', life said to me, 'I am that *which must always overcome itself*.
>
> 'Certainly, you call it will to procreation (*Wille zur Zeugung*) or drive towards a goal, to the higher, further, more manifold: but all this is one and one secret.' (Ibid.)

Accordingly, if '*all* active force' is will to power and will to power is a procreative life force that perpetually overcomes itself (a dialectical dynamic to be closely examined in Chapter 3), then what we are being presented with here is not just an ontological theory of becoming, but becoming as a metaphysical principle.

Having divulged life's secret regarding its inherent destructive-generative will,[20] Zarathustra goes on to extol another destructive-generative will, the type of will famously depicted by William Blake in his 'Proverbs of Hell' as the will to 'Drive your cart and your plough over the bones of the dead'.[21] In the words of Zarathustra:

> Truly, I say to you: good and evil that would be everlasting – there is no such thing! They must overcome themselves out of themselves again and again.
>
> With your values and words of good and evil you inflict violence (*Gewalt*), you appraisers . . .
>
> But a stronger violence (*Gewalt*) grows out of your values and a new overcoming: it breaks (*zerbrechen*) egg and eggshell.
>
> And whoever must be a creator in good and evil – truly, he must first be a destroyer (*Vernichter*) and shatter (*zerbrechen*) values. (Z2 'On Self-Overcoming', KSA 4:149)

Note the reiteration of *Gewalt* and *zerbrechen* plus the added destructive force of the verbal prefix *zer*, meaning 'into pieces'. Note too how the 'stronger violence' of the 'new overcoming' breaks not only the shell but also the egg of the old values, the egg connoting the self qua internalised and entrenched Christian moral values that must be broken by the destroyer-creator of new values (cf. the 'punitive destroyer of whitewashed sepulchres', Z3 'On the Three Evils' 2, KSA 4:238). This far more destructive violence is to be wielded by the new 'creator in good and evil', who has transposed the metaphysical principle of overcoming into 'a new overcoming' that, as indicated above, entails a wholesale destruction/*Untergang* of the old Christian values.

As noted in Chapter 1, Zarathustra's epithet for these creator-destroyers is '*der Erkennenden*' (the knowers), who reappear a year later in *Beyond Good and Evil* as the 'genuine' (*wirklich*) or 'real' (*eigentlich*) philosophers:

> Real philosophers . . . reach for the future with a creative hand and everything that is and was becomes for them a means, a tool, a hammer. Their 'knowing' (*Erkennen*) is *creating*, their creating is legislating, their will to truth is – *will to power*. (BGE 211, KSA 5:145)

What is crucial to note in this pronouncement is the following: the implicit qualitative relation between will to truth and will to power; the equivalence of knowing, creating and legislating; and the scare-quoted verb 'knowing'. The qualitative relation suggests that the destructive-generative quality of the metaphysical will to power is commensurate with the destructive-generative quality of a rational will to truth. The equivalence of knowing, creating and legislating supports my contention that the creative will in *Zarathustra* bears comparison with the legislative rational will in Kant. And the scare-quotes around 'knowing' alert the reader to two types of philosophical knowing: on the one hand, the passive, retrospective type of knowing which Nietzsche ascribes to the classifying and systematising 'philosophical labourers in the noble mould of Kant and Hegel' (ibid., KSA 5:144); on the other hand, the active-creative, future-oriented type of knowing which Nietzsche ascribes to the hammer-wielding 'real philosophers'.[22] Here then is the other destructive-generative will to power and the crux of my argument, namely will to power transposed into will to truth, or, in Zarathustra's formulation, the universal law of becoming transposed into the practical law of self-overcoming. It is this new law or doctrine of self-overcoming which on my reading of *Zarathustra* functions as a binding and tyrannical moral imperative.

Nietzsche's notorious attack on what he refers to as the will to truth has in recent years been the subject of a number of scholarly articles.[23] These latter revolve around two key

Nietzsche passages, both written in 1887: the first is from *The Gay Science*; the second is from *On the Genealogy of Morals*. In the first passage, Nietzsche asks why science presupposes that '*truth* is necessary'. Ruling out utility or prudence 'since the disutility and dangerousness of the "will to truth" of "truth at any price" is constantly proven', Nietzsche concludes that science's presupposition that '*nothing* is *more* necessary than truth' is a vestigial life-negating piety dating back to Plato and perpetuated by Christianity. Elaborating further on this insight, Nietzsche avers that if this will to truth is both 'hostile to life and destructive', then

> the one who is truthful in that audacious and ultimate sense, as presupposed by belief in science, *thereby affirms another world* than that of life, nature and history; and insofar as he affirms this 'other world', must he not thereby deny its counterpart, this world, *our* world? ... But you will have understood what I am getting at, namely that it is still a *metaphysical faith* on which our faith in science rests – that even we knowers of today, we godless anti-metaphysicians, still take *our* fire too from the brand ignited by a thousand-year old faith, that Christian faith, which was also Plato's faith, that God is truth; that truth is divine. (GS 344, KSA 3:574–7; see also GS 357, KSA 3:600)

The second passage appears in the third essay ('What do Ascetic Ideals Mean?') of Nietzsche's *Genealogy of Morals*. Citing the GS 344 passage above, Nietzsche declares of both philosophers and scholars:

> These negators and outsiders of today, those who are unconditional in one thing, in their demand for intellectual cleanliness, these hard, severe (*streng*), abstinent, heroic minds who make up the honour of our time, all these pale atheists, Antichrists, immoralists, nihilists ... the latest idealists of knowledge in whom alone the intellectual conscience lives and is incarnate today – they actually believe that they are all as detached as possible from the ascetic ideal, these 'free,

very free spirits' ... They are by no means *free* spirits: *because they still believe in truth* ... Perhaps I know all of this too closely: that venerable philosopher's abstinence to which such a belief commits one, that stoicism of the intellect ... that *wanting* to stand before the factual, the factum *brutum*' (GM III 24, KSA 5:398-9)

What interests me here is the phrase 'Perhaps I know all of this too closely'. The rhetorical 'perhaps' does little to dispel the suspicion that despite Nietzsche's critique of the will to truth as modernity's secularised confession of faith and, as such, the latest incarnation of the ascetic ideal, he views himself as an idealist of knowledge, driven by an unconditional will to truth.[24] It is this kind of irritably honest (self-)critique that attests to Nietzsche's 'intellectual cleanliness at any price' (GS 357, KSA 3:600). As a self-professed immoralist and Antichrist, he is acutely aware of his simultaneous entanglement in and resistance to the Christian belief in truth, of being both its heir and its most outspoken critic.

To return to *Zarathustra*, the will to power of the knowers' will to truth compels them to become creator-destroyers. Heirs to the rational rigour of the Enlightenment and the precursive Christian virtue of truthfulness, the truthful and truth-seeking knowers are 'hard, strict, narrow, cruel and inexorable' in their honesty (Z4 'The Leech', KSA 4:311-12 - see the conscientious of spirit caricature cited towards the end of Chapter 1).[25] This inexorable cruelty takes the form of a self-imposed law to which the knowers must freely submit:

> You call yourself free? Your ruling thought I want to hear and not that you have escaped from a yoke ...
>
> Can you give yourself your evil and your good and set up your will as a law over you? Can you be judge of yourself and avenger of your laws?
>
> Dreadful is the loneliness of the judge and avenger of one's own law. (Z1 'On the Way of the Creator', KSA 4:81)

In *The Metaphysics of Morals*, Kant refers to this kind of voluntary submission to one's own law as 'free self-constraint' (AA 6:383) and 'the principle of freedom of internal lawgiving' (AA 6:378).[26] And in his earlier *Groundwork of the Metaphysic of Morals* (1785),[27] he had described this law-making rational will as 'not merely subject to the law, but is so subject that it must be considered as also *making the law* for itself and precisely on this account as first of all subject to the law (of which it can regard itself as the author)' (AA 4:431).[28] This authorship is not, however, to be taken literally. As Allen Wood points out, 'the [Kantian] moral law ... has neither a legislator nor an author' since the content of that morality 'is the rational will itself'.[29] Similarly, the law of self-overcoming which the knower imposes on himself is not the product of a residual reverence for custom and tradition or what Nietzsche refers to as unpurified opinions and values (GS 335, KSA 3:563). Nor is it the product of prejudice and weakness: a mere 'sign language of the affects' (BGE 187, KSA 5:107). Predicated on the universal law of becoming, the new practical law of self-overcoming decrees the wholesale destruction of the old moral law predicated on Being – a concept which Nietzsche wittily dismisses as 'a fabrication by the man suffering from becoming' (WLN 2[110]:80, KSA 12:115). It is to this new practical law that the knower voluntarily submits out of respect for the universal law of becoming. Accordingly, as judge and avenger of this law, the knower's 'internal lawgiving' is neither affectively nor self-interestedly willed.[30]

Shattering the Christian Table of Values

As noted above, the imperative of Nietzsche's *Zarathustra* is the eradication of Christian morality and the creation of new values and new laws. 'Are you a new strength and a new right? A prime mover (*erste Bewegung*)? A self-rolling wheel?' demands Zarathustra (Z1 'On the Way of the Creator', KSA 4:80). To be that strength and to claim that right, however, requires an almost impossibly high pain threshold. Witness Zarathustra's spectral shadow, the last in a long line of Zarathustra *Doppelgängers*, who catches up with his flesh and blood counterpart in

Part 4 of *Zarathustra* and forces him to confront the debilitating after-effects of self-overcoming:

> With you I strove towards everything forbidden, worst, farthest: and if there is anything of virtue in me, it is that I felt no fear before the forbidden.
>
> With you I shattered whatever my heart revered . . .
>
> With head and heart I plunged myself into the coldest water. Ah, how often did I stand there naked and consequently red as a crab! . . .
>
> What is left of me? A weary and insolent heart, an unstable will, fluttering wings, a broken spine. (Z4 'The Shadow', KSA 4.339–40)

The 'everything forbidden' of which Zarathustra's shadow speaks is the destruction of long-revered and deep-rooted Christian values. Not until this has been accomplished can the work of self-re-creation begin: 'negation and *destruction*', asserts Nietzsche, 'is a precondition of yes-saying' (EH 'Why I am a destiny' 4, KSA 6:368).

The evaluative as opposed to visceral work of destruction is showcased in a Part 3 chapter of *Zarathustra* entitled 'On the Three Evils' (KSA 4:235–40). In this chapter, Zarathustra 'negates' the three Christian evils of voluptuousness (*Wollust*), lust for power (*Herrschsucht*) and selfishness (*Selbstsucht*), in a bid to attenuate and reverse the 'evil' effects that Christianity's demonisation of these affects has purportedly had on man's natural vigour. While acknowledging the vicious ends to which each of these affects is often willed as a means, Zarathustra seeks to recover the vitality and creative potential inherent in each. He begins with voluptuousness (*Wollust*), the 'evil' most demonised by the clerical community and the one most easily debunked.[31] Gleefully glossed by Zarathustra as 'Sex: for all hair-shirted body-despisers, stake and thorn (*Stachel und Pfahl*)'; 'for the lion-willed, the great fortifier of the heart (*Herzstärkung*)'. Remove the stigmatic shame of carnal pleasure, as well as the brutish rutting of the libertine, and what remains is the procreative urge instinct in all living creatures and 'to free hearts, something innocent and free' (Z3 'On the Three Evils' 2, KSA 4:237).[32] Equally fertile and free is the erstwhile philologist's love of wordplay, which in Zarathustra's re-evaluation of the three Christian evils can be seen in the root-word *Lust* in *Wollust* and which denotes not merely sensuality, but also pleasure and desire.

Pleasure, or what Zarathustra in this discourse refers to as 'self-joy (*Selbst-Lust*)', is the joy one naturally feels in a healthy, robust body. Renaming it the virtue of selfishness (*Selbstsucht* – the third Christian evil), Zarathustra opposes it to the selfishness of cowardice that disguises its low self-esteem as a patient, servile, humility.[33] In place of this type of selfishness, Zarathustra celebrates 'the sound, healthy selfishness, which springs from a powerful soul' (Z3 'On the Three Evils' 2, KSA 4:238). As Nietzsche never tires of telling us, human instincts are neither good nor bad per se but pronounced so by a given value system. Thus, when a particular table of values demonises the natural human drives and thereby saps, suppresses and vitiates them, a new set of values is needed to replace it and, in theory at least, to reinvigorate the depleted affects. On the evidence of Zarathustra's shadow (see above), however, the eradication of the old system of values induces an even greater diminution of desire's affective power, leaving in its wake etiolation and enervation.

Desire is another meaning of the root-word *Lust* in *Wollust* and in *Zarathustra* is linked to becoming:

> Oh, you sentimental hypocrites, you lechers (*Lüsternen*)! Your desire lacks innocence: and now therefore you malign all desiring!
>
> Truly, not as creators, begetters, enjoyers of becoming (*Werdelustige*) do you love the earth!
>
> Where is innocence? Where there is a will to beget (*Wille zur Zeugung*). And whoever wants to create over and beyond himself has for me the purest will. (Z2 'On Immaculate Perception', KSA 4:157)

'Will to beget' carries a dual figurative freight here, beyond the literal reproductive meaning. It connotes both metaphysical becoming qua will to power and an 'ardent creator-will' (*inbrünstiger Schaffens-Wille*)' (Z2 'On the Blissful Isles', KSA 4:111) to beget new values and new laws. In *Zarathustra*, this 'ardent creator-will' is the defining quality of the knowers who want to create 'over and beyond' themselves – hence the *Übermensch* (*über* meaning beyond, *Mensch* meaning man) – in accordance with the laws of becoming and overcoming. 'Even in knowing (*Erkennen*)', says Zarathustra, 'I feel only my will's lust to beget and become; and if there is innocence in my knowledge (*Erkenntniss*) that is because there is will to procreation in it' (Z2 'On the Blissful Isles', KSA 4:111). Without this knowledge of becoming and, most importantly, a will to overpower (*Herrschsucht*) the former Christian paradigm of Being, such 'knowing' remains arid scholasticism, mere system-building for the philosophical labourers.

Wedged between *Wollust* and *Selbstsucht* in Zarathustra's critique of the three Christian 'evils' and the active property of all three is *Herrschsucht*. Re-examined and re-evaluated, *Herrschsucht*, here translated as lust for power, is 'the earthquake which breaks and breaks open all that is rotten and most hollow; the rolling, rumbling, punitive destroyer of whitewashed sepulchres' (Z3 'On the Three Evils' 2, KSA 4:237–8). In this metaphor, lust for power clearly denotes the hammer blows of the real philosophers whose task it is to destroy the 'whitewashed sepulchres' of 'rotten' and rotting values. These are the knowers whose knowledge of the destructive-generative law of becoming begets creator-destroyer legislators whose will to truth is will to power. This type of destruction requires mental strength, the 'stronger violence' (Z2 'On Self-Overcoming', KSA 4:149) cited in the previous section, and is a semantic property of the compound noun *Herrschsucht*. The masculine noun *Herr* connotes the virile qualities with which Zarathustra seeks (*suchen*) to rule over (*herrschen*) and ultimately supplant what he reviles as the 'feminine and servile nature' of Christian virtue (Z3 'On the Three Evils' 2, KSA 4:239). Ecclesiastical 'teachers of resignation', rails Zarathustra, have emasculated virtue, which 'for them is what makes modest and tame: thus they make the wolf a dog and man himself man's best domestic animal' (Z3 'On the Diminishing Virtue' 2 and 3, KSA 4:214–15). But if the mind is to assert its mastery over the 'feminine' virtues of humility, meekness and self-abasement and to give 'men back the *courage* for their natural drives' (WLN 9[121]:161, KSA 12:406), it will need to emulate the drives' innate tenacity and ferocity as exemplified in the ancient warrior virtues of courage and audacity. This transposition of animal strength into spiritual strength, which is similar to the knower's transposition of will to power into will to truth and of destructive-generative becoming into destructive-generative self-overcoming, is emblematised in the 'lion spirit'. To be discussed in Chapter 3, the lion spirit is Zarathustra's epithet for the spirit that tears into the affective manifold and possesses the necessary strength of mind to resist and conquer its formerly humble and venerating Christian mindset, connoted in *Zarathustra* by the 'camel spirit' epithet (see Z1 'On the Three Metamorphoses of the Spirit', KSA 4:29–31).

Partially captured in the 'lion spirit' epithet is the courage (*Tapferkeit*) and audacity (*Verwegenheit*) of the type of intrepid, inquiring mind celebrated by Nietzsche in *Daybreak*. 'There are no scientific methods which alone lead to knowledge!', he declares; 'We investigators are like all conquerors, explorers, seafarers, adventurers of an audacious (*verwegenen*) morality' (D 432, KSA 2:266). Kant makes a similar point in his essay on enlightenment (discussed in Chapter 1), exhorting the enlightened thinker to '*Sapere aude!*' (dare to know) and 'have courage to make use of your *own* understanding!' (AA 8:35). Two other *Daybreak* passages highlight the tenacity of such a mind: in one passage, the tenacity of 'the tensest deliberation (*der gespanntesten Besonnenheit*)' is said to be a quality worth cultivating (D 207, KSA 3:187), and in the other, the 'constant tension (*die stete Spannung*)' of a mind that keeps the 'tireless gaze turned inwards' (D 546, KSA 3:316) is likewise commended. The latter resonates with Kant's use of the word fortitude (*fortitudo*) to denote the mind's 'considered resolve' to resist and conquer the natural impulses (AA 6:380) and for which 'herculean strength' is required (AA 6:376).

Erkenntniss and the Hard Labour of Reorienting the Affects

In a notebook entry for autumn 1887, Nietzsche avers that 'the ever more commanding voice of one's "honesty" should shame one into unlearning that shame which would like to deny and lie away the natural instincts' (WLN 10[45]:182, KSA: 12:476–7). Once this shame has been unlearned, the knower must work to harness the instincts and passions to a higher ideal of man – the kind of work that Kant refers to as 'interference with the purposes of inclination' (AA 4:396). Two passions which Zarathustra singles out for harnessing are contempt and desire. 'I love the great despisers', he proclaims, 'because they are the great venerators and arrows of longing for the other shore' – the other shore being an idealised future where the notional *Übermensch* will live and flourish.

> What is the greatest thing that you can experience? It is the hour of the great contempt. The hour when even your happiness becomes as nauseating to you as your reason and your virtue.
>
> The hour when you say: 'What is the point of my happiness? It is poverty and filth and pitiful contentment! But my happiness ought (*sollte*) to justify existence itself!' (ZP 3–4, KSA 4:15–17)

This tethering of the affective will to power to a higher ideal of man, and, in particular, of happiness to a moral imperative ('to justify existence itself'), is reminiscent of Kant's concept of the 'good will', which in his *Groundwork to the Metaphysic of Morals* he holds to be 'the highest good':

> since reason is not sufficiently serviceable for guiding the will safely as regards its objects and the satisfaction of all our needs ... and since none the less reason has been imparted to us as a practical power – that is, as one which is

to have influence on the *will*; its true function must be to produce a *will* which is *good*, not as a *means* to some further end, but *in itself* . . . Such a will need not . . . be the sole and complete good, but it must be the highest good and the condition of all the rest, even of all our demands for happiness. (AA 4:396)

Kant's controversial notion of the highest good continues to elicit critical debate because, as Kant himself concedes in the *Critique of Practical Reason*, it combines two distinct elements, namely virtue and happiness (AA 5:113). Numerous defences of the concept have been mounted, including the following by Walter James Lowe:

Kant is a rationalist, no doubt; but a rationalist of a peculiarly chastened sort. He knows full well that while the formal imperative (and the will which is determined to act according to the imperative) must be the basis for an act's morality, they are not enough to assure the act's accomplishment. To accomplish the act, the will must needs enlist the cooperation of *desire*; and for that, right principles are not enough. If desire is to be stirred, there must be an object.[34]

Lowe's defence rests on an appeal to what he refers to as Kant's 'moral realism', by which he means Kant's acknowledgment of the flawed nature of man (cf. 'the spirit is willing, but the flesh is weak', Matthew 26:41). Ever prey to the importunate demands of the affects in both their raw (drives) and culturally conditioned (passions) state,[35] man's reason is more often slave to rather than master of the passions. In the words of Zarathustra, 'Behind your thoughts and feelings, my brother, stands a powerful commander, an unknown wise man – he is called self. He lives in your body, he is your body' (Z1 'On the Despisers of the Body', KSA 4:40). Kant also underscores the fact that an act exhibiting conformity to a moral law is far more likely to have been motivated by self-interest than by an unalloyed respect for the law. And yet, despite the ubiquity and intransigence of what Kant mock-indulgently calls 'the dear self' (AA

4:407), and despite the inability of experience to produce one unequivocal example of an act issuing from a 'pure' or 'good will' (i.e., uncontaminated by subjective needs and interests), the establishment of such a will is for Kant the 'highest practical function' of reason (AA 4:396). It is also, I submit, the highest practical function of Zarathustra's doctrine of self-overcoming, which commands that the rational will to truth and becoming destroys the Christian 'truth' of Being.

However, if desire is to be ardent for a rationally determined higher good, its habitual objects will need to be displaced. Zarathustra makes this abundantly clear in his paean to the 'hour of the great contempt':

> The hour when you say: 'What matters my reason! Does it crave knowledge as the lion its food? It is poverty and filth and pitiful contentment!'
>
> The hour when you say: 'What matters my virtue! It has not yet made me rage. How weary I am of my good and my bad! It is poverty and filth and pitiful contentment!'
>
> The hour when you say: 'What matters my justice! I do not see that I am ember (*Gluth*) and coal (*Kohle*). But the just person is ember and coal!' (ZP 3, KSA 4.15-16)[36]

This fusing of desire with the moral objects of desire (i.e., reason, virtue and justice) is presented here as the goal to be pursued once contempt for what had formerly passed as virtue has spent itself. But if reason is to 'crave', virtue to 'rage' and justice to 'burn', the passions will first have to be coerced into serving a higher purpose:

> Let your virtue be too high for the familiarity of names: and if you must speak of it, be not ashamed to stammer about it.
>
> Speak and stammer thus: 'That is *my* good, that which I love, thus does it please me entirely, thus alone do I want the good . . .

Once you had passions and called them evil. But now you have only your virtues: they grew out of your passions.

You planted your highest aim into the heart of these passions: there they became your virtues and joys. (Z1 'On the Joyful and Painful Passions [*Von den Freuden- und Leidenschaften*]', KSA 4:42–3)

As intimated in the rather clumsy chapter title, this planting is going to be a painful exercise. Just how painful can be gauged from a confession made by Zarathustra much later in the text: 'What have I not sacrificed that I might have one thing: this living plantation of my thoughts and this dawn of my highest hope!' (Z3 'Involuntary Bliss', KSA 4:203). Before the planting can commence, however, the ground must be prepared by the cognitive tool of '*Erkenntniss*', the discerning faculty (Z1 'On the Three Metamorphoses', KSA 4:29 and *passim*).

Before the affects can be pressed into the service of higher virtues and a higher ideal, the mind must first be able to discriminate between good and bad virtues, which in *Zarathustra* translates as virtues predicated on the law of becoming and virtues rooted in sloth and 'pitiful contentment'. Kant, for example, affirms that true virtue is 'morality stripped ... of all the spurious adornments of reward or self-love' (AA 4:426), the kind of self-love, say, of those who exclusively seek their own redemption. Zarathustra likewise affirms that 'there is no reward-giver, no paymaster ... I do not even teach that virtue is its own reward' (Z2 'On the Virtuous', KSA 4:120). This discriminatory work, a necessary prerequisite to any revaluation of values and the creation of a higher good, is to be undertaken by the mental faculty of *erkennen*, meaning to know, to identify, to discern, distinguish, perceive, detect and discover (Langenscheidt). Subtly distinct from the more passive verb *kennen* (to know), *erkennen* denotes an act of discovery (cf. *notio* and *cognitio* in Scholastic Latin). What is significant here is the prefix *er*. Like the verbs *erfassen* (to grasp or apprehend), *erforschen* (to investigate) and *ermitteln* (to determine), the prefix in *erkennen* implies *active* cognition: a striving towards knowledge and truth rather than a passive absorption of freely circulating opinions and values.

This faculty, to which Zarathustra repeatedly appeals, plays a cardinal role in his demand for a more discerning, more truthful morality. The knowing or discerning one cannot properly begin the process of overcoming Christian morality until he has distinguished between a wholesome affect or virtue and an unwholesome one – an exercise on full display in the 'Three Evils' chapter discussed in the previous section. Such evaluative discrimination, one might assume, given Nietzsche's famous dictum 'There is *only* a perspectival seeing, *only* a perspectival "knowing" (*Erkennen*)' (GM III 12, KSA 5:365), will inevitably be coloured by one's cultural milieu or affective propensities. But for Nietzsche's Zarathustra, the discerning one is deemed to be in possession of superior evaluative powers – powers, however, that in the naturalist reading of Nietzsche cannot be pure because, to re-quote Robertson, 'Nietzsche denies that practical deliberation can be *pure* (which Kant thinks it must be if a person is to govern himself autonomously).'

Pace Robertson et al., it is my contention that the evaluative capacity of *der Erkennende* is indeed 'pure' in the Kantian sense insofar as it is uncompromised by either inclination or subjective need. As Nietzsche protests in an 1885 notebook entry, perspectivism is by no means synonymous with a democratic relativism: '*my* valuation or condemnation of someone does not give another man the right to value or condemn the same way – unless he is my equal and of equal rank ... To be truthful is a distinction' (WLN 34[121]:8, KSA 11:461).[37] This truthfulness arguably suggests some measure of objective reasoning, uncontaminated by the affects. And when Nietzsche claims that unlike the objectivity exercised by scientists, 'all great philosophy hitherto has been the self-confession of its author and a kind of inadvertent and unconscious memoir' (BGE 6, KSA 5:19), his implicit acknowledgment that his own philosophy is not exempt from the charge is itself a truth-driven departure from the great philosophies that preceded him. It also marks the advent of those 'philosophers of the future' who will demand not only of themselves, but also of others, 'critical discipline (*kritische Zucht*) and every habit which leads to cleanliness (*Reinlichkeit*) and severity (*Strenge*) in matters of the spirit' (BGE 210, KSA 5:143).

Ranking himself as a truth-seeking and truth-bearing *Erkennender*, Zarathustra assumes the right to pronounce upon wholesome and unwholesome virtues and to equate unwholesome with cowardly, cowardly with servile, servile with feminine, and feminine with Christian morality. Submissiveness, obsequiousness, piety, humility and passivity must all be vanquished by 'the sword of judgement', admonishes the prophet of self-overcoming, 'And he who pronounces the "I" wholesome and holy, and selfishness blessed,[38] who also speaks what he knows, is truly a prophet' (Z3 'On the Three Evils' 2, KSA 4:240). The status of the 'I' is interesting here in that it appears to denote the rational 'I' of the intellect which 'knows' and which, on the basis of this knowledge, pronounces the affective, 'selfish' 'I' as blessed. Thus, despite Zarathustra's claim in Part 1 of *Zarathustra* that the 'small reason' of man is largely directed and manipulated by the 'great reason' of the body (Z1 'On the Despisers of the Body', KSA 4:39), without the mind's ability to examine and appraise the affective springs of human action and without the mind's courage, cruelty and fortitude to eviscerate those affects which do not further a higher earthly goal, the affective manifold is doomed to remain an anarchic tyranny of chaotically competing drives. 'Are you the victorious one, the self-conqueror, the ruler of the senses, the master of your virtues?' harangues Zarathustra. 'Or do the animal and necessity speak out of your wish? Or loneliness? Or discord with yourself?' (Z1 'On Children and Marriage', KSA 4:90)

Implicit in Zarathustra's reiterated references to *erkennen* and *Erkenntniss* is the type of analytic rigour common among scholars and scientists, but with that 'constant tension' of the mind directed inwards rather than outwards. Without this invasive probity, insists Zarathustra, without spirit cutting into life, self-mastery cannot be achieved. Self-administered, it demands a constitution strong enough to withstand vivisection:

> You only know the spirit's sparks: you see not the anvil which it is, nor the cruelty of its hammer! . . .

> In all respects, however, you make too familiar with the spirit . . .

> You are tepid, but all deep realisation (*Erkenntniss*) flows cold. Ice-cold are the innermost wells of the spirit. (Z2 'On the Famous Wise Men', KSA 4:134)

Compare these lines with the following from *Beyond Good and Evil*:

> There can be no doubt that [the philosophers of the future] will be the least permitted to disregard those severe and far from innocuous qualities which distinguish the critic from the sceptic: I mean the certainty in measures of value, the conscious employment of a unity of method, the shrewd courage, the standing alone and the capacity for self-responsibility; indeed, they confess to taking a *delight* in nay-saying and dissection and to a certain cold-blooded cruelty which knows how to direct the knife confidently and delicately, even when the heart bleeds. (BGE 210, KSA 5:142–3)

This 'certainty' in measures of value, this 'shrewd courage', this 'nay-saying and dissection' and this 'capacity for self-responsibility' are all qualities that one might arguably associate with the Kantian 'good will'. Good in the sense that it 'does not serve my inclination, but outweighs it' (AA 4:400), the Kantian good will is governed solely by an unconditional respect for and iron duty towards one's own rationally determined moral law:

> Every one must admit that a law has to carry with it absolute necessity if it is to be valid morally – valid, that is, as a ground of obligation . . . here consequently the ground of obligation must be looked for, not in the nature of man nor in the circumstances of the world in which he is placed, but solely *a priori* in the concepts of pure reason. (AA 4:389)

As the ground of obligation, reason acts in opposition to 'the nature of man', to external forces and to the self-appointed guardians and indoctrinators to whom Kant refers in his essay on enlightenment (discussed in Chapter 1). In much the same way, Nietzsche's discerning free spirit or real philosopher acts as both hammer and scalpel to his own entrenched and internalised values. It is this probing and negating dissection of the 'knowing' one that constitutes 'the higher man, the higher soul, the higher duty, the higher responsibility' (BGE 212, KSA 5:147) and affords them the 'new right' to forge and disseminate new virtues and new laws.[39] And while the Kantian-inflected word 'duty' finds no place in the metaphor-saturated rhetoric of *Zarathustra*, it is arguably part of what impels Zarathustra to 'bestow and distribute' (ZP 1, KSA 4:11) his wisdom. The ideal philosopher, writes Nietzsche, is 'the man of the most comprehensive responsibility, who has the conscience (*Gewissen*) for the overall development of man' (BGE 61, KSA 5:79). This is the same responsibility, I submit, that Kant in his essay on enlightenment assigns to the rare, enlightened individual, whose duty it is to impart the fruits of his reason to the wider public. And just as the Kantian good will 'has its full value in itself' (AA 4:394), so too does Zarathustra's 'bestowing virtue' (Z1 'On the Bestowing Virtue', KSA 4:97–102).

Reverence and Martyrdom: Willing the *Übermensch*

In his *Groundwork*, Kant holds 'that reverence for a mere Idea – should function as an inflexible precept for the will' (AA 4:439). In *Zarathustra*, that idea is the *Übermensch* and it is one which 'the great despisers' venerate and long for (ZP 4, KSA 4:17). More visionary ideal than idea, the *Übermensch* is repeatedly invoked by Zarathustra as an objective principle of volition and hence in Kantian terms a practical law. At the close of *Zarathustra* Part 1 the protagonist-prophet declares: '*Dead are all the gods: now we want the Übermensch to live*' and with a valedictory flourish leaves his disciples with the following injunction: 'Let this be our last will at the great noontide!' (Z1 'On the Bestowing Virtue' 3, KSA 4:102). As I aim to demonstrate in this brief final section, Zarathustra's will to the *Übermensch* is commensurate with Kant's concept of the 'good will' in three particulars. As an 'absolute value' in itself it takes no account of utility (AA 4:394); as a practical law it is to be self-imposed and submitted to without any regard for inclination and self-love (AA 4:400-1); and as a will to an idea of moral perfection, the 'true Original' of that idea resides in reason and not in any living exemplars ('Imitation has no place in morality', AA 4:409). I will also show that these three particulars are figuratively represented in *Zarathustra* as a type of martyrdom.

'I teach you the *Übermensch*. Man is something that ought (*sollen*) to be overcome', announces Zarathustra early in his prologue; 'Let your will say: the *Übermensch shall be* (*sei*) the meaning of the earth!' (ZP 3, KSA 4:14). The modal verb *sollen* (should/ought) and the imperative *sei* are important here: the first clearly denotes a duty or obligation, while the second carries the weight of a moral command. That the *Übermensch* is 'a mere Idea' is clear from the literary tropes used to depict it: it is a sea in which man is to drown his 'great contempt' for the debased notions of reason, virtue, and justice (ZP 3, KSA 4:15-16); it is 'lightning out of the dark cloud man' (ZP 7, KSA 4:23); and it is 'rainbow' (ZP 9, KSA 4:26), 'dancing star' (ZP 5, KSA 4:19) and 'the beam of a star' (Z1 'Of Little Old and Young Women', KSA 4:85).[40] It is towards this astral, notional, ideal goal that man is commanded to direct his will:

> – That I may one day be ready and ripe in the great noontide: ready and ripe like the red-hot ore, the lightning-bearing cloud, and the swelling milk-udder: –
>
> – Ready for myself and my deepest will: a bow burning for its arrow, an arrow burning for its star: –
>
> – A star, ready and ripe in its noontide, glowing, pierced, blessed by annihilating sun-arrows: –
>
> – A sun itself, and an inflexible (*unerbittlicher*) sun-will, ready for annihilation in victory! (Z3 'On Old and New Tablets' 30, KSA 4:269)

Sun, star, rainbow and lightning all connote the intangible luminosity of the will's goal, an unattainability reinforced by Zarathustra's oxymoronic noontide star. Often invoked by Zarathustra, 'the great noontide' signifies the epiphanic moment when man, the 'sun of his knowledge' directly overhead (Z1 'On the Bestowing Virtue' 3, KSA 4:102), acknowledges the *Übermensch* as his goal and thereupon embarks upon an inner journey towards that goal. It is a journey that entails the interminable overcomings of one's old submissive, conformist self (the aforementioned 'camel spirit') and the hitching of one's affective wagon to a dancing star: 'Thus goes the body through history, a becomer and a fighter' (Z1 'On the Bestowing Virtue' 1, KSA 4:98). A sufferer too as suggested by the red-hot ore reminiscent of a cauterising iron and the piercing, annihilating arrows of a Sebastian-like martyrdom.

Kant's good will and Zarathustra's will to the *Übermensch* both require the sacrifice of ease and self-gratification to a higher moral goal. Zarathustra loves those who 'keep holy [their] highest hope!' (Z1 'On the Tree on the Mountain', KSA 4:54), a holiness which demands the type of martyrdom indicated in the indented citation above. Unlike the martyrdom of one who 'first seek[s] a reason beyond the stars to perish and become a sacrifice', the knower 'sacrifices himself to the earth, so that the earth of the *Übermensch* may one day come' (ZP 4, KSA 4:17). To die for a transcendent Being whose kingdom is reputed to lie beyond the stars is in Zarathustra's opinion to die for 'a celestial nought' (Z1 'On the Hinterlanders', KSA 4:36). But is there not a strong family resemblance here between the steadfast fidelity of the martyr's will to an idea of goodness and virtue and Zarathustra's will to a 'higher goal'?[41] As Zarathustra confesses, 'We [firstlings] all bleed on secret sacrificial altars, we all roast and burn in honour of ancient idols' (Z3 'On Old and New Tablets' 6, KSA 4:250–1). And while the *Übermensch*, to which man is exhorted to sacrifice himself, is no deity, it is an idea that is intended to inspire the same all-consuming reverence. Moralist or immoralist, Christ or Antichrist, he who sacrifices himself to a higher ideal does so at the behest of a ruling thought. And whether this higher ideal is articulated as a practical law to which the will freely submits in its dutiful obedience to the law it enacts, or is figuratively rendered as sun, star or the great noontide, as a 'ruling thought' it is to command the will absolutely.

In the man who strives towards a higher ideal, commanding and obeying are òne and indivisible. Such a man, asserts Zarathustra, is 'obedient in commanding' (Z2 'On Self-Overcoming', KSA 4:147). Unlike the fickle and divided will driven by the incessant flux of the 'bad drives' (Z1 'On the Tree on the Mountain', KSA 4:53), a good will, or a will to the *Übermensch*, is a single will commanded by a single goal: 'Where is beauty? Where I *must desire* with my whole will, where I desire to love and perish so that an image remains not merely an image' (Z2 'On Immaculate Perception', KSA 4:157). The stressed imperative is noteworthy here, suggesting that the union of love and perishing, of the ardent will's voluntary submission to a ruling thought or image (the *Übermensch*), is a form of loving obedience and self-sacrifice:

> An experiment and a risk seemed all commanding to me; and when it commands, the living thing risks itself in doing so.
>
> Indeed, even when it commands itself, it must also atone for its commanding. Of its own law must it become judge and avenger and sacrifice. (Z2 'On Self-Overcoming', KSA 4:147)

It is this self-imposition of the law by a commanding-obeying will that in Kant's moral philosophy lends to man 'a certain sublimity and *dignity*'.

> For it is not in so far as he is *subject* to the law that [a dutiful person] has sublimity, but rather in so far as, in regard to this very same law, he is at the same time its *author* and is subordinated to it only on this ground. (AA 4:440)[42]

And it is in this shared concept of an individual who freely submits to a self-imposed practical law and does so through the agency of an autonomous rational will that Kant and Zarathustra can be seen as kindred spirits.

Notes

1. R. Kevin Hill references Olivier Reboul's *Nietzsche, critique de Kant* (Paris: Presses universitaires de France, 1974), but notes that whereas Reboul's monograph focuses exclusively on the late Nietzsche, the first of Hill's two-part book focuses on the relationship between Kant's *Critique of Judgement* and Nietzsche's *The Birth of Tragedy*. R. Kevin Hill, *Nietzsche's Critiques: The Kantian Foundations of his Thought* (Oxford: Oxford University Press, 2003), p. 8 (footnote).
2. Hill, *Nietzsche's Critiques*, p. 6.
3. Ibid. pp. 6–32.
4. Charles Larmore rejects on heteronomous grounds Kant's conception of an autonomous or self-legislating reason. He notes that for Kant, self-legislation means that 'principles of thought and action acquire their authority by virtue of rational beings imposing them upon themselves, instead of supposing them endowed with an independent validity to which they must simply assent'. According to Larmore, however, when we impose principles on ourselves 'we presumably do so for reasons: we suppose that it is fitting for us to adopt them, or that adopting them will advance certain of our interests. Self-legislation, when it does occur, is an activity that takes place in the light of reasons that we must antecedently recognize, and whose own authority we therefore do not institute but rather find ourselves called upon to acknowledge.' He concludes, 'in a very un-Kantian spirit, that reason at bottom is a *receptive* faculty'. Thus, while acknowledging that 'Reason does have an inherent connection to freedom . . . it must be freedom conceived, not as autonomy, but rather as the ability to be *moved* by reasons instead of by mere causes' (my emphasis). Charles Larmore, *The Autonomy of Morality* (New York: Cambridge University Press, 2008), pp. 43–5. Whether one endorses Larmore's position will depend on how one interprets his use of the word 'interests'. On my reading of Zarathustra's doctrine of self-overcoming, the agent of that overcoming is a self-legislating rational will that acts exclusively in the light of an idea, a thought, a goal that goes against all other interests except the 'interest' dictated by a higher ideal of humanity.
5. Immanuel Kant. *The Metaphysics of Morals*, trans. Mary Gregor (1991).

6. R. Lanier Anderson, 'What is a Nietzschean Self', in Janaway and Robertson, p. 202.
7. 'Nietzsche's own moral psychological apparatus', writes Lanier Anderson, 'is populated by an impressive array of attitude-types – drives, affects, instincts, desires, wills, feelings, moods, valuations, sensations, concepts, beliefs, convictions, fictions, imaginings, cognitions, and so on'. It may be entirely coincidental, but it is striking that 'cognition' appears at the end of the list and directly after 'fictions' and 'imaginings'. Ibid. p. 210.
8. Ibid. pp. 223–5.
9. *The Metaphysics of Morals* is divided into two parts: the Doctrine of Right, followed by the Doctrine of Virtue.
10. Brusotti et al. (2017).
11. Simon Robertson, 'Normativity and Moral Psychology: Nietzsche's Critique of Kantian Universality', in Constâncio and Bailey, pp. 58–63.
12. Ibid. pp. 71–7.
13. Tom Bailey, 'Nietzsche's Kantian Ethics', *International Studies in Philosophy*, 35:3 (2003), pp. 7–9. See also Tom Bailey 'Nietzsche the Kantian?', in Gemes and Richardson, pp. 134–59.
14. Garrath Williams, 'Nietzsche's Response to Kant's Morality', *The Philosophical Forum*, 30:3 (1999), p. 204.
15. '[T]o think causally . . . to fix with certainty what is end and what is means; above all, to reckon, to be able to calculate – and for that to be possible, man must himself have become *calculable, regulated, necessary*, even for himself and his own self-perception.' But note the incredulous disclaimer with which Nietzsche prefaces this passage: 'But what a lot of preconditions there are!' (GM II 1, KSA 5:292).
16. Hill, *Nietzsche's Critiques*, p. 216.
17. I am indebted to Mark Timmons's lucid explication of Kant's three formal constraints in 'The Categorical Imperative and Universalizability', in *Groundwork for the Metaphysics of Morals*, eds. Christoph Horn and Dieter Schönecker (Berlin: Walter de Gruyter, 2006), pp. 187–9. Simon Robertson also offers a defence of Kantian universality in Nietzsche's thought. While acknowledging that Nietzsche rejects the Kantian requirement that the 'oughts' generated by a moral law apply universally across all agents, Robertson goes on to demonstrate that Nietzsche's conception of self-legislation coheres in all other respects with the 'law-like character of moral reasons' (the first formal constraint) in the Kantian model:

(1) Nietzschean laws govern and constrain conduct 'in a systemic and systematic way'; (2) these self-legislative demands represent 'deep-seated, whole-hearted *commitments*'; and (3) these commitments may be experienced as having 'the force of *practical necessity*' in the same way that Kantian rational agents experience the rational demands of the moral law. Thus, Robertson concludes, 'there is nothing to preclude the *form* of Nietzschean laws being universal – even if their *scope* or jurisdiction is restricted to higher types. As a result, Nietzsche need not deny the thesis that practical normative laws are universal in form.' Simon Robertson, 'Normativity and Moral Psychology', in Constâncio and Bailey, pp. 66–7.
18. This quotation opens my 2013 article on Kant and Nietzsche, out of which article the current chapter evolved. See Francesca Cauchi, 'Nietzsche and Kant: Self-legislation and the rational will in Zarathustra's ethics', *Oxford German Studies*, 42.3 (2013), pp. 280–95.
19. I agree with Peter Sjöstedt that Nietzsche's use of 'hypothetical' here reflects the fact that he was still in the process of developing his doctrine of will to power, a development to which his numerous notebook entries on the subject amply attest. Peter Sjöstedt, 'Metaphysical Doctrine of Nietzsche's Will to Power: Critique of Maudemarie Clark's Position', <www.philosopher.eu/metaphysical-doctrine-of-nietzsches-will-to-power/> (last accessed 7 April 2022). For an overview of the most authoritative interpretations of Nietzsche's concept of will to power, including Maudemarie Clark's, see Bernard Reginster, *The Affirmation of Life: Nietzsche on Overcoming Nihilism* (Cambridge, MA: Harvard University Press, 2006), pp. 126–33. It is worth noting, however, that many of these exegeses draw heavily on *The Will to Power* – a compilation of selected fragments from Nietzsche's notebooks which Nietzsche's sister, Elisabeth Förster-Nietzsche, edited, organised and, in some cases, redacted prior to publication. Reginster's own definition of will to power as the basis of Nietzsche's 'revaluation of life-negating values' is 'will to the overcoming of resistance ... So defined, the concept of power is, in and of itself, devoid of any *determinate content*. It gets a determinate content only from its relation to some determinate desire or drive.' Ibid. pp. 131–2.
20. Lawrence Hatab also refers to the destructive-generative dynamic of will to power and traces it back to the Apollo-Dionysus dynamic as staged by Nietzsche in *The Birth of Tragedy* and to the Greek

agōn. In respect of the latter, Hatab refers us to Nietzsche's early essay 'Homer's Contest', in which Nietzsche characterises the Greek *agōn* as a competitive struggle that 'emerged as a *cultivation* of more brutal natural drives' and aimed at excellence rather than the obliteration of opposition. But while Hatab acknowledges 'the flux and force of natural life energies' and depicts the will to power as 'an "agonistic" force field', he does not explicitly refer to will to power as a metaphysical doctrine. Instead, he refers us to Nietzsche's ungrounded immanent or 'existential naturalism', which 'includes forces, instincts, passions, and powers that are not reducible to objective, scientific categories'. Lawrence J. Hatab, *Nietzsche's Life Sentence: Coming to Terms with Eternal Recurrence* (New York and London: Routledge, 2005), pp. 7-17. For a brief but sound refutation of the postmodernist reading of Nietzsche's doctrine of will to power as a *non*-metaphysical doctrine see Peter Sjöstedt's article cited in the previous note. Daniel Harris also notes the agonic dynamic of self-overcoming, 'The strength of the *agōn*, and so of self-overcoming, is the strength to have being, to know and trust and affirm oneself, and then to express that strength by plunging oneself into becoming out of an affirmation of the finite, revisable, and workable products of human striving.' But whereas Harris's emphasis is on the ideal of affirmation, mine is on the lived reality of the finite 'plunging' and on the superhuman strength that such plunging or *Untergang* entails. Daniel I. Harris, 'Compassion and Affirmation in Nietzsche', *Journal of Nietzsche Studies*, 48:1 (2017), p. 22.

21. William Blake, *The Marriage of Heaven and Hell*. For a reading of the parallels between Blake and Nietzsche's response to Christian morality, see Francesca Cauchi, 'Blake and Nietzsche on self-slaughter and the moral law: A reading of *Jerusalem*', *Journal of European Studies*, 45:1 (2014), pp. 1-18.
22. J. Keeping similarly notes that the creative aspect of Nietzsche's concept of will to power is not limited to procreation but also extends to the creation of 'new philosophies, and new scientific theories.' J. Keeping, 'The Thousand Goals and the One Goal: Morality and Will to Power in Nietzsche's *Zarathustra*', *European Journal of Philosophy*, 20:1 (2011), p. 78.
23. A representative selection of these articles is: Ken Gemes, '"We Remain of Necessity Strangers to Ourselves": The Key Message of Nietzsche's *Genealogy*', in *Nietzsche's 'On the Genealogy of Morals': Critical Essays*, ed. Christa Davis Acampora (Lanham, MD: Row-

man & Littlefield, 2006), pp. 191–208; Charles Larmore's chapter entitled 'Nietzsche and the Will to Truth', in Larmore, *Autonomy*, pp. 223–45; Scott Jenkins, 'Nietzsche's Questions Concerning the Will to Truth', *Journal of the History of Philosophy*, 50:2 (2012), 265–89; and Daniel I. Harris, 'Nietzsche on Honesty and the Will to Truth', *Journal of the British Society for Phenomenology*, 51:3 (2020), pp. 247–58.

24. Gemes, Larmore, Jenkins and Harris (see previous note for publication details) all agree that Nietzsche not only values, but extols truth and advances his own truth claims. As Jenkins (p. 265) succinctly puts it, 'Nietzsche's own views on the value of truth do not follow from his critique of the will to truth.' In their respective analyses of this contradiction or incoherence in Nietzsche's stance towards truth, each of the above commentators cites instances of Nietzsche's clear commitment to truth. Larmore (p. 241, n26) cites Nietzsche's contrast between Christian faith and the ancients' '*fact-sense*, the last and most valuable of all senses' (A 59, KSA 6:247–8); Jenkins (p. 286) cites Nietzsche's assertion that the 'service of truth is the hardest service' and one that 'requires greatness of soul' (A 50, KSA 6:230); Jenkins (p. 265) and Harris (p. 249) both cite Nietzsche's claim that for him the 'true measure of value' increasingly came to be 'how much truth can one *endure*, how much truth does a spirit *dare*?' (EH F 3, KSA 6:259); and Harris (p. 249) refers us to Nietzsche's admiration for those who 'have trained themselves to sacrifice all desirability to truth, to *every* truth, even plain, bitter, ugly, unpleasant, unchristian, immoral truth ... For there are such truths.' (GM I 1, KSA 5:258). As Larmore argues (pp. 237–8), Nietzsche failed to differentiate between truth as a goal and truth as a standard, adding that 'Thinking itself would be unintelligible without a respect for the demands of truth.' Harris's incisive account (p. 249) will serve to clarify the current position among Anglo-American philosophers on the status of Nietzsche's commitment to truth: 'Nietzsche, at least by the *Genealogy of Morality*, clearly believes in truth, puts forward truth claims, and decries the falsity of numerous widespread beliefs. Indeed, he believes that his philosophy tracks certain truths about human beings obscured by other philosophies ... Rather than questioning the existence of truth, Nietzsche questions its value.'

25. Cf. 'any insistence on profundity and thoroughness is a violation, a desire to hurt the basic will of the spirit, which incessantly

strives for surface and sheen – in all desire to know there is a drop of cruelty' (BGE 229, KSA 5:167).

26. In his discussion of the relationship between law and freedom in Kant's concept of the moral law, Walter Lowe cites the following passage from Jean-Luc Nancy's *L'Impératif catégorique*: 'the law is *addressed to* a freedom, and is *not founded by* that freedom. Conversely, freedom consists not of following one's own law ... but of initiating something by oneself: it is a freedom to inaugurate, in advance of any law. And yet it is this very freedom which is, from the very beginning, engaged by the law. In short, there are always two "origins" here, which do not overlap and each of which seems endlessly, in its turn, to take precedence over the other: the address by the law and the free beginning.' See Walter Lowe, *Theology and Difference: The Wound of Reason* (Bloomington and Indianapolis: Indiana University Press, 1993), p. 110.

27. Immanuel Kant, *Groundwork of the Metaphysic of Morals*, trans. H. J. Paton (New York: Harper & Row, 1964). In his meticulously researched archival study on Nietzsche's intellectual influences, Thomas Brobjer notes that while there is no evidence of Nietzsche ever having read Kant's *Groundwork*, Schopenhauer's critique of the latter text was 'closely read' by Nietzsche in 1884. Brobjer, *Nietzsche's Philosophical Context*, pp. 36–9.

28. Peter Berkowitz also draws a link between *Zarathustra* and Kant's *Groundwork*, remarking that Zarathustra's ethics of creativity 'should be seen as a radicalization of the characteristically modern doctrine according to which the good is equated with freedom and freedom is understood in terms of living under laws that one makes for or gives to oneself' – to which he adds a footnote reference to Rousseau's *Social Contract* and Kant's *Groundwork*. Berkowitz, *Nietzsche*, pp. 149–53. But while Berkowitz describes Zarathustra's ethics as one which 'conceives of the creator as one who makes his own will a law' (Z1 'On the Way of the Creator'), he does not identify that law as the law of becoming, nor does he associate this law with Zarathustra's doctrine of self-overcoming.

29. Allen W. Wood, 'The Moral Theory of German Idealism', in *The Routledge Companion to Nineteenth Century Philosophy*, ed. Dean Moyer (Oxford: Routledge, 2010), p. 111.

30. Cf. the following passage from Kant's *Groundwork*: 'human reason, with this compass [i.e., judgement] in hand, is well able to distinguish, in all cases that present themselves, what is good or evil, right or wrong ... the power of judgement first begins to show what

advantages it has in itself when the ordinary mind excludes all sensuous motives from its practical laws. Then ordinary intelligence becomes even subtle . . . in trying to determine honestly for its own instruction the value of various actions' (AA 4:404).

31. Cf. 'The passions become evil and insidious if they are regarded as evil and insidious. This is how Christianity succeeded in transforming Eros and Aphrodite – great ideal-befitting powers – into diabolical goblins and sprites' (D 76, KSA 3:73).

32. In a late notebook entry, Nietzsche denounces the '*dissolute and licentious*' not for their 'immorality' but for 'their depressing influence on the *value of the desires*' (WLN 11[153]:230, KSA 13:72).

33. Cf. 'The weak in courage is strong in cunning'. William Blake, *The Marriage of Heaven and Hell.*

34. Lowe, *Theology and Difference*, p. 113. A more recent defence has been mounted by Pauline Kleingeld who lays particular emphasis on Kant's precise definition of happiness. Her first point is that Kant defines happiness 'in terms of the harmony between an agent's ends and the state of the world, not in terms of how the agent feels'. Her second is that when happiness is conceived 'as [an] element of the highest good, that is, as the happiness of *virtuous* agents, it also includes the realization of their *moral* ends'. Pauline Kleingeld, 'Kant on "Good", the Good, and the Duty to Promote the Highest Good', in *The Highest Good in Kant's Philosophy*, ed. Thomas Höwing (Berlin and Boston: Walter de Gruyter, 2016), p. 40.

35. As noted in Chapter 1, Kant draws a distinction between affects (*Affekten*) and passions (*Leidenschaften*) (AA 6:407–8). In this study, however, I use the term 'affects' to denote both the drives and the passions, except where otherwise stated.

36. These lines evoke a kind of Blakean marriage between the 'Thunder of Thought, & flames of fierce desire'. See William Blake, *Jerusalem* (plate 3), in *The Complete Writings of William Blake with all the variant readings*, ed. G. Keynes (London: Nonesuch Press, 1957), p. 621.

37. I agree with Larmore that 'Nietzsche was no "value-pluralist" in any fundamental sense.' Larmore, *Autonomy*, p. 242.

38. Cf. '[W]e shall give back to men their courage for actions decried as egoistic and restore to these actions their value – *we shall rob the latter of their bad conscience!*' (D 148, KSA 3:140).

39. Robert B. Louden also notes that in several places Nietzsche explicitly acknowledges 'that duty and ought are central concepts

in his own system of values'. Citing as examples BGE 226 (KSA 5:162) and D Pref. 4 (KSA 3:15–16), Louden further notes that 'Nietzschean oughts share [the] core feature of inescapability with Kantian categorical imperatives.' Robert B. Louden, 'Phantom Duty? Nietzsche versus Königsbergian Chinadom', in Constâncio and Bailey, pp. 202–3.

40. The ideality of the *Übermensch*, as evinced in the metaphorical language to which Zarathustra resorts in his depiction of the same, brings to mind Lowe's emphasis on the necessarily abstract nature of Kant's concept of the 'highest good': 'This necessary . . . indirectness of the notion of the Highest Good is of cardinal importance because it thwarts the human, all-too-human impulse to give content to the notion by looking to what one happens to find fulfilling; by hitching one's wagon to whatever "inevitable march of history" is currently in vogue.' Lowe, *Theology and Difference*, p. 125. Lowe's borrowing of the Nietzschean term 'human, all-too-human' as the self-interested element expressly excluded in Kant's notion of the 'highest good' lends further support to my claim of commonality in the ethical thought of both philosophers.

41. Karl Jaspers makes a similar point concerning the fervour of Nietzsche's will to sacrifice: 'Quite possibly everything that Nietzsche denies has been denied before, but . . . without endangering the denier existentially because of the secret safety of some obvious existent standing in the background. In Nietzsche's case, on the other hand, dissatisfaction gives rise to such a passionate and self-sacrificing impulse to deny that it seems to come from the source that impelled the great religious leaders and prophets.' Karl Jaspers, *Nietzsche: An Introduction to the Understanding of His Philosophical Activity*, trans. Charles F. Wallraff and Frederick J. Schmitz (South Bend, IN: Regnery/Gateway, Inc., 1979), p. 434.

42. Note, however, Allen Wood's interpretation of what Kant means by the 'author' of the moral law (cited at the end of the 'Creator-destroyers and hammer-wielding legislators' section of this chapter).

3
Hegel's 'Labour of the Negative' and the Lacerations of Self-Negation

> Ours is a birth-time and a period of transition to a new era. Spirit has broken with the world it has hitherto inhabited and imagined, and is of a mind to submerge it in the past, and in the labour of its own transformation.
>
> (PhS §11, W 3:18)

Dissenters notwithstanding, Hegel and Nietzsche have long been held to be fundamentally irreconcilable,[1] not least because of Nietzsche's hostility towards all philosophical systems – 'The will to system is a lack of integrity' (TI 'Maxims and Arrows' 26, KSA 6:63) – and his animus towards those late eighteenth-century philosophers who delayed 'the victory of scientific atheism' and with it the death of God. According to Nietzsche, Hegel 'was a delayer *par excellence*, with his grandiose attempt to persuade us of the divinity of existence by finally enlisting the help of our sixth sense, the "historical sense"' (GS 357, KSA 3:599). In recent years, however, renewed attempts at a rapprochement between the two philosophers have been made.[2] Robert R. Williams, for example, has sought to establish points of convergence in the specific areas of tragedy, recognition and the 'death of God', while Will Dudley finds common ground in the two thinkers' positing of true freedom in the practice of philosophy.[3] I shall also touch on the latter by highlighting

Hegel and Nietzsche's common calls for a practice of philosophy uncontaminated by moral bias – although, as I have endeavoured to show in the previous two chapters, Nietzsche's re-purposing of the Christian virtues of honesty, obedience, self-control and self-denial evinces a clear moral bias, albeit one predicated on the law of becoming rather than on any divinely ordained law.

My main contention in this chapter is that Nietzsche's principle of affirmative negation, which in *Zarathustra* is figured as both lion spirit and *Untergang* (destruction), is an iteration of Hegel's 'labour of the negative' (PhS §19, W 3:24). In section 1, I shall underscore the destructive force of the collocation 'affirmative negation'. In section 2, I will show how the lion spirit of negation, the second stage in what Zarathustra refers to as the three metamorphoses of the spirit from camel to lion to child (Z1 'On the Three Metamorphoses', KSA 4:29–31), unwittingly recuperates Hegel's assertion that 'Spirit is not the life that shrinks from death and keeps itself untouched by devastation' (PhS §32, W 3:36). In section 3, I shall draw out the affinity between Hegel's notion of practical freedom and Zarathustra's goal of planting the 'highest thought of life' (Z1 'On War and Warriors', KSA 4:59) into the soil of the passions. And in the final section, I shall look at the ramifications of spirit's tyrannical demand for 'much bitter dying' (Z2 'On the Blissful Isles', KSA 4:111) in a life dedicated to self-overcoming.

Affirmative Negation and Deleuzian Derision

For Gilles Deleuze, affirmative negation is quite simply an oxymoron. In his seminal 1962 study *Nietzsche et la philosophie* (not translated into English until 1986), he derides what he loosely and reductively understands as Hegel's dialectical negation-of-a-negation and, on the basis of this simplification, declares Nietzsche's philosophy of affirmation to be 'resolutely anti-dialectical'.[4] Equally resolute, however, is Deleuze's negative construal of the Hegelian dialectic. Denouncing the latter as a 'combination of reactive forces and nihilism', as '*Ressentiment* [which] needs negative premises, two negations, in order to produce a phantom of affirmation', Deleuze rapturously affirms

Nietzsche's 'affirmation of affirmation'.[5] Unless we recognise the 'anti-Hegelianism [that] runs throughout Nietzsche's work as its cutting edge', writes Deleuze, 'Nietzsche's philosophy remains abstract and barely comprehensible'.[6] This is a very large, if not preposterous claim and one which flies in the face of Walter Kaufmann's earlier characterisation of Nietzsche as a 'dialectical monist'. Drawing parallels between Hegelian 'spirit' and Nietzsche's 'will to power', and between Hegel's '*aufheben*' and Nietzsche's '*sublimieren*', Kaufmann contends that 'Nietzsche's sublimation actually involves, no less than does Hegel's *aufheben*, a simultaneous preserving, cancelling and lifting up', by means of which the metaphysical principle of spirit or will to power transforms itself from matter into form while retaining its essential force throughout its successive transformations.[7] In the previous chapter, I also focused on the essential force of will to power and showed how Nietzsche transposes this force from the metaphysical realm of becoming to the spiritual realm of self-overcoming.

Deleuze's chief textual support for his anti-dialectical Nietzsche is the passage in *Ecce Homo* where Nietzsche sniffs out the 'offensively Hegelian' whiff of his first publication, *The Birth of Tragedy*, in which 'the opposition between Dionysian and Apollonian . . . [is] sublated (*aufgehoben*) into a unity in tragedy' (EH 'BT' 1, KSA 6:310). As depicted in the young Basel professor's inaugural publication, Dionysus and Apollo respectively emblematise the Schopenhauerian-imbued concepts of the primordial One and the principle of individuation ('*principium individuationis*'), or in Hegelian terms, undifferentiated substance and subject. But if Nietzsche was soon to discard Schopenhauer's metaphysics of Being, the *agōn* between aesthetic form and tragic insight (Apollo and Dionysus) is still very much alive in *Gay Science* 107, tellingly entitled 'Our ultimate gratitude to art' (see Chapter 1) and in the quasi-satyr play of Part 4 of *Zarathustra*.[8] In both of these texts, art either performs or is said to perform the redemptive role of safeguarding either author or protagonist against the abyss of negation. But whereas in *The Birth of Tragedy* Nietzsche claims that it is 'only as an aesthetic phenomenon that existence and the world are eternally justified', in GS 107 the earlier claim is modified to read: 'As an aesthetic phenomenon existence is still *endurable for us*' (KSA 3:464). In other words, art is no longer seen by Nietzsche as a justification of life but rather as a life-sustaining ruse for enduring it.[9]

In *Ecce Homo*, the creative tension between Apollonian form and Dionysian Being that had constituted the core dynamic of *The Birth of Tragedy* is replaced with the dialectical tension between destruction and becoming, negation and affirmation:

> The affirmation of passing away *and destruction* that is crucial in a Dionysian philosophy, a yea-saying to opposition and war, *becoming* along with a radical repudiation of the very concept of 'Being' – in all cases, I must acknowledge these as being closer to me than to what has been thought hitherto. (EH 'BT' 3, KSA 6:313)[10]

It is this cognitive act of affirmative negation, which typifies Nietzsche's hammer-hard real philosophers and Zarathustra's creator-destroyer *Erkennenden*, that in this chapter I shall map onto Hegel's concept of '*determinate* negation'. Determinate negation is the second stage in the Hegelian dialectic and denotes the critical work of negation in thought's progressive journey towards knowledge.[11] The negation is determinate in the dual sense of having content and of generating a new form: 'It is a new concept but one higher and richer than the preceding – richer because it negates or opposes the preceding and therefore contains it, and it contains even more than that, for it is the unity of itself and its opposite' (SL 33, W 5:49). Put another way, the discarding of a particular conceptualisation yields a more accurate articulation of that concept, which would not have been possible without the prior articulation.[12] Zarathustra views this *Aufhebung*, this negation and transformation of the flawed ideas of the revered 'great men' as one of his primary tasks:

> I walk among people as the fragments of the future: that future which I look towards.

And all my concentration and endeavour is to compose and collect into one what is fragment and riddle and dreadful accident . . .

To redeem those past ones and transform every 'it was' into 'thus I willed it!' (Z2 'On Redemption', KSA 4:179)

In this chapter, I shall argue that dialectical negation, as the immanent driving force of the Hegelian spirit's 'progressive unfolding of truth' (PhS §2; W 3:12), is pivotal to Zarathustra's doctrine of self-overcoming, the first precept of which is the negation of the Christian moral paradigm and all erroneous, fragmentary, partial thought that has hitherto passed for knowledge. To insist, therefore, as Deleuze insists, that 'Nietzsche's "yes" is opposed to the dialectical "no"; affirmation to dialectical negation; . . . [and] lightness, dance, to dialectical responsibilities',[13] is to celebrate Nietzsche's affirmative ideal while disregarding the '*crooked* ways' (Z2 'On Self-Overcoming', KSA 4:148) of negation by which such an ideal is to be reached. In short, Nietzsche's 'yes' is inseparable from a ruthlessly destructive 'no', a 'no', moreover, to the binary mode of argumentation displayed in Deleuze's critique.

In the opening aphorism of *Human, All Too Human*, Nietzsche dismantles the type of binary opposition routinely employed by metaphysicians and substitutes organic relation for crude opposition. 'How can something emerge from its opposite', he asks, 'for example, rationality from irrationality, the sentient from the dead, logic from unlogic (*Unlogik*) . . . living for others from selfishness, truth from errors?' Such seeming oppositions, he argues, 'are only sublimations (*Sublimirungen*) in which the basic element appears to have almost evaporated and which crystallises only under the keenest observation' (HH 1, KSA 2:23-4). Accordingly, the exultant 'yes' which Deleuze opposes to Hegel's dialectical 'no' needs to be approached with considerable circumspection. As Nietzsche cautions, a philosophical ideal must always be viewed in light of the physiological need of the person promoting it: '"Is it hunger or abundance that have become creative here?"' (GS 370, KSA 3:621) – the same hunger to which Nietzsche admits in his late preface to Volume 1 of *Human All Too Human*, confiding to his readers that the need to alleviate the burden of 'sickness, loneliness, strangers, *acedia*, inactivity' was what spawned his idealised 'free spirit' (HH I P2, KSA 2:15).

From observations/confessions such as these, one can justifiably infer that Nietzsche's customary rhetorical flourishes and Zarathustra's hectic *joie de vivre* often mask an underlying need – a need which Nietzsche's intellectual conscience was bent on unmasking and quashing through a ferocious discipline of probity and self-negation. This discipline, we learn in *Zarathustra*, is the secret of life that life itself once imparted to the preacher of self-overcoming:

> 'Behold', life said to me, 'I am that *which must always overcome itself* . . .
>
> I must be struggle and becoming and purpose and the conflict of purpose – alas, whoever guesses my will guesses too on what *crooked* ways it must go!
>
> Whatever I create and however much I love it, soon must I oppose it and my love: so wills my will.' (Z2 'On Self-Overcoming', KSA 4:148)

This inner conflict and negation, I contend, is a re-articulation of Hegel's 'labour of the negative'. It is a labour, moreover, that Nietzsche claims to have begun while writing his fourth *Untimely Meditation*, 'Richard Wagner in Bayreuth' (1876). In his 1886 preface to Volume II of *Human, All Too Human*, Nietzsche asserts that 'The composure needed to be able to speak of an innermost aloneness (*Alleinsein*) and austerity over the long intervening years first came to me with the book *Human, All Too Human*' (HH II P1, KSA 2: 370–1). It was in these years, 'lonely now and severely mistrustful of myself', that 'I took sides, not without anger, *against* myself and *for* everything hard and hurtful precisely for me'. (HH II P4, KSA 2:373)

Spirit's 'Labour of the Negative'

In his preface to the *Phenomenology*, Hegel writes of 'the seriousness, the suffering, the patience, and the labour of the negative', of a life lived not *in itself* but *for itself* (PhS §19, W 3:24) – a life in which the 'reflection in otherness within itself . . . is the process of its own becoming' (PhS §18, W 3:23). *In itself*, spirit is substance. In order for it to be *for itself*, 'it must be . . . the knowledge of itself as Spirit, i.e. it must be an *object* to itself, but just as immediately a sublated object, reflected into itself'. This reflexivity is the means by which spirit's undifferentiated substance actualises and differentiates itself. It is the moment when spirit '*relates itself to itself* and is *determinate*' (PhS §25, W 3:28). In this 'moment of the "I" which is for itself pure negativity' (PhS §21, W 3:25), substance posits itself as subject and in 'the objectivity negative to knowing' (PhS §36, W 3:38) becomes conscious of its internal subject-object bifurcation.[14] Rephrased, it is the 'moment' of spirit's rite of passage from consciousness to self-consciousness, when spirit's internecine but transformational battle within itself commences. As Hegel avers, self-consciousness is spirit's 'judgment of its own nature and, at the same time, the operation of coming to itself, to produce itself, to make itself (actually) into that which it is in itself (potentially)' (RH 23, W 12:31).[15]

In *Zarathustra*, this notion of transformative negation as the necessary (but, as we shall see, far from sufficient) condition for spirit's creative act of self-realisation, lies at the heart of Zarathustra's doctrine of self-overcoming. Literalising spirit's 'operation of coming to itself' as a form of invasive surgery ('Spirit is life that itself cuts into life'), Zarathustra echoes the following trope in Hegel's *Phenomenology*:

> the life of Spirit is not the life that shrinks from death and keeps itself untouched by devastation, but rather the life that endures it and maintains itself in it. It wins its truth only when, in utter dismemberment, it finds itself. (PhS §32, W 3:36)

The same trope anticipates Nietzsche's concept of a 'Dionysian' type of philosopher who 'can allow himself every luxury of destruction, disintegration, negation' (NCW 'We Antipodeans', KSA 6:425). Through violent confrontation with itself – the tyranny to which the title of this monograph refers – spirit can begin to tackle the existential imperative of 'mak[ing] itself (actually) into that which it is in itself (potentially)', of learning 'how to become what you are' (to borrow the subtitle to Nietzsche's *Ecce Homo*).

Before making itself into that which it is in itself, spirit's first task is to purge itself of any predisposition or 'complacency (*Genügsamkeit*)' (PhS §10, W 3:17). A fact often overlooked by Nietzsche scholars is that Hegel, just as forcefully as his successor, railed against the propensity of philosophers towards moral edification rather than rational insight. In his prefatory preamble to the *Phenomenology of Spirit*, Hegel censures the 'rapturous haziness' of indeterminate abstractions such as 'the holy' and 'the eternal' as an appeal to feeling rather than understanding (PhS §7–10, W 3:16–17). In remarkably similar terms, Nietzsche declares that philosophers who are wedded to the 'holy task [of] improving, saving, or redeeming mankind' know nothing about the demands of 'intellectual integrity' (A 12, KSA 6:178). With characteristic excess, however, Nietzsche did not stop there. Diagnosing 'the most abstruse metaphysical assertions of a philosopher' as symptomatic of an unconscious moral disposition, he notoriously dismissed *all* philosophical works as affective will to power tricked out in epistemological finery (BGE 6, KSA 5:19–20).

Both thinkers also sought to recall philosophy to its proper earthly sphere. Bewailing spirit's impoverished 'sense of solid and substantial being', Hegel criticises his peers for 'shroud[ing] in a mist the manifold variety of ... earthly existence and of thought' instead of confining the spirit of inquiry to 'Notion and Necessity as products of that reflection which is at home only in the finite' (PhS §9–10, W 3:17). In a similar vein, Nietzsche's wittily concise 'history of an error' dismisses as mere fabrication the Platonic, Christian and Kantian notions of a so-called true world. Duly noting the recent dispersal of the 'mist and scepticism' shrouding the Kantian concept of the noumenal, Nietzsche announces 'The first yawn of reason. The cockcrow of positivism' (TI 'How the "true" world became a fable', KSA 6:80). In short, the only world with which a genuine philosopher ought to concern himself is the earthly one: 'Remain true to the earth' (ZP 3, KSA 4:15), implores Zarathustra, and ignore those priestly types whose 'infatuated spirit' beats its head against the walls of the finite world in a desperate attempt to escape into another world – a world which Zarathustra mockingly refers to as '"that world"' (Z1 'On the Hinterlanders', KSA 4:36).[16]

In purging itself of all otherworldly traces, spirit invariably finds itself in conflict with the regnant moral or ethical paradigm, the destruction of which, according to Hegel, is inevitable. All moral systems, he claims, are intrinsically unstable since the universal which each purports to manifest is a flawed particularisation of that universal (cf. Nietzsche's repudiation of Christian morality as a degraded, decadent, herd-animal type of morality). As Hegel argues,

> a moral whole, as such, is limited. It must have above it a higher universality, which makes it disunited in itself. The transition from one spiritual pattern to the next is just this, that the former moral whole, in itself a universal, through being thought (in terms of the higher universal), is abolished as a particular. (RH 38, GL 74)

It is at this transitional moment, continues Hegel,

> that appear those momentous collisions between existing, acknowledged duties, laws, and rights and those possibilities which are adverse to this system, violate it, and even destroy its foundations and existence. (RH 39, W 12:44–5)

The agents of this spiritual progression, writes Hegel, are those 'world-historical individuals'[17] who are able to grasp 'a higher universal, make it their own purpose, and realize this purpose in accordance with the higher law (*Begriffe*) of the spirit' (RH 39,

GL 75). For Nietzsche, who viewed himself as the nonpareil of world-historical violators, the higher law of the spirit is intellectual integrity and has its highest embodiment in those 'real philosophers' whose greatness lies in their ability to apply 'the vivisector's knife directly to the breast of the *virtues of the age*' (BGE 211–12, KSA 5:145). For Zarathustra, they are the truthful knowers who, like Nietzsche, have a sufficiently developed intellectual conscience to see the Christian moral paradigm as a debased universal and, more importantly, to recognise its residual precepts and proscriptions rooted in their own breast (see GS 344, 357 and GM III 24, previously cited in Chapters 1 and 2).

As outlined at the start of this section, this recognition is the moment when spirit relates itself to itself and becomes an object of reflection. In *Zarathustra*, this moment is referred to as 'the hour of the great contempt' (briefly addressed in Chapter 2) – the hour when the docile, venerating spirit takes a good look at itself and de(s)cries a stinking rag of 'poverty and filth and pitiful contentment!' (ZP 3, KSA 4:15).[18] Here in the desert of solitary introspection, spirit embarks on its brutal but transformative journey towards self-realisation, a journey famously allegorised in *Zarathustra* as a threefold metamorphosis of spirit from camel to lion to child. The first stage in this process occurs when the 'camel spirit' takes upon itself a new burden: the burden of incisive self-scrutiny. 'What is the heaviest thing?' asks the truthful spirit:

> Is it not this: to humiliate oneself in order to mortify one's pride? . . .
>
> Or is it this: to feed on the acorns and grass of knowledge (*Erkenntniss*) and for the sake of truth suffer hunger of soul?
>
> Or is it this: to be sick and forgo comforters, and make friends with the deaf who never hear what you want?
>
> Or is it this: to wade into filthy water when it is the water of truth and not balk at cold frogs and hot toads? (Z1 'On the Three Metamorphoses', KSA 4:29)

To the truthful spirit, mortifying one's pride and starving one's soul for the sake of herd-like truths is to submit to outmoded Christian values. Upon recognition of its sickness and the long convalescence that lies ahead in the insalubrious swamp of ugly truths,[19] the truthful and awakened spirit must submit to an even greater mortification: that of a savage self-critique. To cite the Hegel sentence once again, '[Spirit] wins its truth only when, in utter dismemberment, it finds itself' (PhS §32, W 3:36).

In *Zarathustra*, this savage self-critique is symbolised by the lion. Representing the second stage in spirit's transformation, or what Hegel refers to as 'determinate negation', the naysaying lion spirit performs the role of negative reason (EL §79, W 8:168) in its negation of the venerable Christian virtues of humility, self-abasement and pity.[20] The sanctimonious pride of hair-shirted mortification is to be humiliated by a more discerning pride mortified by its self-denigration. The emaciated soul, long fed on a (starvation) diet of transcendent Truth, is to hunger after less palatable ('acorns and grass') earthly truths (Z1 'On the Three Metamorphoses', KSA 4:29).[21] Liberated from the 'fetters of false values' (Z2 'On Priests', KSA 4:117) and its former infatuation with the infinite, spirit can return to a body no longer reduced to a spectral counterpart of the soul. And lastly, the succour of 'comforters' is to be abjured (Z1 'On the Three Metamorphoses', KSA 4:29) so that the purging of false values can be effected. Meanwhile, there is to be no shrinking from the 'cold frogs and hot toads' (ibid.) lurking in the swamp of ugly earthly truths. Implicit in these transvaluations of pride and truth is spirit's transition (to use Hegel's taxonomy) from one particularised universal to a higher species of the same, a transition that entails the negation of conceptual husks within which a flawed universal has ossified. '[S]triving and urging towards itself' (RH 39, W 12:45), spirit's truth must now succumb to a higher truth, its laws and duties to higher laws and duties,[22] and its revered concepts to newly created concepts that spirit itself must forge.[23]

As noted above, spirit's transition from one particularised universal to a higher articulation of that universal is figured in *Zarathustra* as a threefold metamorphosis of spirit. The second stage in this transformative process is the negation of the proscriptive and prescriptive tenets of Christian dogma to which the venerating or unreflecting conformist 'camel' spirit has long been in thrall:

> Spirit becomes a lion; freedom will it capture and be master in its own desert.
>
> Its last Lord it seeks here: inimical will it be to Him and to its last God; for victory will it wrestle with the great dragon.
>
> What is the great dragon which spirit no longer cares to call Lord and God? 'Thou shalt' is the name of the great dragon. But the lion spirit says 'I will'.

By vanquishing the great dragon 'Thou shalt', with its implicit prohibition of 'I will', spirit frees itself from error and illusion and thereby 'creates itself freedom for new creating'. It is crucial to grasp here the leonine ferocity involved in this work of negation, the work of vanquishing God through the deracination of Christian values one has long revered. As Zarathustra warns:

> To seize the right to new values – that is the most terrible seizing for a laden and reverential spirit. Indeed, it is preying and the act of a predatory animal.
>
> It once loved 'Thou shalt' as its most sacred thing: now it must find illusion and despotism in the most sacred in order to wrest itself free from its love: for this the preying lion is needed. (Z1 'On the Three Metamorphoses', KSA 4:30-1)

This desecration recalls the *Daybreak* passage (cited in Chapter 1) in which Nietzsche speaks of the 'spiritual and bodily tortures' endured by those who tread the path of truth and of freedom of thought (D 18, KSA 3:31). But if the role of the lion spirit is to clear the ground for the creation of new values, that creation, in the fullest sense of their fructification within the body, is the exclusive right and privilege of spirit in its third and final metamorphosis from lion to child.[24]

In contrast to the will of the lion spirit, a fundamentally reactive force driven by the single aim of extricating spirit from the jaws of the dragon 'Thou shalt', the will of the child spirit has neither goal nor final state. It simply wills its own freedom in an endless process of becoming: 'Aye, for the game of creating, my brethren, a holy yea-saying is needed: *its own* will the spirit now wills; *its own* world the world-bereft one wins' (Z1 'On the Three Metamorphoses', KSA 4:31).[25] This figurative child, I would argue, connotes the higher universal of the idea of freedom. Like a child creating its own world in the act of playing, the 'child' spirit wills *its own* will and creates *its own* world anew through continual self-recreation. 'Innocence is the child and forgetting', teaches Zarathustra, 'a new beginning, a game, a self-rolling wheel, a holy yea-saying' (ibid.). And just as Hegel's Idea of freedom is a transposition into the human spirit of God's willing 'nothing but Himself, His own will' (RH 25, W 12:33), so too is Zarathustra's figurative representation of freedom. Insofar as the child spirit wills nothing but its own will and insofar as its 'self-rolling' is *causa sui* – its eternally recurring first movement a Prime Mover, the Zarathustran child spirit can be read as a secular iteration of Divine self-creation. 'Once spirit was God', recalls Zarathustra, 'then it became man' (Z1 'On Reading and Writing', KSA 4:48); now it must become child or *Übermensch*.[26]

Before spirit can liberate itself from its bondage to 'Thou shalt'[27] and will itself towards humanity's 'highest hope' (ZP 5, KSA 4:19), it first must recognise its inner freedom. For Hegel, this freedom is spirit's essence and goal:

> it is Freedom in itself that comprises within itself the infinite necessity of bringing itself to consciousness and thereby, since knowledge about itself is its very nature, to reality. Freedom is itself its own object of attainment and the sole purpose of Spirit. (RH 25, W 12:33)

The lion spirit *affirms* this freedom by saying 'I will'. But as we shall see in the final section of this chapter, if freedom brings itself to consciousness and to the reality of its nature, there is a yawning abyss between the affirmation of freedom and its actualisation. This gulf between freedom *for* and freedom *in*, between the lion's 'nay' and the child's 'yea', between the *Untergang* (going under) and *Übergang* (going over) of self-transformation, is all too visible in Zarathustra's troubled *Bildung*. 'I will', says the lion, but in this second phase of spiritual metamorphosis, the leonine 'I will' is less a performative act than an 'I am willing' declaration of intent. As Nietzsche wryly remarks in the *Genealogy of Morals*, there is an immeasurable gulf 'between the original "I will", "I shall do" and the actual discharge of the will, its *act*' (GM II 1, KSA 5:292).

Practical Freedom and the Planting of Thought into the Passions

If spirit is to be able to will its own will in terms of action, it must first enlist the support of the passions – a point on which Hegel and Nietzsche are in full accord. Without 'the need, the instinct, the inclination, and passion of man' (RH 28, W 12:36), argues Hegel, the Idea will remain an abstract universal rather than a universal with living content. By making spirit dependent on the affects for its objective realisation, both thinkers flesh out Kant's abstract concept of an autonomous will. In doing so, however, both are equally careful to differentiate between blind animal instinct and desires that have been informed by reason. Only Idea-driven desires, avers Hegel – desires which in Zarathustra's words are driven by 'a ruling thought' – can mediate a higher universal.[28] Unlike the instinct-driven animal that cannot, in Hegel's words, 'represent to itself what it desires' (PR §4, 36; W 7:47), the animal desires in man can be imbued with a ruling thought.[29] In *Zarathustra* these animal desires are figured as 'wild dogs' and are to be taught how to sing like birds (Z1 'On the Joyful and Painful Passions', KSA 4:43).

In discussing the need for the practical engagement of desire in the actualisation of the Idea, Hegel draws our attention to the 'interest' a man necessarily has in any volitional act and to the anticipated 'satisfaction' consequent upon such an interest being met. But as Hegel explains, there is a distinction to be made between interest *in* and self-interested 'private advantage'. With regard to the first, the relation between interest and satisfaction is intrinsically connected to that between Idea and its realisation, whereas in the case of the second, advantage is pursued solely for its own sake. Distinct from naked instinct, interest *in*, insists Hegel, is subsequent to reflection, understanding and the awakening of reason (RH 28, W 12:36–7). Similarly in *Zarathustra*, 'the hour in which even your happiness becomes loathsome to you and likewise your reason and your virtue' (ZP 3, KSA 4:15) is the hour of critical self-reflection. This is the moment when happiness, reason and virtue, now viewed in the light of a higher universal, are seen as expressions of complacency and self-gratifying ease.

A parallel distinction between interest *in* and self-interest is implicit in Zarathustra's contrast between a sickly and a healthy selfishness. Driven by the idea of freedom and the will to create life-affirming (as opposed to afterlife-affirming) values, a healthy selfishness 'thirsts to heap all riches in [its] soul'. Replete with the riches of reflective understanding, spirit can afford to bestow its wealth in the form of new values. A sickly selfishness, on the other hand, robs from those whose abundance it lacks and consequently covets (Z1 'On the Bestowing Virtue' 1, KSA 4:98). As Zarathustra teaches, the satisfaction sought by these covetous types is vengeance:

> That which we discern (*erkennen*) in a man, we also inflame in him. Therefore beware of the small ones!
>
> They feel small before you and in invisible vengeance their baseness glimmers and glows at you. (Z1 'On the Flies of the Market-Place', KSA 4:67–8)

What these 'small ones' suffer from is the type of resentment that Nietzsche refers to as *ressentiment* and ascribes to the Church Fathers, namely the vengeful resentment of those who chafe against the yoke of their impotence, especially when confronted by those who, unlike themselves, are free to act upon their reaction.[30] What these 'degenerate' small ones lack is the ability to generate, to create beyond themselves: 'Upward goes our way, from genus (*Art*) to super-genus (*Über-Art*)', proclaims Zarathustra, 'but a horror to us is the degenerate sense, which says "All for me"' (Z1 'On the Bestowing Virtue' 1, KSA 4:98). Such sickly, selfish men are neither interested *in* a higher idea(l) nor capable of 'transforming it into action, into actuality' (RH 28, W 12:36). They are merely the conduit for their base instincts.

Hegel's rationale for equating 'interest' with 'passion' deserves particular attention:

> We assert then that nothing has been accomplished without an interest on the part of those who brought it about. And if 'interest' be called 'passion' [it is] because the whole individuality is concentrating all its desires and powers, with every fibre of volition, to the neglect of all other actual or possible interests and aims.

By 'passion', Hegel continues,

> I mean here nothing more than human activity resulting from private interest, from special or, if you will, self-seeking designs – with this qualification: that the whole energy of will and character is devoted to the attainment of one aim and that other interests or possible aims, indeed everything else, is sacrificed to this aim. This particular objective is so bound up with the person's will that it alone and entirely determines its direction and is inseparable from it. It is that which makes the person what he is. For a person is a specific existence. He is not man in general – such a thing does not exist – but a particular human being. (RH 29, W 12:37-8)

Described here and with startling clarity is what Nietzsche more than half a century later would term 'will to power'. What Hegel in his *Philosophy of Right* refers to as 'a *dialectic* of drives and inclinations', whereby 'the satisfaction of one demands that the satisfaction of the other be subordinated or sacrificed'

(PR §17, 50; W 7:68), is commensurate with Nietzsche's definition of will to power as the will's domination of one affect over all other competing affects in its discharge of power. To reiterate, it is crucial to distinguish here between a thought-driven desire and an instinct-driven desire. The 'particular objective' of Hegel's proto-will to power is not the blind satisfaction of raw desire but the satisfaction of a rationally considered aim duly realised through the passions. In its exclusive surge towards a 'particular objective', this combined rational and non-rational will constitutes the will of 'the whole individuality'. This will, writes Hegel, is the thinking will: 'the will is a particular way of thinking – thinking translating itself into existence, thinking as the drive to give itself existence' (PR §4, 35; W 7:46–7). It is this type of thinking will that Zarathustra has in mind when he reminds his disciples at the close of Part 1 of *Zarathustra* that '*Dead are all the gods: now we want the Übermensch to live* – Let this be our last will at the great noontide!' (Z1 'On the Bestowing Virtue' 3, KSA 4:102).[31]

But if the *Übermensch* is ever to materialise, this 'ruling thought' or higher universal must first be planted into the passions so that they will voluntarily serve the *übermenschlich* ideal.[32] 'I love the one who makes his virtue his inclination (*Hang*) and his destiny (*Verhängniss*)', declares Zarathustra; 'thus for the sake of his virtue he wants to live on [i.e., in the *Übermensch*] and live no more' (ZP 4, KSA 4:17). In the *Hang-Verhängniss* wordplay[33] resides the putative marriage between the rational and non-rational wills, between thought and passion. Towards this single aim, this one goal[34] – 'It is time for man to fix his goal. It is time for man to plant the seed of his highest hope' (ZP 5, KSA 4:19) – all else must bend 'with every fibre of volition'. Labour, invention, virtue and passion must all be yoked to the one thought-driven goal. And when the will is so bound up with desire and with the object of that desire, to the extent 'that it alone and entirely determines its direction and is inseparable from it' (see indented Hegel citation above), any desire which is not aligned with the higher universal must be sacrificed to it. As we saw in the previous section, 'for the sake of truth' spirit must prey upon its former loves and comforts.

If spirit is to actualise the Idea of freedom as a higher universal, it must first submit to this higher universal:

> What is great in man is that he is a bridge and not a goal: what is lovable in man is that he is a *going over* (*Übergang*) and a *going under* (*Untergang*).
>
> I love those who do not know how to live except as under-goers (*Untergehende*), for they are the over-goers (*Hinübergehenden*). (ZP 4, KSA 4:16-17)

The German verb *untergehen* means *to go under* or *to perish*, both of which meanings connote the determinate negation stage in the Hegelian dialectic. If spirit is to entertain any hope of realising its immanent freedom, it must first negate itself. Without the negative *Untergang* of spirit, no transformative *Übergang* can be effected. But in order for this *untergehen* or self-negation to be willingly undergone so that 'the particular and definite and its negation' can bring about the higher universal (RH 43, W 12:49), man's highest aim must be grafted onto the passions. This is what Zarathustra means by self-conquest and self-overcoming:

> Are you the victorious one, the self-conqueror, the ruler of the senses, the master of your virtues? Thus I ask you.
>
> Or do the animal and necessity speak out of your wish? Or loneliness? Or discord with yourself? . . .
>
> A higher body you shall create. (Z1 'On Children and Marriage', KSA 4:90)

In this higher body, the Idea of freedom will be hungered after – with every fibre of its being – as both inclination and destiny. Only when the higher universal has been made the 'distinct object of desire and interest' (RH 31, W 12:40),[35] will reason crave, virtue rage and justice burn for the Idea of freedom. Spirit first, passion second. Nietzsche and Hegel are adamant on this point: 'first, the Idea, secondly, the complex of human passions', writes Hegel; 'the one the warp, the other the woof of the vast tapestry of world history' (RH 29, W 12:38).

Spirit's Vicious Cycle of Bitter Deaths and Interminable Resurrections

'I love the one who is of a free spirit and a free heart: thus is his head only the bowels of his heart, but his heart drives him on to his destruction (*Untergang*)' (ZP 4, KSA 4:18). Thus pronounces Zarathustra in his prologue, but in the ensuing narrative it becomes increasingly evident that when spirit attempts to incorporate a higher ideal or higher universal, the anticipated synthesis of head and heart, of the rational and the non-rational will, remains elusive. Instead of a movement of progression, the dialectic short-circuits leaving only the labour of the negative. Caught within the snares of its violent self-critique, spirit turns bitter, sceptical and self-pitying:

> I no longer trust myself since I sought out the heights and no-one trusts me any longer . . .
>
> When aloft, I find myself always alone. No-one talks with me, the frost of loneliness makes me shiver. What do I want on the heights?
>
> My contempt and my longing wax together; the higher I climb, the more I despise him who climbs. What does he want on the heights?
>
> How ashamed I am of my climbing and stumbling! How I jeer at my heavy breathing! How I hate the man who can fly! How weary I am on the heights! (Z1 'On the Tree on the Mountain', KSA 4:52)

The *Zarathustra* narrative is littered with similar testaments to the debilitating consequences of what Hegel celebrates as the 'tremendous power of the negative' and 'the energy of thought' (PhS §32, W 3:36).[36] Post-*Untergang*, thought's energy is all too often depicted as despondent and depleted – a spent spirit. Witness the humbling of pride and the quailing of courage before the inner demons that lurk in the caverns and forests of self-knowledge (Z1 'On the Way of the Creator', KSA 4:80–3). Witness the keenness of the knife with which spirit severs the umbilical cord to metaphysical comforts (Z2 'On the Famous Wise Men', KSA 4:132–5). Witness the glaring light of enlightenment and the resentful hunger of one who endlessly gives and never receives (Z2 'The Night Song', KSA 4:136–8). Witness the residual remorse over spirit's voluntary slaughter of its fondest illusions (Z2 'The Grave Song', KSA 4:142–5). Witness the quailing of courage (again) on the abyss of compassion for the higher men (Z2 'The Soothsayer', KSA 4:172–6). And witness the shame of knowing that one lacks the commanding voice and requisite inner strength for the *Übergang* to the third and final metamorphosis of spirit (Z2 'The Stillest Hour', KSA 4:187–90). As Nietzsche acknowledges, 'the accumulated force which compels the creating man to feel that what has gone before is untenable, awry, deserving of negation' is 'inseparable from pain' (WLN 2[106]:79, KSA 12:113).

'Much bitter dying must there be in your life' (Z2 'On the Blissful Isles', KSA 4:111), warns Zarathustra in another circumlocution of the labour of the negative. But what he fails to disclose until the fourth and final part of *Zarathustra*, the part which Nietzsche privately circulated among friends and acquaintances, is the far more bitter resurrections. In the clash between universal and particular, between thought and desire, that which is resurrected or *aufgehoben* is the negated particulars. Lying in the path of every aspiring creator-legislator, teaches Zarathustra, are one's 'seven devils' or inner demons, and it is these which must be overcome before any *Übergang* can be effected: 'You must want to burn yourself in your own flame; how could you become new if you did not first become ashes!' (Z1 'On the Way of the Creator', KSA 4:82). In Part 4, Zarathustra's seven inner demons are seen to be indestructible: his compassion for the broken higher men (Z4 'The Cry of Distress', KSA 4:300–3); his disgust and nauseous loathing of the rabble (Z4 'Talk with Kings', KSA 4:304–8); his hypertrophic will to truth at the cost of life itself

(Z4 'The Leech', KSA 4:309–12); his penitential spirit which, having plunged the knife into its own entrails, almost bleeds to death from intellectual honesty (Z4 'The Magician', KSA 4:313–20); his residual guilt and bad conscience despite having slain his belief in God (Z4 'Out of Service', KSA 4:321–6); his shame for having murdered God and for visiting on others the suffering consequent upon a world bereft of otherworldly comforts (Z4 'The Ugliest Man', KSA 4:327–32); and his rabble spirit that intransigently rejects his own hard-won gift of wisdom (Z4 'The Voluntary Beggar', KSA 4:333–7).

As the *Zarathustra* narrative shows, spirit's dialectically driven *Untergang* has led not to the longed for *Übergang* but to a broken spirit which, as we saw in Chapter 2, takes the form of Zarathustra's spectral shadow. Wan, sickly and downcast, it resembles the 'meagre, ghastly and famished' Christian soul (ZP 3, KSA 4:15) that Zarathustra had set out to expunge. What Hegel refers to as 'pure negativity or, when reduced to its pure abstraction, *simple becoming*' (PhS §21, W 3:25), is presented in *Zarathustra* as a ceaseless, restless, internecine dialectic which admits of no progression, no *Übergang*.[37] Whereas in the Hegelian dialectic it is 'the positive (*Affirmativen*) elements in which [the] negative element disappears as something subordinate and vanquished (*Überwinden*)' that carry the spirit forward (RH 18, W 12:28),[38] in the Zarathustran dialectic it is the negated elements which reassert their dominance in a vicious cycle of eternal return. These failed overcomings are prefigured in the rope-dancing episode at the start of *Zarathustra*, where the bold attempt of the ropedancer to advance towards the *Übermensch* is scotched by jeers of self-doubt. We encounter the same self-derision towards the end of Part 2 in a Gothic nightmare in which Zarathustra appears as the guardian of death's coffins. Holding silent vigil over what appear to be the graves of his own 'bitter dying', Zarathustra is violently interrupted by a thunderous wind which tears through the graveyard gates and deposits at his feet a black coffin spewing forth roaring, mocking, shrieking laughter (Z2 'The Soothsayer', KSA 4:173–4).

What the ropedancer parable and the Gothic vignette symbolise is a self-defeating rather than self-overcoming dialectic.

Instead of a self-consummating scepticism which for Hegel dialectically generates an ever-higher form of spirit, Zarathustra experiences a self-consuming scepticism which threatens to foreclose any further spiritual development. Locked into what Hegel refers to as the '*Unhappy Consciousness*', Zarathustra evinces 'the consciousness of self as a dual-natured, merely contradictory being' (PhS §206, W 3:163). Thus, while the innocence of becoming qua child spirit recalls the Hegelian dialectic of 'unfolded becoming' (PhS §22, W 3:26), and while Zarathustra's positive construal of 'eternal self-fleeing and self-returning' as a new beginning (Z3 'On Old and New Law Tables' 2, KSA 4:248) mirrors Hegel's equally positive rendering of 'unrest that is the self' as the 'immediacy and simplicity of the beginning because it ... has returned into itself (PhS §22, W 3:26), the existential reality for Zarathustra is a relentless labour of the negative without any felt sense of a new beginning.[39] In closing out this chapter, I wish to suggest that what Zarathustra idealises as the innocence of becoming but viscerally experiences as ever-recurring bouts of the same bitterness, disgust and self-doubt is both a striking precursor of Freud's return of the repressed and a lived reality of Nietzsche's speculative notion of eternal return.[40]

The first mention of eternal return in Nietzsche's published works is in *Gay Science* 341.[41] Under the heading 'The greatest weight', Nietzsche asks us to imagine how we would react to being told that 'This life as you now live it and have lived it, you will have to live once more and countless times more ... and [with] everything in the same order and sequence' (KSA 3:570). The same idea resurfaces in Part 3 of *Zarathustra* in a two-part chapter entitled 'On the Vision and the Riddle' (KSA 4:197–202). In this chapter, Zarathustra converses with the 'spirit of gravity, my devil and arch-enemy', here objectified as 'half-dwarf, half-mole'. In the first part of the chapter, Zarathustra tells the dwarf that courage is the best death-slayer because it is able to look back on life and say 'Was *that* life? Well! One More Time!' In the second part, Zarathustra revisits the subject of death and return by asking the dwarf in hushed tones whether the two of them, standing there in the moonlight beside a gateway called Moment in which the eternal paths of past and future come together, have lived that precise moment before. If so, he speculates, 'must we not return eternally?' The sudden howling of a dog derails Zarathustra's fearful (*fürchten*) thoughts and sends them hurtling back to a moment in his childhood when the sound of a dog howling in terror at the full moon had filled the young Zarathustra with pity (*Erbarmen*).[42] The memory erases both dwarf and gateway, leaving Zarathustra 'alone, desolate, in the most desolate moonlight' (the same loneliness and desolation of which Nietzsche speaks so poignantly in his two late prefaces to *Human, All Too Human*), wondering whether the dwarf, the gateway and his whispered musings on eternal return had all been just a dream.

The second allusion to eternal return occurs towards the end of Part 3 in another two-part chapter, 'The Convalescent' (KSA 4:270–7). In the first part of this chapter, Zarathustra summons up his 'most abysmal thought' (eternal return) only to recoil with such 'Disgust, disgust, disgust' that he is left prostrate for seven days. Emerging from his affliction at the start of second part of the chapter, the 'convalescent' Zarathustra is greeted by his 'animals': an eagle and a serpent, which in *Zarathustra* function as objective correlatives of the protagonist's pride and cunning. Having watched over him for seven days, his animals set about lifting his spirits with a hurdy-gurdy song about eternal return:

> Everything goes, everything comes back; the wheel of existence rolls eternally. Everything dies, everything blossoms again, eternally runs the year of existence.
>
> Everything breaks, everything is joined anew . . . Everything parts, everything greets itself again; the ring of existence eternally remains true to itself.

'Oh, you jokers and barrel organs!' exclaims Zarathustra. Whereupon he immediately counters their 'rainbow' rendition of eternal return with a visceral account of his own seven-day encounter with the concept, the mere thought of which had sent him reeling:

> Alas, man returns eternally! The small man returns eternally!
>
> Naked I once saw them both, the greatest human and the smallest human: all too similar to one another – even the greatest one still all too human!
>
> All too small the greatest one! – That was my sickness with people! And the eternal return of the smallest! That was my weariness with all existence.
>
> Oh, Disgust! Disgust! Disgust![43]

The above lines recall Zarathustra's words in his earlier discourse 'On Redemption' (cited at the start of this chapter), in which he had spoken of the all too flawed and fragmentary great men of the past and how he wished 'To redeem those past ones and transform every "It was" into "Thus I willed it!"' At present, however, he is still 'a cripple on this bridge', crippled with resentment towards time. In order to redeem the fragments and accidents of the past, spirit must teach its creative will to say to the past: 'I will it thus! Thus shall I will it!'[44] In the meantime, however, spirit's resentment towards the past and its 'antipathy towards time' continues to punish itself either through guilt and bad conscience or by succumbing to a Schopenhauerian nihilism that counsels the cessation of willing altogether:

> And now cloud upon cloud rolled over the spirit, until at last madness preached: 'Everything passes away, therefore everything deserves to pass away! . . .
>
> Alas, where is redemption from the flux of things and from the punishment of existence?' Thus preached madness. ('Z2 'On Redemption', KSA 4:180–1)

Zarathustra concludes by asking whether there might not be something 'higher' than teaching the will how to unlearn its revenge against time. That something higher is presumably a veiled reference to eternal return, the thought of which fills him with such abject horror (ibid., KSA 4:177–82).

Returning to the 'Convalescent' chapter, upon hearing Zarathustra's exclamation of 'Disgust! Disgust! Disgust!' his animals hastily renew their blandishments in a bid to avert an imminent relapse. With touching solicitude, they urge their patient to learn singing from the birds so that he can compose new songs with which to heal his soul and bear his 'great destiny':

> For your animals know well, oh Zarathustra, who you are and must become; behold, *you are the teacher of the eternal return* – that now is *your* destiny!
>
> That you must be the first to teach this doctrine – how should this great destiny not be your greatest danger and affliction! (Z3 'The Convalescent' 2, KSA 4:275-6)

Twittering on in this vein for nigh on a page, matching in length Zarathustra's pained account of his nauseating thought experiment of eternal return, his animals finally fall silent to await their patient's response. Deep in thought, with eyes and ears closed, Zarathustra remains oblivious to their 'rainbow-coloured' fables.[45]

What are we to make of these three *Zarathustra* chapters? To my mind, all three conspire to suggest that the so-called doctrine of eternal return is one for which Zarathustra lacks both strength and courage. Admittedly, three chapters later he declares his love for eternity 'and for the nuptial ring of rings – the ring of return!' (Z3 'The Seven Seals (Or: the Yes and Amen Song)' (KSA 4:287-91). But this refrain, repeated seven times, strikes my ear at least as an egregious instance of the kind of pretty, meretricious words that enable one to dance blithely over things and that Zarathustra had gently chided his animals for doing in their hurdy-gurdy song of return. As intimated above, the mere thought of eternal return induces in Zarathustra such a tidal wave of disgust that it threatens to plunge him into an abyss of weariness as nihilistic and all-consuming as the one preached by the Schopenhauerian soothsayer: 'Everything is the same, nothing is worthwhile, knowledge chokes' (Z3 'The Convalescent' 2, KSA 4:274). We can also infer from the troubled aftermath of

Zarathustra's several *Untergangs*, inventorised at the start of this section, that his disgust at the smallness of even the greatest of men is directed as much at himself as it is at the great or higher men whom he deems to be beneath him.

In short, the progression of spirit at the heart of the Hegelian dialectic is presented in the *Zarathustra* narrative as a vicious and debilitating cycle of all too human returns and relapses. Be it spirit's thought experiment of eternal return, its savage leonine nay-saying that tears the heart out of its long-cherished illusions, or the frost and fire of desolate loneliness, the devastating after-effects as recounted by Zarathustra in such heart-rending detail loudly attest to the 'tremendous' but inherently tyrannical power of the negative.

Notes

1. For a list of scholars who view Hegel and Nietzsche as philosophically opposed see Daniel Breazeale, 'The Hegel-Nietzsche Problem', *Nietzsche-Studien*, 4 (1975), p. 146, n2. For a more detailed survey and incisive critique of those commentators who have sought to bridge the Hegel-Nietzsche divide, see the opening chapter of Stephen Houlgate's 1986 study, *Hegel, Nietzsche and the Criticism of Metaphysics* (Cambridge: Cambridge University Press).
2. The first anglophone scholar to discern Hegelian elements in Nietzsche's thought was Walter Kaufmann, whose authoritative monograph on Nietzsche, first published in 1950, a year after the end of the Second World War, went a long way towards rehabilitating Nietzsche's thought after its flagrant misappropriation by the National Socialist propaganda machine. Walter Kaufmann, *Nietzsche: Philosopher, Psychologist, Antichrist* (Princeton: Princeton University Press, 1974).
3. Robert R. Williams, *Tragedy, Recognition, and the Death of God: Studies in Hegel and Nietzsche* (Oxford: Oxford University Press, 2012); Will Dudley, *Hegel, Nietzsche, and Philosophy: Thinking Freedom* (New York: Cambridge University Press, 2002). I also contributed to the commentary on the affinity between Hegel and Nietzsche in a 2016 essay out of which the current chapter evolved. See Francesca Cauchi, 'Hegel and Nietzsche on thought, freedom, and "the labour of the negative"', *Journal of European Studies*, 46.2 (2016), pp. 1-16.

4. Gilles Deleuze, *Nietzsche et la philosophie* (Paris: Presses Universitaires de France, 1962); *Nietzsche and Philosophy*, trans. Hugh Tomlinson (London: Continuum, 2002), p. 8. All quotations are taken from the English-language edition. For a detailed and convincing refutation of Deleuze's anti-Hegelian reading of Nietzsche see Breazeale, who accuses Deleuze of rhetorical excess and concludes that his interpretation of Hegel is 'uninformed and derivative, as are his criticisms'. Breazeale, 'The Hegel-Nietzsche Problem', pp. 158–61. Houlgate takes a similar stance, describing Deleuze's reading of Hegel and of dialectical negation in particular as 'a distortion'. As Houlgate notes, 'Dialectical negation for Hegel is not [as Deleuze contends] something brought to bear on a positive premise from the outside, but is inherent in that premise from the start.' Houlgate, *Hegel, Nietzsche*, p. 7.
5. Deleuze, *Nietzsche and Philosophy*, p. 196.
6. Ibid. p. 8. 'The Deleuzian assumption that Nietzsche saw Hegel as his great antagonist must contend with the lack of much evidence of Nietzsche's reading Hegel and with the generic nature of the majority of Nietzsche's comments about Hegel.' Elliot L. Jurist, *Beyond Hegel and Nietzsche: Philosophy, Culture, and Agency* (Cambridge, MA: The MIT Press, 2000), p. 27.
7. Kaufmann, *Nietzsche*, pp. 235–6.
8. See note 24 in Chapter 1.
9. Hatab revisits the creative tension between Apollo and Dionysus in *The Birth of Tragedy* to remind us that for Nietzsche, Greek tragedy afforded an example of affirmation in the midst of tragic insight, which on Hatab's reading corresponds to Nietzsche's concept of eternal recurrence. Hatab, *Nietzsche's Life Sentence*, pp. 23–37.
10. By 'Being', Nietzsche is referring to the concept of being as something fixed, static and permanent. In *Twilight of the Idols*, Nietzsche endorses the Heraclitean concept of becoming and pillories *all* other philosophers for their 'lack of historical sense, their hatred towards the very idea of becoming ... What is, does not *become*; what becomes, *is* not ... So they all believe, desperately even, in being' (TI '"Reason" in Philosophy' 1, KSA 6:74). As Houlgate notes regarding Hegel's concept of becoming as expounded in the *Science of Logic*, 'all coming-to-be entails a ceasing-to-be of *some* kind and ... all ceasing-to-be entails a coming-to-be. There is no pure genesis that does not involve a process of corruption and no pure destruction that is not a process

of generation.' He goes on to add that such a concept of becoming finds its echoes in Nietzsche's philosophy. Stephen Houlgate, *The Opening of Hegel's Logic: From Being to Infinity* (West Lafayette, IN: Purdue University Press, 2006), p. 286.

11. For Hegel, as Robert Pippin notes, 'none of the fundamental positions in the history of Western philosophy are simply in error or mistaken but are all only partial views of "the truth," where the truth itself is not an independent substantive position but the right synoptic view of all possible positions explained in terms of their partiality and interconnection'. Robert B. Pippin, *Hegel's Practical Philosophy: Rational Agency as Ethical Life* (Cambridge: Cambridge University Press, 2008), p. 122.

12. 'Negation ... requires content in order to be negation, to negate a fixed determinacy. Conversely, the positive that results from negation is an alternative determination. Hegel's notion of determinate negation establishes that determinacy radically *depends* on the other.' Rocío Zambrana, *Hegel's Theory of Intelligibility* (Chicago: University of Chicago Press, 2015), p. 95.

13. Deleuze, *Nietzsche and Philosophy*, p. 9.

14. It is worth mentioning Jacob Böhme here, the seventeenth-century cobbler-mystic whom Hegel studied in considerable detail and whose theosophy is predicated on a dialectical principle of negativity, namely that God mediates himself or becomes manifest to himself through an act of diremption. Here is Hegel's rendition of the same idea in his 1824 'Lectures on the Philosophy of Religion': 'the infinite seeks self-diremption in order to be only the affirmative as negation of negation.... The finite is therefore an essential moment of the infinite in the nature of God; and it may consequently be said that God is the very being who finitizes himself, who posits determinations within himself ... he determines himself, he posits for himself an other over against himself so that there is God and there is the world ... Without the moment of finitude there is no life, no subjectivity, no living God. God creates, he is active: therein lies the distinguishing, and with distinction the moment of finitude is posited' (LPR 307–8, W 16:191). As Elizabeth Haldane observed at the turn of the last century, 'Diversity in identity, the fact that the element of negativity is essential in any conception we form of what is infinite or absolute, – this is the lesson that Böhme has to teach us, and this is the dialectic which ... throws a flood of light on the contradictions that puzzle us in life.' Elizabeth S. Haldane, 'Jacob Böhme and his Relation

to Hegel', *The Philosophical Review*, 6:2 (1897), p. 153. For a comprehensive study of Hegel's reading and interpretation of Böhme, see Cecilia Muratori, *The First German Philosopher: The Mysticism of Jakob Böhme as Interpreted by Hegel*, trans. Richard Dixon and Raphaëlle Burns, in *International Archives of the History of Ideas*, 217 (Springer, 2016).

15. There are three German editions of Hegel's posthumously published *Lectures on the Philosophy of History*. The first edition, by Eduard Gans, appeared in 1837. A revised and enlarged edition by Hegel's son, Karl, was published in 1840. And a third, more comprehensive edition by Georg Lasson was published in 1917 by Felix Meiner. Robert S. Hartman's translation of *Die Vernunft in der Geschichte: Einleitung in die Philosophie der Weltgeschichte* (*Reason in History: A General Introduction to the Philosophy of History*) follows the second edition, which is generally considered to be the most authoritative. Hartman's text, however, also includes interpolations from Gans's first edition and Lasson's third edition. I have referenced my citations from the second edition as 'W 12' (denoting volume 12 of the Suhrkamp imprint of Hegel's *Werke*), and from the third edition as 'GL'.

16. As Max Gottschlich points out, however, even the finite world of appearances is problematic for Nietzsche. In Gottschlich's discussion of Hegel and Nietzsche's respective critiques on the limitations of Kant's transcendental logic, he points out that while Nietzsche 'is one of the few philosophers to comprehend the hidden teleological character of formal logic, for example, in asserting that formal logic is an "imperative, *not* to know the true, but to posit and arrange a world *that shall be called as true by us*"' (WLN 9[97]:157, KSA 12:389), Nietzsche's insistence on the illusoriness not only of being but also of appearance undermines his own doctrine of will to power. As Gottschlich argues, if formal logic is merely a tool to enable us to dominate and domesticate actuality, without a system of appearances (the 'modelled actuality' of Kant's transcendental logic), Nietzsche's principle of will to power would have no means of realising itself in space and time. Max Gottschlich, 'The Necessity and Limits of Kant's Transcendental Logic, with Reference to Nietzsche and Hegel', *The Review of Metaphysics*, 69:2 (2015), pp. 308-10.

17. Although Hegel asserts that in world history 'individuals' are peoples, he repeatedly alludes to 'great men', and to Alexander

the Great and Julius Caesar in particular, as those through whom the Idea is progressively realised.
18. Cf. '*Exceptional vanity* –This person has the consolation of possessing one supreme quality: over the rest of his being – and it is almost all the rest! – his gaze glides contemptuously' (D 521, KSA 3:300).
19. Cf. the ascetic spirit which, having returned from the dark forest of knowledge, is 'draped in ugly truths, his hunter's spoils, and rich in tattered clothes; many thorns also stuck to him' (Z2 'On the Exalted Ones', KSA 4:150).
20. On the debilitating effects of pity, Nietzsche writes, 'Pity is the opposite of the tonic affects which increase the energy of vital feelings: it has a depressive effect. One loses strength when one pities' (A 7, KSA 6:172).
21. Cf. Nietzsche's idealised free spirits: 'explorers to the point of cruelty, with unflinching fingers for the incomprehensible, with teeth and stomach for the most indigestible ... ready for any risk, thanks to an excess of "free will"' (BGE 44, KSA 5:62).
22. In BGE 212 (KSA 5:147), already cited in Chapter 2, Nietzsche refers to the war waged by the 'herd animal' on 'the higher soul, the higher duty, the higher responsibility, on creative power and mastery'.
23. Cf. 'What dawns on the philosophers last of all: they must no longer merely let themselves be given concepts, no longer just clean and clarify them, but first of all must *make* them, *create* them, present them and persuade in their favour. Up to now, one generally trusted in one's concepts as a miraculous *dowry* from some miracle world ... This *filial respect* towards *what is to be found in us* is perhaps part *of the moral component* in *knowing*. What's needed first is absolute scepticism towards all received concepts' (WLN 34[195]:12-13, KSA 11:486-7).
24. That dialectical negation is necessary but not sufficient for self-determination is clearly articulated in the following passage from Richard Dien Winfield's article on negation and truth: 'This negative freedom to deny is only one side of the negativity and autonomy required for truth. In theory and practice, naysaying by itself leaves only doubt and destruction. To provide self-determination, negation must involve not just liberation from the given, but also the positive autonomy to establish new determinacy by a subject who therein remains at one with itself.' Richard Dien Winfield, 'Negation and Truth', *The Review of Metaphysics*, 64:2 (2010), pp. 288-9. As I have shown, this positive autonomy is figured in *Zarathustra* as a child.

25. I agree with Gooding-Williams that the tendency among Nietzsche commentators to interpret the 'child' symbol in *Zarathustra* in Romantic terms is problematic. Citing Erich Heller's representative Romantic reading of this symbol as a vision of 'pure unselfconscious being' in the tradition of Rousseau, Schiller, Kleist, Wordsworth and Hegel, Gooding-Williams reminds us that the child, as depicted in *Zarathustra*, 'wills his own will' and cannot therefore symbolise pure unselfconscious being. Adopting Hegelian terminology, Gooding-Williams argues that since the child's willing 'bears a *reflexive* relation to itself: the will of the child wills itself', then 'the child exists *for-itself* as will'. Robert Gooding-Williams, *Zarathustra's Dionysian Modernism* (Stanford, CA: Stanford University Press, 2001), pp. 40–1. See also Erich Heller, *The Disinherited Mind* (New York: Harcourt Brace Jovanovich, 1975), pp. 321–6.
26. The kinship between Böhme and Hegel in respect of dialectical negativity is relatively well documented (see note 14 above). What has not, to my knowledge, been noted before is just how closely Böhme's account of the ontological dialectical will prefigures the dialectical transformation of spirit or thought as preached by Zarathustra. '[E]very life ... is based on will', asserts the Silesian mystic in the opening sentence of his 1620 work *Six Theosophic Points* – a statement which, aside from any question of influence, irrefutably anticipates Nietzsche's philosophy of will to power. In the ensuing exposition, Böhme describes the 'ungrounded' and undifferentiated will as 'a dumb existence without comprehension or life' until kindled by the 'fiery essences' immanent within it. Once enkindled, will 'enters into itself, grasps itself in itself, and makes the centre in itself; but with that which is grasped passes out of itself, manifests itself in the brightness of the eye, and thus shines forth out of the essence in itself and from itself'. Jacob Böhme. *Six Theosophic Points and Other Writings*, trans. John Rolleston Earle (New York: Alfred A. Knopf, 1920), pp. 13–16. As my reading of the three metamorphoses discourse has shown, Zarathustra advocates a kindred dialectical process. Cribbed and confined by two millennia of Christian conditioning, the human spirit, weighed down by its 'dumb existence without comprehension or life', burns to release its inner freedom. To do so, it must first emulate the camel and carry its burden of prolonged genuflecting submission into the desert of interiority. There, upon entering into itself, spirit must will the courage to grasp itself in itself by means of a lacerating, lion-spirited self-negation before passing out of itself as a child-like spirit recreating the world in its own image.

27. While Hegel attributes to Christianity the realisation that 'man as man is free and that freedom of Spirit is the very essence of man's nature' (RH 24, W 12:31), in an early essay entitled 'The Spirit of Christianity and its Fate' (1798), he mounts a blistering attack on the Judaic spirit's 'thoroughgoing passivity' and abject 'servitude' to Mosaic Law, against which he sets Jesus's Sermon on the Mount. Friedrich Hegel, *On Christianity: Early Theological Writings*, trans. T. M. Knox (New York: Harper, 1961), p. 194.
28. 'Hegel is as much interested in the significance of the "urge" [*Drang*] for knowledge', asserts Pippin, 'as he is interested in the dependence of the practical on the theoretical or on thinking.' Pippin, *Hegel's Practical Philosophy*, p. 133.
29. Houlgate makes a similar point: 'Hegel is adamant that we are not to eradicate natural desire – but that we must render our natural desires intelligent by incorporating them into a life of understanding and freedom.' Stephen Houlgate, 'Religion, Morality and Forgiveness in Hegel's Philosophy', in *Philosophy and Religion in German Idealism*, eds. William Desmond, Ernst-Otto Onnasch, and Paul Cruysberghs (New York: Kluwer Academic Publishers, 2004), p. 84. It is my contention that Hegel's position is entirely commensurate with Zarathustra's when he exhorts man to instil his 'highest aim into the heart of [the] passions' (Z1 'On the Joyful and Painful Passions', KSA 4:43).
30. 'The slave revolt in morality begins when *ressentiment* itself becomes creative and gives birth to values: the *ressentiment* of those who, being denied the actual reaction, namely the act, compensate for it only with imaginary revenge' (GM I 10, KSA 5:270).
31. Houlgate's claim that the 'central tenet' of Nietzsche's 'antimetaphysical philosophy . . . is that we are wholly natural, physiological beings, that we are nothing other than a complex of primitive and sublimated bodily desires' is a clear articulation of the naturalist Nietzsche with which I take issue in my Introduction. See Houlgate, *Hegel, Nietzsche*, p. 56. *Pace* Houlgate, my argument in this and the previous chapter is that the role of rational thought in orienting the bodily desires towards a higher universal or higher ideal is pivotal to Zarathustra's teaching on the *Übermensch*.
32. Cf. Nietzsche's delighted discovery of Spinoza, whose 'whole tendency like my own [is] to make knowledge the most *powerful passion*' (letter to Franz Overbeck postmarked 30 July, 1881; KSB 6:111). *Selected Letters of Friedrich Nietzsche*, ed. and trans.

by Christopher Middleton (Indianoplis: Hackett, 1996), p. 177. Nietzsche's remark about Spinoza sits rather uneasily with the earlier-cited statement (see Chapter 1, n6) by John Richardson regarding Nietzsche's view of agency: 'So Nietzsche rejects agency's picture of itself as properly independent of the drives ... We need to watch for what distinguishes us in our drives and passions, and learn to subordinate our agency ... to this.' Richardson, 'Nietzsche's Freedoms', in Gemes and May, p. 143.

33. To a philologist like Nietzsche, these clever but revealing puns are stock in trade. Take, for example, the following puns from one of his 1885 notebook entries: *beten* (to pray) and *bitten* (to ask); *Schicksal* (destiny) and *geschickt* (sent). The first discloses the self-interested nature of prayer, which Socrates in the *Euthyphro* (14d–e) had mocked as a type of business transaction between gods and men, while the second adverts to the Christian belief in a God-sent destiny as opposed to the destiny that a 'free spirit' quite literally carves out of and for itself (WLN 34[241]:14, KSA 11:501).

34. 'A thousand goals have there been until now, for there have been a thousand peoples. Only the fetter for the thousand necks is lacking, the one goal is still lacking' (Z1 'On the Thousand and One Goals', KSA 4:76).

35. Cf. 'By fulfilling their own great purpose in accordance with the necessity of the universal Spirit, these world-historical men also satisfy themselves' (RH 42, GL 80).

36. In his fascinating study *Postponements*, David Farrell Krell locates the source of the aporia between Zarathustra's *Untergang* and *Übergang* in the problematic concept of the *Übermensch*: 'The entire book is caught in the tension and pull of "over" man, "down" going, and going "over": *Übermensch, Untergang, Übergang*. The meaning of the *über* is itself bifurcated along vertical and horizontal axes. *Übermensch* is somehow *above* mankind and *beyond* human history; *Übergang* is a crossing *over* or going *across* the bridge of the future to a new kind of humanity. No wonder commentators today are wrestling with the problem of the relation between historical mankind and overman! For the ambiguity, the double axis of the project, is ineluctable and irreducible ... *Thus Spoke Zarathustra* commences with downgoing. Each of its four parts tries to *end* with downgoing. Tries but fails. Postpones the *Untergang*.' David Farrell Krell, *Postponements: Woman, Sensuality, and Death in Nietzsche* (Bloomington: Indiana University Press, 1986), p. 53. Another possible reason for the irreconcilability

between *Untergang* and *Übergang* might be the indisputably autobiographical nature of *Zarathustra*. If, as Thomas Brobjer asserts, '*Z[arathustra]* is based on Nietzsche's own life and his view of *Bildung* and self-development' (Brobjer's essay does not elaborate upon Nietzsche's view of *Bildung*), then Zarathustra's inability to cross over the bridge to the *Übermensch* may, I submit, be a reflection of Nietzsche's own inability to do so on account of his being ineluctably afflicted with the decadence of late modernity. Thomas Brobjer, '*Thus Spoke Zarathustra* as Nietzsche's Autobiography', in *Nietzsche's 'Thus Spoke Zarathustra': Before Sunrise*, ed. James Luchte (London: Continuum, 2008), p. 30.

37. Karl Jaspers reached the same conclusion fifty years ago: 'But overcoming and self-overcoming – this penetration of all possibilities – *appears to have no goal*. In what will this path end – this dialectic that is experienced as real, kept in motion as it is by the constant sacrifice of what is one's own? If the last overcoming . . . is mere movement impelled by the most extreme requirements of truthfulness, without a clearly conceived ideal, without creation and actualisation of man himself, and hence without reconciliation and without any decision other than denial, then it would appear to be simply a matter of constant self-crucifixion terminating in nothingness. But where Nietzsche cannot confront us with a visible ideal, he finds the positive meaning of overcoming *in the way* itself: he *affirms endlessness*.' Jaspers, *Nietzsche*, pp. 393–4.

38. Gooding-Williams correctly points out that while the *Phenomenology* is retrospective and 'represents as ineluctable a movement that has already occurred', *Zarathustra* is prospective and 'articulates a speculative (hypothetical) account of a possibility that has yet to be realized'. Gooding-Williams, *Zarathustra's Dionysian Modernism*, p. 30. But whereas for Gooding-Williams that possibility is realised at the end of Part 4 of *Zarathustra* when Zarathustra allegedly 'becomes a child' (ibid. p. 44), it is my contention that the eternally returning inner demons which haunt Zarathustra in Part 4 attest to his inability to progress to the final metamorphosis.

39. This eternal return of contradiction is well expressed by Maurice Blanchot in his essay 'On Nietzsche's Side' in which he endorses Jaspers's affirmation of the necessary and *sui generis* contradictions in Nietzsche's work: 'Knowledge, says Jaspers, wants to commit itself to all its possibilities, to go beyond each one of them, and cannot linger over them. First it seems to touch, seize something,

as if it were absolute ... Then, by a reversal to the opposite, it rejects what it has just affirmed, does so with the same passion and the same force ... There is no reconciliation of opposites: oppositions, contradictions do not get to rest in some higher synthesis, but hold themselves together by an increasing tension'. Maurice Blanchot, *The Work of Fire*, trans. Charlotte Mandell (Stanford, CA: Stanford University Press, 1995), p. 290.

40. I have opted for the experientially freighted 'return' over the more abstract 'recurrence'.
41. For a book-length study of Nietzsche's experience of eternal return see Hatab, *Nietzsche's Life Sentence*. While Hatab addresses the five most common interpretations of eternal recurrence to be found in Nietzsche scholarship, namely cosmological, existential, normative, symbolic and ontological, the primary focus in his monograph is the existential nexus between the thought of eternal recurrence and life-affirmation.
42. This reminiscence, here attributed to Zarathustra, is uncannily proleptic in light of Nietzsche's tearful breakdown in January 1889 over the sight of a horse being brutally flogged close to his Turin lodgings.
43. Pippin reminds us that what most intrigued Nietzsche about Montaigne was how he managed 'to exhibit such a thoroughgoing skepticism and clarity about human frailty and failings (the virtue of *Redlichkeit* so often praised by Nietzsche) *without* Pascal's despair and eventual surrender, or La Rochefoucauld's icy contempt for the "human all too human"'. As Pippin observes, Montaigne's ability to wed honesty to cheerfulness was, for Nietzsche, the mark of a man 'who had succeeded at what seems a supreme Nietzschean goal, the task, "to make oneself at home on the earth" [UM 'Schopenhauer as Educator' 2, KSA 1:348]'. Robert Pippin, 'How to Overcome Oneself: Nietzsche on Freedom', in Gemes and May, pp. 74–5. Indeed, it is precisely this ability to make oneself at home in the world that Zarathustra signally lacks and that a whole-hearted affirmation of eternal return would seem to entail.
44. An alternative formulation for this is Nietzsche's concept of *amor fati*: 'My formula for human greatness is *amor fati*: that one does not want anything else, not forwards, not backwards, not for all eternity. Not just to endure what is necessary, still less to conceal it – all idealism is mendaciousness before what is necessary – but to *love* it' (EH 'Why I Am So Clever' 10, KSA 6:297).

45. Heinrich Meier also points out that it is Zarathustra's animals who address Zarathustra as 'the teacher of the eternal return' and that we never actually see Zarathustra proclaim the teaching of the eternal return. Heinrich Meier, *What is Nietzsche's Zarathustra?: A Philosophical Confrontation*, trans. Justin Gottschalk (Chicago and London: The University of Chicago Press, 2021), p. vii.

4
The Bitter Cup of Pure Love: Feuerbach and Zarathustra

> Beyond yourselves shall you love some day! So first *learn* to love! And for that you must drink the bitter cup of your love.
>
> (Z1 'On Children and Marriage', KSA 4:92)

Ludwig Feuerbach 'slew' God some forty years before Nietzsche's madman entered the market square of modernity, lantern in hand and the following lament on his lips: 'God is dead. God remains dead. And we have killed him. How shall we console ourselves, the murderers of all murderers?'[1] Rising out of the darkness of an apocalyptic void, the madman's dirge-like *'requiem aeternam deo'* (GS 125, KSA 3:480-2) could not be further removed from the glad tidings of Feuerbach's *The Essence of Christianity* (hereafter *'Christianity'*), proclaiming that the divine attributes of the Christian God are human perfections projected onto an illusory Divine Being. These perfections, avers Feuerbach, are the human powers of reason, will and love, which are intrinsically and respectively related to the human faculty of understanding, the moral law and the human heart.[2] In *Zarathustra*, it is the same three human powers, or what Feuerbach refers to as 'the divine trinity *in* man' (EC 3, GW 5:31), that Zarathustra is seeking to revitalise in man through the *übermenschlich* ideal: 'Let your love for life be love for thy highest hope: and let your highest hope be the highest thought of life!' (Z1 'On War and Warriors', KSA 4:59).

Although dismissed towards the end of Part 2 of *Zarathustra* as a consolatory fiction – 'on [fleecy clouds] we sit our motley puppets and call them gods and *Übermenschen*' (Z2 'On the Poets', KSA 4:164) – the *Übermensch* is presented at the start of *Zarathustra* as both practical law and normative ideal (discussed at length in Chapter 2). As law, it is the rod with which Zarathustra goads the apathetic human specimen of late modernity to overcome his Christianity-induced limitations. As ideal, it is rainbow, lightning and dancing star. The incorporation of this practical law through self-overcoming entails not only the combined powers of reason, will and love, but their harmonious integration. Not until the 'highest thought of life' (the *Übermensch*) has become man's 'highest hope' and the exclusive object of his love will man voluntarily submit to the law of self-overcoming as decreed by practical reason. The combined agency of reason and will in the rational will's evaluative-legislative and negative-transformative roles was discussed in Chapters 2 and 3, respectively. Here in Chapter 4, the role of love as the third power in the dynamic of self-overcoming will be examined and an argument made for the qualitative affinities between the delineations of love in Feuerbach's *Christianity* and Nietzsche's *Zarathustra*. I shall begin, however, with a brief, contextualising exposition of Feuerbach's anthropological genealogy of Christian theology and concomitant objective of restoring to man his innate human perfections.

Reclaiming the 'Divine' Powers of Human Greatness

Feuerbach's twofold argument in *Christianity* is that '*The divine being is nothing else than* the human being, or, rather, *the human nature* purified, freed from the limits of the individual man' (EC 14, GW 5:48); and that this 'reduction' of the Divine to the human, or in Feuerbach's formulation, of theology to anthropology, is a simultaneous exaltation of man's innate perfections. This dual dynamic of lowering God into man and making man into God is exemplified for Feuerbach in the Incarnation, save that 'this human God was by a further process made a transcendental, imaginary God, remote from man' (EC xviii, GW 5:20). What Christian dogma designates as predicates of God, contends

Feuerbach, are nothing more than a projection and magnification of the three immanent powers constitutive of man: reason (omniscience), will (omnipotence) and love (Christ). In other words, it was not God who created man in his own image, but man who created God in a 'purified' image of man.

Feuerbach's 'projection' thesis is a direct inversion of Hegel's philosophy of spirit.[3] But whereas in Hegel, Absolute Spirit comes to self-knowledge through its objectification of itself in the finite world, in Feuerbach's inversion, finite spirit (human consciousness) acquires knowledge of itself through God qua objectification of man's innate perfections. 'Man – this is the mystery of religion – projects his being into objectivity (*vergegenständlicht sich*), and then again makes himself an *object* to this projected image of himself thus converted into a subject' (EC 29–30, GW 5:71). Unlike the Greek or Indian deities, 'mere products of men or deified men' (EC 56, GW 5:113) in which man's self-objectification was broadly speaking an exaltation of human qualities, the self-objectified Christian God gives rise to self-abasement and self-alienation. Man thus appears to himself not merely as 'the object of an object' (ibid.), but as a debased object to an exalted object of worship. Nietzsche makes a strikingly similar observation in one of his late notebooks (note the repeated phrase 'product of man'):

> All the beauty and sublimity we've lent to real and imagined things I want to demand back, as the property and product of man: as his most splendid vindication. Man as poet, as thinker, as God, as love, as power – oh, the kingly prodigality with which he has given gifts to things, only to *impoverish* himself and *himself* feel miserable! That has been man's greatest selflessness so far, that he admired and worshipped and knew how to conceal from himself the fact that it was *he* who created what he admired. (WLN 11[87]:215, KSA 13:41)

For both Feuerbach and Nietzsche then religion is a form of man's unwitting self-objectification in God.[4] It is also for Feuerbach a positive source of human self-knowledge, the elucidation of which is the substance of Part 1 of *Christianity*, entitled 'The True or Anthropological Essence of Religion'.[5] This concept of self-objectification qua self-knowledge is not only pivotal to Feuerbach's hermeneutic in *Christianity*, but is lifted directly from Hegel's theory of knowledge.[6] As explicated in Chapter 3, self-objectification is the first 'moment' in the Hegelian dialectic. It is the moment of the 'I', when consciousness, as undifferentiated substance (*in itself*), becomes conscious of its own consciousness and becomes thereby an object to itself (*for itself*). In Hegel's formulation, when consciousness '*relates itself to itself* and is *determinate*', it is simultaneously *in itself* and *for itself* (PhS 25). Feuerbach paraphrases and augments this as follows:

> Consciousness consists in a being becoming objective to itself; hence it is nothing apart, nothing distinct from the being which is conscious of itself ... *Consciousness* is *self-activity* (*Selbstbetätigung*), *self-affirmation* (*Selbstbejahung*), *self-love* (*Selbstliebe*) – self-love not in the brutish sense, *joy in one's own perfection. Consciousness is the characteristic mark of a perfect nature; it exists only in a self-sufficing, complete being.* (EC 6, GW 5:36)[7]

The crucial thing to note here is that the unmediated 'self-activity' of reflexive consciousness is described not merely in speculative terms, but also in affective terms. By referring to this reflexivity as the type of 'self-affirmation', 'self-love' and 'joy in one's own perfection' that only 'a self-sufficing, complete being' experiences in the act of self-consciousness, Feuerbach underscores and contradistinguishes the materialism of his account from the 'immaterial, self-sufficing speculation' of idealist philosophy. Signalling here his departure from Hegel, Feuerbach insists that his theoretical philosophy in *Christianity* 'corresponds to the real, complete nature of man':

> it declares *that* alone to be the true philosophy which is converted *in succum et sanguine*, which is incarnate in Man.... It generates thought from the *opposite* of thought, from Matter, from existence, from the senses; it has relation to its object first through the senses, i.e., passively, before defining it in thought.' (EC xiv–xv, GW 5:16)

As discussed in the previous chapter, reflective consciousness is fundamental to Zarathustra's doctrine of self-overcoming: without the self-knowledge generated by reflexivity, no attempt at self-overcoming would ever be essayed. The greatest thing we can experience, declares Zarathustra, is 'the hour of the great contempt' – doubly great because in the epiphanic flash of self-clarity, the full human potential of each of man's three innate powers – reason, will and love – illuminates the understanding. In the light of this new understanding: reason's *raison d'être* emerges as a craving for knowledge that is as instinctual as the lion's craving for food (ZP 3, KSA 4:15), or what Feuerbach describes as 'the power of the instinct for knowledge (*die Macht des Wissentriebs*) – an *absolutely irresistible, all-conquering power*' (EC 4, GW 5:32); will's becoming is cognitively grasped as both ontological principle and a dynamic model for self-overcoming (Z1 'On the Three Metamorphoses', KSA 4:29–31); and love appears as self-love, the kind of self-love that for Feuerbach is '*joy in one's own perfection*' and for Zarathustra belongs to one whose 'soul is so overfull that he forgets himself, and all things are in him: thus all things will be his destruction (*Untergang*)' (ZP 4, KSA 4:18).

Feuerbach reminds us, however, that the self-consciousness of the understanding is oblivious to the anguish of the human heart:

> The pure, perfect, flawlessly divine nature is *the self-consciousness of the understanding*, the consciousness which the understanding has of *its own perfection*. The understanding knows nothing of the sufferings of the heart; it has no desires, no passions, no wants and, for that reason, no deficiencies and weaknesses, as the heart has. (EC 34, GW 5:76)

Hence the gulf between the consciousness of human perfection and its potential realisation in the individual, between the 'children' of Zarathustra's hope and his ability to become the type of child spirit that will ideally and dialectically emerge out of the battle between the camel spirit and the lion spirit. Thus, when Zarathustra teaches that 'fundamentally (*von Grund*) one loves only one's child and work; and where there is great love for oneself, that is a symbol of pregnancy: so have I found it' (Z3 'On Involuntary Bliss', KSA 4:204), the normative freight of 'fundamentally', implying that one ought to be wedded exclusively to the goal of self-overcoming, and the figurative triad of child–work–pregnancy, effectively mask the hard, interminable labour of self-overcoming. As I noted early in the Introduction, *Zarathustra* closes with the protagonist still striving towards his children and his work.

But if the reclamation and actualisation of human greatness is the shared objective of Feuerbach's *Christianity* and Nietzsche's *Zarathustra*, the two texts present markedly divergent humanistic visions. I shall briefly mention three, each of which has a direct bearing on the love–suffering–compassion theme of this chapter. First, whereas Feuerbach sought to eliminate God but to leave Christian values intact, Nietzsche's professed aim was to eradicate all Christian traces from the human psyche – but as discussed in Chapters 1 and 2, the Christian values of obedience, self-mastery, self-denial and self-sacrifice feature prominently in Nietzsche and Zarathustra's table of values. Second, one of the Christian values that Feuerbach wished to retain was particularly anathema to Nietzsche, namely the interpersonal I–thou values of communality and neighbourly love (*agape*) in which the Christian ideal of man's humanity to man is enshrined.[8] It was values such as these which no doubt prompted Engels's famous quip that '[Feuerbach] by no means wishes to abolish religion; he wants to perfect it'.[9] Third, whereas Feuerbach believed that the actualisation of the perfections of the human species could be effected only through the bond between self and other,[10] Nietzsche's vision of human perfection takes the form of a self-sufficing, self-legislating individual who requires no 'other', no 'thou', for self-completion. It is all the more surprising, therefore, to discover at the moral heart of Nietzsche's *Zarathustra* the same Christ-like qualities of love, sacrificial suffering and compassion that lie at the moral and material 'heart' of Feuerbach's account of 'divine' human love.

Love, sacrificial suffering and compassion are the sequential foci of the remaining three sections of this chapter. The first section will focus on Feuerbach's assertion that love qua 'absolute' human power can never be the predicate of a proposition but always only the subject, and will take Zarathustra as a case in point. The second section will map Zarathustra's impulse to sacrifice himself for an ideal of human perfection onto Feuerbach's representation of 'pure' love as the impulse to sacrifice self to another, and will draw out the suffering intrinsic to both. The third and final section will provide a detailed examination of Zarathustra's compassion, a subject rarely discussed by Nietzsche scholars.[11] That examination will disclose how love's suffering is presented in *Zarathustra* as constitutive not only of a centrifugal love for a higher human being, but of a centripetal love, or *amour propre*, that is perpetually humiliated by an indomitable, affective will to power. It will also disclose how Zarathustra's compassion for the inexorable and ineluctable suffering of self-love is engendered on the one hand by the universal and reciprocal relations between I and thou and on the other by the fundamental innocence of the affects. In respect of the latter, it will be seen how envy, malice, vengeance and all the other symptoms of *ressentiment* are sympathetically diagnosed by Zarathustra as involuntary defence mechanisms triggered by a beleaguered self-love.

Love as a Human Absolute

The critical objective of an early chapter in *Christianity* entitled 'The Mystery of the Incarnation; Or God as Heart-Essence (*Herzwesen*)' is to demonstrate that the religious concept of Divine Love is the objectification of a love that is intrinsic to the human heart. This argument is implicit in the titular phrase 'God as '*Herzwesen*'. – the compound noun is an epithet for love, which as 'heart-essence' is identified as a uniquely human 'God'. By 'God', Feuerbach appears to mean absolute – not in the idealist, speculative, abstract sense of absolute, but absolute in the sense of an innate and inviolable human power:[12]

> The divine trinity *in* man, *above* (*über*) the individual man, is the unity of reason, love, will. Reason, will, love or heart

are not powers which man *has* – for he is nothing without them, he is what he is only through them – they are the constituent elements of his nature, which he neither *has* nor *makes*, the *animating, determining, governing powers – divine, absolute powers* to which he can oppose no resistance. (EC 3, GW 5:31-2)[13]

As an animating, determining, governing power, love is emphatically not in man's power. 'Is it man that possesses love', asks Feuerbach, 'or is it not much rather love that possesses man?' (EC 4, GW 5:32). Love, he argues, is an essence, an ontological given. It cannot therefore be a predicate of either God or man; it is always only subject. Hence Feuerbach's objection to the subject-predicate form of the Christian dictum 'God is Love', which in its transposition of love from an *impersonal* essence to a *personal* attribute leaves love at the mercy of hate, baying for 'the *blood* of heretics and unbelievers' (EC 52, GW 5:107). This salutary warning against the dangers of religious fanaticism is brought sharply into view in Feuerbach's rehearsal of Socrates' distinction in the *Euthyphro* (10a) between a deed that is loved by the gods because it is holy and a deed that is holy because it is loved by the gods. 'Love is not holy, because it is a predicate of God', writes Feuerbach; 'rather, it is a predicate of God because it is through and for itself divine' (EC 273, GW 5:448). What makes this love divine, according to Feuerbach, is its 'absolute', irresistible quality.

Love's inexorability grounds Feuerbach's interpretation of the doctrine of Incarnation. He asserts that the love that impelled God to renounce his Godhead and vest it in his Son was an 'absolute, pure love' in the sense of being an impulsion rather than a volitional act. 'Love conquers (*überwinden*) God' – a paraphrase of St Bernard's '*Amor triumphat de Deo*' which Feuerbach cites in a footnote – because love is 'a higher power and truth than deity' (EC 53, GW 5:107-8). Like thought and will, pure love is a higher power by virtue of being an 'absolute' essence over which man has no control. Entirely *in itself*, love is always only subject and therefore not subject to human (or divine) volition. 'It was love to which God sacrificed his divine majesty', declares Feuerbach. 'And what sort of love was that?' It was love for man, he answers. 'And what kind of love was that?' Human love, retorts Feuerbach. 'Has love a plural? Is it not everywhere like itself?' He applies the same argument to Christian prayer, observing that the devout Christian in his supplications to God presupposes that God feels as the supplicant feels: 'God is to him a heart susceptible to all that is human. The heart can betake itself only to the heart; feeling can appeal only to feeling.' Thus, Feuerbach concludes, the type of love evinced in God's self-renunciation and sacrifice of his Son can be none other than a human kind of love. More importantly, it is for Feuerbach the highest form of human love, namely 'the true human love ... which impels the sacrifice of self to another' (EC 53–5, GW 5:108–11).

It is my contention in this chapter that Nietzsche's Zarathustra, a parodic Christ-like prophet preaching an ostensibly anti-Christian creed, is paradoxically impelled by a Christ-like love to sacrifice himself for the redemption of mankind. This is not, of course, a bid to redeem the 'sins' of mankind, but rather to induce man to redeem himself from the concepts of sin and guilt and the concomitant fear of divine retribution. In the figure of Zarathustra, we are confronted with a modern-day prophet who preaches redemption from Christianity through the same type of sacrificial love embodied in and epitomised by Christ. An overt parallel between Christ and Zarathustra is made in the opening sentence of *Zarathustra*: 'When Zarathustra was thirty years old, he left his home and the lake of his home and went into the mountains', just as Christ is said to have begun his ministry at the age of 30 (Luke 3:23). Technically speaking, Zarathustra does not begin his 'ministry' until he is 40, after a decade spent in meditative mountain solitude. These two details suggestively link Zarathustra to his creator, who wrote Part 2 of *Zarathustra* in the Alpine village of Sils Maria[14] and published Part 3 at the age of 40. And just as the forty-year-old Nietzsche wrote *Zarathustra* as a vehicle for the propagation of his ideas, so its forty-year-old protagonist leaves his mountain refuge to bestow the fruits of his wisdom upon the world of men. Zarathustra refers to this bestowal as a 'bestowing love' (Z1 'On the Bestowing Virtue', KSA 4:98), the type of love which, as I shall argue below, is commensurate with Feuerbach's definition of 'true human love' as that which sacrifices itself to another.

'I love mankind', announces Zarathustra in response to an anchorite whom he encounters in his descent to the lowlands. It is the same anchorite who ten years earlier had seen Zarathustra carrying his 'ashes to the mountain' – the metaphor signalling Zarathustra's *Untergang* status, namely his having burned himself/his former metaphysical comforts in his own flame. The hermit is curious to learn what Zarathustra thinks he can possibly hope to achieve 'among the sleepers':

> Why ... did I go into the forest and the desert? [asks the anchorite]. Was it not because I loved man too much?
>
> Now I love God: man I do not love. Man is to me an imperfect thing. Love for man would kill me.

To which Zarathustra testily replies, 'What spoke I of love! I bring mankind a gift' (ZP 2, KSA 4:12–13), an answer and a gift which marks the subtle but important difference between the two hermits' respective love for man. Whereas the anchorite's love had been a philanthropic love for post-lapsarian man, Zarathustra's love is for the constitutive perfections of man – in other words, for species man viewed as an ideal and a goal.[15] The first kind of love, in Zarathustra's view, is tainted by dogma and fear: on the one hand, the dogmatic belief that human beings are fundamentally incorrigible (a Christian prejudice buttressed by the mythical transgression of Adam and Eve and consequent transmission to mankind of 'original sin'); on the other, the selfish fear of being sucked into a vortex of pity. Zarathustra's love, by contrast, is love for an ideal man whose innate human powers/perfections have been disinterred from the Procrustean bed of Christian indoctrination. As outlined above, these perfections are reason, will and love, which in *Zarathustra* respectively translate into the following: self-reflective thought, which reveals to the knowing ones the self-debilitating and self-diminishing effects of internalised Christian values (the same effects, ironically, as those produced by Zarathustra's self-imposed doctrine of self-overcoming); the rational will, which compels the knowers to sacrifice the 'poverty and filth' of their happiness, reason, virtue and justice (ZP 3, KSA 4:15-16) on the altar of a higher ideal qua higher articulation of happiness, reason, virtue and justice; and a bestowing love, which impels the reflexively enlightened one to sacrifice himself to that higher ideal.

Feuerbach's account of this self-reflexive moment, when the ego becomes simultaneously aware of the perfection of the species and of the imperfections under which it lies buried, anticipates the element of contempt in Zarathustra's rendition.

> It is true that the human being, as an *individual*, can and must ... feel and recognise himself to be limited; but he can become conscious of his limits, his finiteness, only because the perfection, the infinitude (*Unendlichkeit*) of his species, is perceived by him, whether as an object of feeling, or conscience, or of the thinking consciousness. If he makes his *own* limitations the *limitations of the species*, this arises from the mistake that he identifies himself *immediately* with the species – a mistake which is intimately connected with the individual's love of ease, sloth, vanity and egoism ... *Every being is sufficient to itself*. No being can deny itself, i.e., its own nature (*Wesenheit*); no being is a limited one to itself. Rather, every being is *in itself* and *for itself* infinite – has its God, its highest conceivable being, *in itself*. (EC 7, GW 5:37-8)

In *Zarathustra*, it is the prospect of resurrecting and re-appropriating the species perfections of reason, will and love that catapults Zarathustra out of his mountain sequestration and fires the fledgling prophet's inaugural address to the people in the market square. Having reflexively perceived the infinite *in itself* quality of the three perfections, Zarathustra feels compelled to bestow this gift of self-knowledge and self-potential upon the world. 'I teach you the *Übermensch*', he begins. 'Man is something that ought to be overcome. What have you done to overcome him?' (ZP 3, KSA 4:14). It is a rhetorical question, of course, and one which implicitly scorns the individual's 'love of ease, sloth, vanity and egoism' as noted by Feuerbach above and against which Zarathustra is wont to rail. Take, for example, the following blistering harangue:

> All beings hitherto have created something beyond themselves and you want to be the ebb of this great flood and prefer to go back to animals than overcome man?
>
> What is the ape to man? A laughing-stock or a painful object of shame. And so shall man be to the *Übermensch*: a laughing-stock or a painful object of shame.
>
> You have made your way from worm to man and much within you is still worm. Once you were apes and even now man is more ape than any ape. (Ibid.)

In other words, despite being endowed with cognitive and reflexive abilities far beyond those of his hominoid ancestors, man is content to pluck knowledge from the nearest low-hanging branch and swallow it whole.

Christ's Passion and Zarathustra's Sacrificial Love

As discussed at length in Chapter 2, Zarathustra preaches the type of love that impels the sacrifice of self to an idea(l). This type of sacrificial love is the subject of Zarathustra's discourse 'On the Bestowing Virtue'. 'It is your thirst to become sacrifices and gifts', he declares, the same thirst, I would argue, that induces him to leave the relative comfort of his mountain refuge to undergo the rigours of peripatetic teaching. The central tenet of this teaching is self-overcoming and the restitution to man of his three innate powers of reason, will and love. But in order for these uniquely human perfections to be realised, the heart must be ardent for them: 'a bow burning for its arrow, an arrow burning for its star' (Z3 'On Old and New Tablets' 30, KSA 4:269). To love the potential within man, teaches Zarathustra, is simultaneously to despise in him the 'ape' and the 'worm', the 'plant' and the 'ghost' (ZP 3, KSA 4:14). 'You go the way of the lover (*Liebenden*)', exhorts Zarathustra; 'you love yourself and that is why you despise yourself as only lovers despise' (Z1 'On the Way of the Creator', KSA 4:82).

Zarathustra's love is a much-laboured point in his market-square oration before a jeering crowd. Comprising eighteen successive declarations, this remarkable litany of love and the objects of this love impress upon the reader love's unconditional demand for suffering and sacrifice in the service of the *übermenschlich* ideal. It is the same unconditional demand as the one made by the destructive-generative rational will to power (discussed in Chapter 2) in its demand for suffering and sacrifice out of reverence for the universal law of becoming.

> I love the great despisers, because they are the great venerators and arrows of longing for the other shore.
>
> I love the one who does not first seek a reason beyond the stars to perish (*unterzugehen*) and become a sacrifice, but instead sacrifices himself to the earth so that the earth of the *Übermensch* may one day come.
>
> I love the one who lives in order to know (*erkennen*) and who wants to know so that the *Übermensch* may one day live. Thus he seeks his own destruction (*Untergang*) . . .
>
> I love the one who loves his virtue: because virtue is the will to perish (*Wille zum Untergang*) and an arrow of longing [for the *Übermensch*]. (ZP 4, KSA 4:17)

In the above lines, love for the *Übermensch* is figured as cupidic 'arrows of longing for the other shore', arrows which symbolise not only the upward trajectory, the higher goal of man qua species ideal, but also the suffering inherent in such yearning. To yearn is to love. But to love the *Übermensch*, the higher potential in man, is simultaneously to will one's own destruction (*Wille zum Untergang*) and to suffer thereby the pains of self-sacrifice. In Feuerbachian terms, these arrows of longing connote the suffering of the heart. For Zarathustra, they are the piercing, glowing, 'annihilating sun-arrows' of self-sacrifice (Z3 'On Old and New Tablets' 30, KSA 4:269). This self-sacrifice is described by Zarathustra as a sacrifice 'to the earth' because that which is to be destroyed are the otherworldly hopes and goals that have diminished the value of man and his life on earth. But as Max Stirner convincingly argued in his incendiary polemic *The Ego and His Own* (briefly discussed in the last section of my Introduction), any idealised man or idealised aspect of man – be it the Feuerbachian 'supreme essence' or the Zarathustran *Übermensch* – is an idea by means of which the mind tyrannises over the body.[16]

As noted in the previous chapters, this tyranny is writ large in Zarathustra's concept of *Untergang*. Thrice repeated in the above-cited sacrificial account of self-overcoming, *Untergang* is the act to which reason, will and love are jointly committed in their shared longing for the other shore. 'Loving and perishing (*Untergehn*) have rhymed from eternity' (Z2 'On Immaculate Perception', KSA 4:157), hymns Zarathustra in a rainbow rendition of self-overcoming that is notably similar to his animals' hurdy-gurdy rendition of eternal return. In this *sub specie aeternitatis* version of 'loving and perishing', when the altar of self-sacrifice is ablaze with ardent flames, the heart is said to experience the beatific joy of being 'anointed and consecrated with tears as a sacrificial victim' (Z2 'On the Famous Wise Men', KSA 4:134). In a later discourse, however, Zarathustra employs a less lyrical locution: 'Will to love: that is also being willing for death' (Z2 'On Immaculate Perception', KSA 4:157). It is this *Untergang* kind of love, a love that wills the sacrifice of all its former loves on the altar of an ideal man of the future, that I am construing as an absolute human love in the Feuerbachian sense of a 'pure' love that sacrifices self to other. This absolute love, the third human power operating within Zarathustra's doctrine of self-overcoming, is what drives the knowing ones into the godless wilderness to break their 'venerating heart' (Z2 'On the Famous Wise Men', KSA 4:133), to burn themselves in their own flame (Z1 'On the Way of the Creator', KSA 4:82) and to 'bleed on sacrificial altars' (Z3 'On Old and New Tablets' 6, KSA 4:251).

The world-historical sacrificial victim is Jesus, whose suffering love for man is apotheosised in the gospel narratives of Christ's Passion (the word 'passion' taken from the Latin verb *patior* meaning to suffer or endure). In *Christianity*, Feuerbach reads Christ's suffering on Calvary as an allegory of the heart's essence (*Herzwesen*). Viewed through the lens of his dual hermeneutic of demystifying Christian theology in order to exalt its anthropological foundations, the Passion of Christ, insofar as it raises suffering – 'the *être suprême of the heart*' – to 'the highest metaphysical thought' (EC 59, GW 5:118), emblematises the heart's suffering as a human absolute. By demystifying the Passion in this way, Feuerbach elevates the '*passio pura*, the pure suffering' of Christ (ibid.), to a human universal: 'The material, the source of suffering, is the universal heart, the common bond of all beings' (EC 54 fn, GW 5:111). Rephrased, if suffering constitutes the 'universal heart', then love's suffering is a universal through which the boundary between individual and species can be transcended. Once again, the words 'material' and 'universal heart' register Feuerbach's materialist-humanist departure from the rationalist-idealist philosophy he had imbibed from Hegel's lectures at the University of Berlin. The erstwhile Hegelian no longer takes thought or reason to be the only universal and, by implication, the only conduit through which the individual can overcome his finitude and become one with the species.[17] By adding love to the anthropological universals of reason and will, Feuerbach presents us with the 'divine trinity' in species man that grounds his naturalistic humanism.[18]

The humanism that Feuerbach perceives in the Passion of Christ might be said to lie less in the latter's self-sacrifice for the redemption of mankind than in the abject suffering he endured in common with two criminals. Indeed, one might argue that a large part of what we witness before the Calvaric triptych is the spectacle of shared human suffering. 'The heart is the source, the centre of all suffering', writes Feuerbach; 'A being without suffering is a being without a heart' (EC 62, GW 5:126).[19] It is this suffering of the universal heart and, in particular, of the heart that suffers at the sight of another's suffering, which in

Part 4 of *Zarathustra* is said to be Zarathustra's greatest danger. In a chapter entitled 'The Cry of Distress', Zarathustra hears a cry of distress that he instantly recognises as 'a human cry'. It is, moreover, as he tells the Soothsayer, a cry that may well emanate from 'a black sea'. The metaphor and interlocutor are instructive. The former hints at a Schopenhauerian sea of suffering, which lends additional support to my reading of the Soothsayer as an allegorical representation of Schopenhauerian pessimism. It is in this black sea of suffering that Zarathustra's compassion, his 'final sin', appears to reside (Z4 'The Cry of Distress', KSA 4:301). In the closing section of this chapter, I shall cite various passages from the first two parts of the *Zarathustra* narrative where the protagonist-prophet's compassion can be clearly discerned. These two parts comprise Zarathustra's public discourses. But if at the didactic level of these discourses, love for a higher ideal of man demands the suffering of self-sacrifice; at the sub-textual level, a compassionate love can be heard, a 'pure' love that suffers from the ineluctable suffering of mankind. This suffering, which for Feuerbach constitutes 'the common bond of all beings', is for Zarathustra rooted in man's self-love or *amour propre*.

An Excursus on Self-Love and the I and Thou of Compassion

As discussed in Chapter 1, Nietzsche was acutely aware of the dangers of compassion. As early as *Daybreak* he had warned against *Mitleid*, especially in the case of those who have taken upon themselves the task of being 'physicians' or educators of mankind. Such a man must be continually on his guard against this 'emotion' (*Empfindung*), as 'it will paralyse him at every decisive moment' and hamper both his knowledge and his ability to be the physician he has set out to be (D 134, KSA 3:127-8). It is on account of one's devotion to this task, pronounces Zarathustra, that 'all great love is above even its compassion, because it still wants to create the beloved!' (Z2 'On the Compassionate', KSA 4:116). What Zarathustra means here by creating 'the beloved' is the transformation of man from a deeply flawed individual into a higher human being, or in Hegelian-Feuerbachian terms into a particular that enacts the purity of its constitutive universals of reason, will and love. This transformation will arouse the love and admiration of others rather than compassion for the broken and defeated.

The error of philanthropists, inveighs Nietzsche, is to pity the sick, suffering, poor 'thing' instead of stimulating man's native, '*shaping* powers' (*gestaltender Kräfte*):

> In man, *creature* and *creator* are combined: in man there is matter, fragment, abundance, clay, excrement, nonsense, chaos; but in man there is also creator, builder, hammer-hardness, spectator-divinity and seventh day: – do you understand this contrast? And that *your* pity is aimed at the 'creature in human', at what needs to be shaped, broken, wrought, torn, burnt, tempered and refined – at what needs to *suffer* and *should* suffer? (BGE 225, KSA 5:161)[20]

In contrast to what Nietzsche sees as the presumptuous and intrusive love of the philanthropist which succeeds only in exacerbating the shame and thereby diminishing the self-worth of the one pitied, love for the creative potential in man, albeit a sorely tested love, endeavours to rise above compassion and thereby minimise the individual's shame.[21] 'If I must be compassionate', says Zarathustra, 'I do not want to be called so; and if I am compassionate, then I like it to be from a distance' (Z2 'On the Compassionate', KSA 4:113). In this brief excursus, I will show how Zarathustra's 'great love' for the *Übermensch* is *not* above its compassion; as the 'devil' once confided to Zarathustra, '"Even God has his hell: it is his love for mankind"' (ibid., KSA 4:115). I will also show how Zarathustra's compassion extends beyond those who voluntarily suffer the torment of self-overcoming to the involuntary suffering of *all* human beings. This latter kind of suffering is induced by the daily if not hourly humiliation of man's *amour propre* by the inexorable and indomitable affective will to power.

Any discussion on compassion needs to be prefaced with a few words on the semantic contiguity between pity, compassion, sympathy and empathy. Langenscheidt lists pity, compassion and sympathy under the German noun *Mitleid*, although sympathy is more commonly rendered in German as *Mitgefühl* or *mitempfinden* and contrasted with empathy (*Einfühlung*). Michael Frazer cites the widespread translation of *Mitleid* as 'pity' rather than 'compassion' in English-language editions of Nietzsche's work as partially responsible for the lack of nuance in commentators' stock representation of Nietzsche's stance on *Mitleid*.[22] The received view of the latter is grounded in Nietzsche's sustained and vigorous attack on what he dismisses as the psychologically naïve valorisation of pity as a selfless, hence moral, act of benevolence. Against this view (already discussed in Chapter 1), Nietzsche insightfully demonstrates how the purportedly disinterested act of pity/compassion is fundamentally self-serving, motivated by the emotional needs of the dispenser of pity at the expense of the emotional needs of the one pitied.

Nietzsche's trenchant critique of pity is well documented and requires no rehearsal here.[23] What has received far less attention, however, is his position on what I would term *passive*, as opposed to *active*, pity. By passive pity I mean the involuntary stab of pain that one feels but restrains oneself from acting upon at the sight of another's suffering. This type of involuntary *suffering-with* is etymologically rooted in the words 'compassion' (from the Latin *com-passio*), 'sympathy' (from the Ancient Greek *sum-patheia*), and '*Mitleid*' (*mit-leiden* – with suffering).[24] It is this *suffering-with* that Frazer, correctly in my view, identifies as Zarathustra's unconquerable compassion. As Zarathustra himself declares at the end of Part 4, 'My suffering and my compassion (*Mein Leid und mein Mitleiden*) – what does it matter? Am I striving after *happiness*? I am striving after my *work!*' (Z4 'The Sign', KSA 4:408).[25] As I shall argue in the remainder of this chapter, the psychological root of this *suffering with* emerges in *Zarathustra* as self-love or *amour propre*.

In the previous section, we saw how Feuerbach demystifies the Passion of Christ and presents it as an allegory of 'pure' human love that is pure insofar as it suffers out of compassion for others. Compassion and suffering, asserts Feuerbach, are inextricable: 'As if compassion (*Mitleiden*) were not suffering

(*Leiden*) – the suffering of love ... No love, no suffering' (EC 54 fn, GW 5:111). Zarathustra voices the same belief: 'Compassion (*Mitleiden*) is the deepest abyss; as deeply as one sees into life, as deeply does he see into suffering (*Leiden*)' (Z3 'On the Vision and the Riddle' 1, KSA 4:199). In *Zarathustra*, however, Nietzsche discloses a deeper layer to this pure love that suffers in common. This layer is the suffering of self-love and its noble scion pride (not to be confused with its bastard brother vanity) – the pride and self-love that is routinely savaged by man's irrational and inexorable will to power. Thus, while Zarathustra glorifies the suffering of self-sacrifice as a heroic virtue, he also recognises that for the majority of mankind suffering is a negative principle in the circumvention of which every sinew is reactively bent.[26]

All too well did Nietzsche learn from his educator Schopenhauer that 'the life of the individual is a constant struggle' and that the *individuum principium* 'discovers adversaries everywhere, lives in continual conflict and dies with sword in hand'.[27] Imbued with Schopenhauer's conviction that the root of man's suffering lies in the will's incessant surge towards satisfaction, Nietzsche further apprehended, on the evidence of *Zarathustra* at least, that while the narrow, selfish, self-indulgent type of self-love is the primary beneficiary of the will's blind pursuit of gratification, the other type of self-love – one that is intrinsically connected to man's innate sense of pride – is progressively eroded by the blind inexorability of the affective will to power. What is most striking in *Zarathustra*, however, is that the universal suffering of a buffeted self-love is brought home to Zarathustra through the inter-subjective relation of I and thou.

In a key passage in *Christianity*, Feuerbach enumerates three relational aspects of the thou to the I, namely the universal, the reciprocal and the moral. The 'universal significance' of the human other, holds Feuerbach, resides in the fact that despite being an individual entity, the other is 'the representative of the species' by virtue of being a member of that species. The reciprocal relation manifests itself specularly: 'The other is my *thou* – the relation being reciprocal – my *alter ego*, man objective to me, the revelation of my own nature, the eye seeing itself.' By *alter ego*, Feuerbach simply means a second self, an objective I through which, in accordance with Hegel's dialectical theory of knowledge, man achieves consciousness of his own nature. The third relational aspect of the thou to the I is the moral relation between I and thou: 'My fellow-man is my *objective* conscience; he makes my failings a reproach to me; even when he does not expressly mention them, he is my personified feeling of shame' (EC 158, GW 5:277). Nietzsche would undoubtedly have repudiated the last of these relations on at least three counts: first, because he believes that man's conscience should be activated by self-scrutiny rather than by self-comparison with another; second, because the thou's look of disapproval has in all probability been prompted by socio-cultural norms to which the I does not subscribe; and third, because Nietzsche saw his fellow-man as an inverted 'objective conscience' – the other's myriad failings functioning as a salutary goad to his own conscience to fashion a more inspiring, more self-determining human specimen.

Leaving aside then the moral relation between I and thou, the universal and reciprocal relations are shown in *Zarathustra* to be predicated on the suffering of self-love. This is not the voluntary suffering of self-love engendered by a love of self-perfection and the concomitant desire to realise within oneself the fullness of that perfection – it is not this kind of suffering because the human perfections of reason, will and love manifest themselves through reflexivity and not through the other. Rather, the suffering of self-love that manifests itself in the reciprocal and universal relations between self and other is the *involuntary* suffering of primal self-love. Unlike the former kind of suffering, this kind of suffering self-love is brought home to the I via the suffering of the thou in whom one's own nature is revealed. In its uncompromised state, this primal self-love is depicted by Zarathustra as the 'self-delighting soul (*selbst-lustige*)', supple as a dancer and revelling in its self-delighting body (Z3 'On the Three Evils' 2, KSA 4:238), and by Feuerbach as '*joy in one's own perfection*' (EC 6, GW 5:36), that 'simple, natural self-love which is innate in all beings' (EC 140, GW 5:247). It is this pure self-love that is under constant siege by the affective will to power.

One of the most surprising and rarely noted features of *Zarathustra* is its recognition of the fundamental innocence of all human affects and of the suffering they cause to both self and other. As Nietzsche notes in *Human, All Too Human*: 'man cannot be made accountable for anything, not for his nature, nor for his motives, nor for his actions, nor for the outcome' (HH 39, KSA 2:63). Envy, enmity, vengeance – collectively comprised in Nietzsche's concept of *ressentiment* – are shown by Zarathustra to be the involuntary reflexes of an inherent self-love seeking compensatory relief from its suffering. Take, for example, Zarathustra's discourse on 'The Flies of the Market Place', where the titular flies, emblematic of the small-minded many whose precarious self-love battens on the robust self-love of the magnanimous few, are depicted as a veritable but pardonable plague. 'Blood they would have from you in all innocence; blood their bloodless souls crave – and they sting therefore in all innocence' (Z1, KSA 4:67). What is bloodless here is also blameless, namely the craven pride of 'the sick and pining' (Z1 'On the Hinterlanders', KSA 4:37), which involuntarily craves vengeance.

While urging the noble ones to 'Flee into thy solitude! . . . it is not your lot to be a fly-swat' (Z1, 'On the Flies of the Market Place', KSA 4:66), Zarathustra is far from oblivious to the dangers that beset the solitary. The first of these dangers is self-doubt. Shielded from the 'invisible vengeance' (ibid.) of those afflicted with low self-esteem, the assured self-love of the recluse suffers its own insurrection. Crushed by the insupportable burden of solitude, warns Zarathustra, 'your pride will yield and your courage quail' (Z1 'On the Way of the Creator', KSA 4:81). It is in this erosion of self-love that the invisible, insidious vengeance of self-contempt finds the richest of soils in which to breed. This is not the invigorating kind of self-contempt that is experienced in the epiphanic hour of the great contempt, but the kind of self-contempt that gnaws away at one's self-love and ultimately vitiates it. As Zarathustra confesses in one of his early discourses, 'We are sorest bent and troubled by invisible hands' (Z1 'The Tree on the Mountain', KSA 4:51). More perilous still for the noble soul is the second danger that besets the solitary, namely mean-spirited envy. Out of this emotion arises the same type of peevish vengeance from which it had sought to escape by fleeing into solitude.

> That is my poverty: that my hand never rests from giving; that is my envy, that I see expectant eyes and the brightened nights of longing . . .
>
> I should like to hurt those I illumine; I should like to rob my recipients: – thus do I hunger after malice.
>
> Withdrawing my hand when another is already outstretched to it . . . thus do I hunger after malice.
>
> Such revenge doth my abundance concoct: such spite springs out my loneliness. (Z2 'The Night Song', KSA 4:136-7)[28]

However, regardless of whether the embittered pride of the bloodsucking 'flies' exacts vengeance on the 'silent pride' of those whom they secretly envy, or whether a noble pride seeks to inoculate itself against the sting of the former only to discover within itself a kindred strain of venomous rancour, the respective fight or flight mechanism of each is a natural reflex of self-love. In exhorting the noble soul to withdraw into solitude, Zarathustra's overriding concern is to safeguard the natural love that man has for the innate perfections within the human species from turning into pernicious self-contempt. Even in the face of a friend, he notes, we discover the reflection of our own countenance in a 'coarse and imperfect mirror'. And those who presume to inflict their 'nakedness' on a friend will be cursed for doing so because only a god has sufficient inner beauty to dispense with his clothing (Z1 'On the Friend', KSA 4:71-3). This indiscriminate levelling of the affects, I would argue, is what underpins Zarathustra's compassion (*Mitleid*). Not the philanthropic kind of compassion marked by veiled condescension and the cold hand of charity, but a reserved, fastidious compassion that is prompted by an acute sense of shared suffering (*Mitleid*), of suffering-with.

The greatest danger for the noble soul, asserts Zarathustra, is not the danger of being shamed into reverting to one's Christian roots, but of losing one's 'highest hope' for man and thereby becoming 'a churl, a scoffer, a destroyer' and a cynical slanderer of 'all high hopes' (Z1 'On the Tree on the Mountain', KSA 4:53). This danger is illustrated in Part 3 of *Zarathustra* in a chapter entitled 'On Passing By'. En route back to his mountain refuge, the palpable failure of his teaching having no doubt clouded his highest hope for man, Zarathustra is waylaid by a 'foaming fool' loitering outside the gates of the proverbial 'big city'. Aping Zarathustra's wisdom, but evincing none of his compassion, the fool rails against the filth and stench of human vice clogging up the highways and byways of the city. 'Spit on the city of sunken souls and narrow chests', froths the fool, 'where everything [is] putrid, infamous, prurient, morbid, overripe, [and] ulcerous.' Nauseated by the tirade, Zarathustra stops the fool's mouth, first by chiding him for having tarried so long in the festering sump instead of seeking cleaner air elsewhere, and second by holding up a mirror to show him that 'vengeance, you vain fool, is all your foaming'. Vengeance breeds vengeance, venom, venom. Distance is paramount: without it, self-love degenerates into hypocritical self-blindness and contempt for others. 'Out of love alone shall my contempt and my warning bird soar up', says Zarathustra, 'not out of the swamp!' That is why Zarathustra's love for man qua potential bridge to a higher type of man one minute drives him to exchange the silent contemplation of the hermit for the homiletic exhortation of the prophet and the next minute drives him back into solitude, for 'where one can no longer love, there one should *pass by!*' (Z3 'On Passing-By', KSA 4:224–5).

Zarathustra's compassion is a ubiquitous presence throughout the early discourses. It can be seen in his refusal to disabuse the anchorite of his sentimental love for God (ZP 2, KSA 4:14); in his indulgence towards the 'despisers of the body' who should 'neither unlearn nor unteach', but be free to cherish and bequeath their belief in the sanctity of the soul and the innate depravity of the body (Z1 'On the Despisers of the Body', KSA 4:39–41); and in his gentle mockery, tinged perhaps with a little envy, of the academic purveyors (*Lehrstuhlen*) of 'poppy virtues' who, unlike the tormented Zarathustra, enjoy the peace afforded by a sedated spirit. 'Blessed are the sleepy ones', preaches Zarathustra, 'for they shall soon nod off' (Z1 'On the Academic Chairs of Virtue', KSA 4:32-4). But it is in Zarathustra's heartfelt empathy with the tormented ones that his compassion is most poignant. Unlike the soft, flabby-buttocked behinds of the *Lehrstühlen* snoozing contentedly in their armchairs and academic chairs of sleepy virtue, the backsides of the tormented ones squirm upon the uncomfortable seat of their own passions. As the irrational will's seat of power, it is a hidden cellar of wild dogs (Z1 'On the Joyful and Painful Passions', KSA 4:43) and hissing serpents (Z1 'On the Pale Criminal', KSA 4:46).

'All feeling suffers in me and is in prison', confesses Zarathustra, and it is through the walls of his own prison that he addresses his fellow prisoners. He speaks to those who look to heavenly hinterlands to redeem them from the hellish hinterland of their impotent suffering (Z1 'On the Hinterlanders', KSA 4:35-8); to the young man (one of Zarathustra's many *Doppelgängers*), whose oppressive loneliness and despondent failure to self-overcome tears Zarathustra's heart (Z1 'On the Tree on the Mountain', KSA 4:51-4); to 'the poor soul[s]' who helplessly spread their infectious diseases abroad (Z1 'On the Pale Criminal', KSA 46-7); to the 'terrible ones who carry within them the beast of prey and have no choice but lusts or self-laceration' (Z1 'On the Preachers of Death', 4:56); and to the figurative flies of the marketplace whose famished pride wreaks vengeance on the sound pride of the noble ones. These last, sympathises Zarathustra, 'punish you for all your virtues ... Even when you are gentle towards them, they still feel themselves despised by you; and they repay your benevolence (*Wohlthat*) with veiled malevolence (*Wehthaten*)' (Z1 'On the Flies of the Market-Place', KSA 4:67).

Nietzsche's juxtaposition of the homonymous nouns *Wohltun* and *Wehtun* is illuminating. Forging a link between apparent opposites, the wordplay recalls the opening aphorism of Volume 1 of *Human, All Too Human*, already alluded to in the previous chapter. Under the heading 'Chemistry of concepts and sensations', Nietzsche argues that the two terms in a binary opposition are intrinsically connected, one pole being but an outgrowth or 'sublimation' (*Sublimirungen*) of the other (HH 1, KSA 2:23–4). As we saw above, benevolence gives rise not only to malice in the benefactor: 'to him who forever dispenses, the hand and heart become callous from dispensing' (Z2 'The Night Song', KSA 4:137), but also in the beneficiary: 'Great obligations do not make people grateful, but vengeful; and when a small kindness is not forgotten, it becomes a gnawing worm' (Z2 'On the Compassionate', KSA 4:114). In short, Zarathustra's compassionate reading of *ressentiment* views self-contempt as a natural outgrowth of self-love: 'To the despisers of the body will I speak a word. That they despise (*verachten*) is caused by their esteem (*Achten*)' (Z1 'On the Despisers of the Body', KSA 4:40). Once again, the wordplay serves to reinforce Nietzsche's argument against erroneous moral polarities. A similar correlation is revealed between noble pride and abject humility, the latter emerging as an all-too-human outgrowth of the former's repeated capitulation to the vagaries of the will: 'Truly, you know not the spirit's pride! But still less could you endure the spirit's humility, should it ever wish to speak!' (Z2 'On the Famous Wise Men', KSA 4:134). All too often, laments Zarathustra, the pride with which we greet the morning will have been humbled by the evening (Z1 'On Reading and Writing', KSA 4:49).

Zarathustra's animals – 'the proudest animal under the sun' (eagle) and 'the cleverest animal under the sun' (serpent) (ZP 10, KSA 4:27) – also convey the interrelation between pride and will. This interrelation is illustrated through two kindred images: a serpent-entwined sun and an eagle and serpent locked in a loving embrace. The first image is engraved on the golden-handled staff presented to Zarathustra by his followers at the end of Part 1. The second is introduced towards the end of 'Zarathustra's Prologue' and is explicitly linked to Zarathustra's totemic animals. Common to both compound images is the serpent. A symbol rich in signification, the skin-shedding serpent was adopted by a number of ancient cultures as a symbol of regeneration and rebirth. Taken in this sense, it might plausibly be seen to represent Nietzsche's ontological principle of will to power – a procreative life force that perpetually renews itself through a dialectical movement of destruction and generation. Accordingly, the golden-handled staff with its engraving of 'a golden sun and around it the serpent of knowledge (*Erkenntniss*)' (Z1 'On the Bestowing Virtue' 1, KSA 4:99), could be interpreted as the knowledge or wisdom of the knowers that life is will to power. The second image, that of a serpent coiled lovingly around the neck of a proud eagle, appears to convey the same message. But as we have learned from the foregoing discussion in this section, eagle pride is far more likely to be strangled by the envy, malice and vengeance of man's chthonic will to power than empowered by its creative-transformative potential.

Notes

1. For the multiple ways in which Feuerbach anticipated Nietzsche see Van A. Harvey, *Feuerbach and the Interpretation of Religion* (Cambridge: Cambridge University Press, 1997). Writing in the aftermath of the Second World War, the French Jesuit priest Henri de Lubac identified Feuerbach, Nietzsche and Auguste Comte as the ternary progenitors of diverse forms of atheist humanism then sweeping across the Western world. In his book *The Drama of Atheist Humanism*, Lubac addresses what he saw as an exigent threat to the Christian faith posed by these three philosophers, whose anti-Christian doctrines spawned the positivist (Comte), materialist (Feuerbach) and individualistic (Nietzsche) creeds of late modernity. The danger of these ideologies, for Lubac, lay in the emancipative thrust of their shared basic premise: 'Man is getting rid of God in order to regain possession of the human greatness which, it seems to him, is being unwarrantably withheld by another. In God he is overthrowing an obstacle in order to gain his freedom.' Instead of feeling exalted by God in whose image and likeness man was created, repines Lubac, the dispirited, modern-day Christian feels before God nothing but the chafing of the yoke and an affront to his dignity. Henri de Lubac, *The Drama of Atheist Humanism*, trans. Edith M. Riley (Cleveland and New York: The World Publishing Company, 1967), pp. 5-6. It was in order to remove this yoke and restore to man his essential human greatness that Feuerbach wrote *The Essence of Christianity* and Nietzsche his *Zarathustra*.
2. 'God as a Being of the Understanding'; 'God as a Moral Being or Law'; and 'The Mystery of the Incarnation; or, God as Love,

as Heart-Essence (*Herzwesen*)' are the sequential titles of the first three chapters of *Christianity*.
3. Harvey opens his monograph on Feuerbach with a substantial chapter on the latter's projection thesis. But while acknowledging the dominant role played by Hegel's dialectical model of consciousness in Feuerbach's critique of religion, Harvey also highlights an illuminating existentialist strand, which 'bears the weight of many of Feuerbach's most interesting insights'. These insights are not only independent of and therefore undiminished by 'the now arcane Hegelian philosophy of consciousness', but form the basis of important later developments in Feuerbach's thought. Harvey, *Feuerbach*, pp. 11-12.
4. In her book-length study of Nietzsche's *The Gay Science*, Kathleen-Marie Higgins draws our attention to a number of aphorisms in this pre-*Zarathustra* text that implicitly endorse Feuerbach's argument that man has impoverished himself by projecting his inner powers and potential onto a man-made conception of God. See Chapter 5 ('God is Dead') of Kathleen-Marie Higgins, *Comic Relief: Nietzsche's 'Gay Science'* (New York: Oxford University Press, 2000), pp. 95-122.
5. Feuerbach points out that the Jehovah of ancient Judaism was qualitatively identical to the human individual in all but the duration of existence. Moreover, notes Feuerbach, 'the religious man is not shocked at this identification; for his understanding is still in harmony with his religion' (EC 197, GW 5:336).
6. For a detailed exposition of the extent to which Feuerbach's self-projection thesis is grounded in Hegel's dialectical theory of consciousness, see the section entitled 'The Hegelian Model of Self-Alienation as the Context of Feuerbach's Phenomenology' in Marx W. Wartofsky, *Feuerbach* (Cambridge: Cambridge University Press, 1977), pp. 206-10.
7. The italicised words in all my citations from *The Essence of Christianity* replicate Feuerbach's emphases in the German original. As noted in the 'Abbreviations and Translations' section of this monograph, George Eliot chose to omit most of these emphases from her translation of the second edition of *The Essence of Christianity* – a decision presumably taken with the general reader in mind.
8. What distinguishes Feuerbach from his successor 'masters of suspicion' (Nietzsche, Marx and Freud), writes Harvey, is Feuerbach's belief that 'the new age of which he was the prophet would only

emerge if the deepest values of Christianity were preserved ... If he criticised Christianity, it was in the service of the same human values Christianity itself recognised and fostered. If the Trinity was to be rejected as a reified myth, this rejection was in the name of a genuine human family bound by ties of love and mutuality.' Harvey, *Feuerbach*, pp. 101–2. In a similar vein, Robert Jenson observes that 'Feuerbach dreamed of a universal humanity and so of a shared eternal vision of human value, but therein he remained parasitic on the faith he debunked. Thus Western unbelief has since had to abandon that dream and now knows only classes and genders and races and cultures.' Robert W. Jenson, *Systematic Theology, Volume 1: The Triune God* (Oxford: Oxford University Press, 1997), p. 53.

9. Friedrich Engels, *Ludwig Feuerbach and the End of Classical German Philosophy* (Moscow: Progress Publishers, 1978), p. 33. Engels's quip, as Lawrence Stepelevich points out, was merely a repetition of Max Stirner's epigrammatic 'Our atheists are pious' in *The Ego and His Own*, the work in which Stirner exposed the idealism he found lurking behind Feuerbach's avowedly empiricist-naturalist project and which precipitated Marx and Engels's ideological break with Feuerbach. See Lawrence S. Stepelevich, 'Max Stirner and Ludwig Feuerbach', *Journal of the History of Ideas*, 39:3 (1978), p. 458.

10. Noting that the word 'religion' derives from the Latin *religare* meaning to bind fast, Engels accuses Feuerbach of resorting to 'etymological tricks[,] ... the last resort of idealist philosophy', as a means of elevating the bond between two people into a religion. Engels, *Feuerbach*, p. 34.

11. A noteworthy exception is Michael Frazer, 'The compassion of Zarathustra: Nietzsche on sympathy and strength', *The Review of Politics* 68:1 (2006), pp. 49–78.

12. 'The *absolute* to man is *his own nature*' (EC 5, GW 5:35).

13. Feuerbach's exposition of these 'absolute perfections' constitutive of man is strongly reminiscent of what William Blake in his unpublished verse epic *The Four Zoas* allegorises as the eponymous Zoas. Numbering four rather than three (but see additional comment at the end of this note), Urizen, Luvah, Tharmas and Urthona respectively symbolise reason, love, the senses and imagination. In their prelapsarian form, these primal powers constitute the fourfold unity of man which, once fallen, disaggregates into antagonistic forces. It is this internecine battle which dominates the dramatic action of *The Four Zoas*. Of particular relevance to

the thematic focus of this chapter is Luvah, who in the mythopoeic universe of *The Four Zoas* is named Prince of Love and in later passages of the work is closely identified with Jesus. In Blake's arresting image of Jesus donning Luvah's 'robes of blood', a compound image emblematising Jesus as love, suffering and compassion, the identification between Christ's suffering and that of the human heart is made most explicit. S. Foster Damon, *A Blake Dictionary: The Ideas and Symbols of William Blake* (Providence: Brown University Press, 1965), p. 255. It is also worth noting on the subject of Blake's striking anticipation of Feuerbach's account of the human perfections that Feuerbach also includes the imagination. In his chapter on 'The Mystery of the Logos and Divine Image', which deals with the idea of the second person in the Holy Trinity, Feuerbach explicitly refers to 'the imagination as a divine power'. It is to this power that he attributes the divine image of Christ: 'The Son is, therefore, expressly called the *Image* of God; his essence is that he is an image – the representation of God, the visible glory of the invisible God. The Son is the satisfaction of the need for mental images, the nature of the imaginative activity in man made objective as an absolute, divine activity' (EC 75, GW 5:153–4). Feuerbach also takes as self-evident that the ideas of 'the Transfiguration, the Resurrection, and the Ascension of Christ' are objects of the imagination (ibid.).

14. Cf. the closing couplet from Nietzsche's blushingly poor verse entitled 'Sils Maria': '[There sat I, waiting, waiting . . .] Suddenly, my friend! One turned into Two – / and Zarathustra came into view' (GS 'Appendix: Songs of Prince Vogelfrei', KSA 3: 649).

15. Zarathustra's love for an idealisation of man rather than man as a concrete individual is open to the same charge Max Stirner levelled at Feuerbach's religious anthropology, namely that the individual is being sacrificed to the species, the concrete to an abstraction. As Manfred Vogel observes in the introduction to his translation of Feuerbach's *Principles of the Philosophy of the Future*, 'Feuerbach stops short of fully and completely concretizing man. Sometimes he speaks of man as indeed fully concretized – as the earthly, finite human individual – but at other times he is speaking of generic man, of man in general, of the human species.' Cited in Stepelevich, 'Stirner and Feuerbach', pp. 454–5.

16. See previous note.

17. I am indebted to Marx Wartofsky's extensive and penetrating exegesis of Feuerbach's critique of, but also embroilment in, Hegel's philosophy. Wartofsky, *Feuerbach* (1977).

18. As Wartofsky notes, in revising the rationalist credo that thought is the essence of man by the inclusion in that essence of both will and feeling, Feuerbach was seeking 'to *empiricize* and *voluntarize* the Hegelian *Idea* – to take the *Idea* of the *Logic* and the *Spirit* of the *Phenomenology* and interpret them as much with respect to feeling and will as with respect to reason' (ibid. p. 272).

19. It is surprising, perhaps, that in Feuerbach's visceral account of Christ's suffering he makes no mention of the iconographic Sacred Heart. Depicted as a bleeding heart encompassed by a crown of thorns and surmounted by a rood, its crude anatomical realism could be said to have the unintended effect of foregrounding the human rather than the divine. In his article 'Of metaphoric hearts', Frank Gonzalez-Crussi remarks upon the strikingly explicit anatomical realism of two early images of the Sacred Heart of Jesus: one painted by Pompeo Batoni in 1767, the other by Charles-Joseph Natoire, which forms the frontispiece of Gallifet's devotional work *De Culto Sacro Sancti Cordis Dei* published in 1726. (*Hektoen International* 5.2 (2013): n.p. Available at <https://hekint.org/2017/01/27/of-metaphoric-hearts/> (last accessed 11 April 2022).

20. In his outstanding article on Nietzsche's complex attitude towards compassion and his related ideal of self-overcoming, Daniel Harris directs us to GS 338 (KSA 3:565–8) and Z2 'On the Compassionate' (KSA 4:113–16), which he glosses as follows: 'For Nietzsche, we respond to others in a healthy way when we attend to suffering not as an evil per se, but as potentially, though not necessarily, frustrating the particular potential of those we know and care about. This is why Nietzsche cautions us to exercise compassion selectively, with our friends, whose sufferings we understand and so can treat in its complexity.' Harris also notes Nietzsche's focus on 'friendship's incitement toward joy and shared joy as an antidote to the erasure of compassion's shared suffering', citing in support of the latter claim D 144 (KSA 3:136–7) in which Nietzsche insightfully observes that we can 'neither *aid* nor *comfort* [others] if we want to be the echo of their lamentation'. Daniel I. Harris, 'Compassion and Affirmation in Nietzsche', *Journal of Nietzsche Studies*, 48:1 (2017), p. 24.

21. Nietzsche's view of shame as the most invidious effect of compassion and of compassion as the greatest danger to his love for the higher potential latent within man is succinctly expressed in the five catechistic aphorisms which close out Book Three of *The Gay Science* (GS 271–5, KSA 3:519):

Where lie your greatest dangers? – In compassion.
What do you love in others? – My hopes.
Whom do you call bad? – The one who always wants to shame others.
What is most human to you? – To spare someone shame.
What is the seal of having attained freedom? – No longer being ashamed before oneself.

22. Frazer, 'The Compassion of Zarathustra', pp. 11–12. Frazer's essay contains a comprehensive and incisive account of Nietzsche's complex attitude towards compassion.
23. David Cartwright traces Nietzsche's stance on pity back to Kant and supports his claim by mapping a passage from Nietzsche's *Nachlass* onto a passage from Kant's *The Metaphysical Principles of Virtue*. The *Nachlass* passage is as follows: 'Pity is a squandering of feeling, a parasite harmful to moral health, "it cannot possibly be our duty to increase the evil in the world." If one does good merely out of pity, it is really oneself one really does good to, and not the other. Pity does not depend upon maxims but upon affects; it is pathological [*pathologisich*]. The suffering of others infects us; pity is an infection [*Ansteckung*]' (WP 368, KSA 12:268). The Kant passage is as follows: 'if another person suffers and I let myself (through my imagination) also become infected [*anstecken lasse*] by his pain, which I still cannot remedy, then two people suffer, although the evil (in nature) affects only the one. But it cannot possibly be a duty to increase the evils of the world or, therefore to do good from pity [*Mitleid*].' Cartwright attributes the same 'psychological model' of pity to David Hume and Benedict de Spinoza. David E. Cartwright, 'Kant, Schopenhauer, and Nietzsche on the Morality of Pity', *Journal of the History of Ideas*, 45.1 (1984), pp. 84–5. Michael Ure provides a thorough exposition of Nietzsche's psychological analysis of pity by way of a series of aphorisms in Nietzsche's *Daybreak* in which Nietzsche applies his critical scalpel to the ethics of pity advanced by Jean-Jacques Rousseau and Schopenhauer. Michael Ure, 'The Irony of Pity: Nietzsche contra Schopenhauer and Rousseau', *Journal of Nietzsche Studies*, 32 (2006), pp. 68–91.
24. Cartwright makes the same etymological observation, but takes Nietzsche's use of *Mitleid* to mean pity rather than compassion and concurs with Jean Stambaugh that Nietzsche's work lacks any conception of compassion. Cartwright, 'Kant, Schopenhauer', pp. 96–7 (footnote). Jean Stambaugh, 'Thoughts on Pity and Revenge',

Nietzsche-Studien, 1 (1971), pp. 27–35. Against Stambaugh and Cartwright, the final section of this chapter ('An excursus on self-love and the I and thou of compassion') expatiates on what I consider to be a clearly articulated conception of compassion in *Zarathustra*.

25. Zarathustra's inability to master his compassion is not necessarily a failure; it can also be seen as a mark of his humanity. As Frazer points out by way of *Ecce Homo*, Nietzsche sees compassion as an unavoidable sentiment in those with true insight into the human condition. True strength comes not from extirpating this feeling but from learning how to withstand it: 'my humanity does *not* consist in feeling with (*mitzufühlen*) men how they are, but in *enduring* that I feel with (*mitfühlen*) them' (EH 'Why I Am So Wise' 8, KSA 6:276). Frazer, 'The Compassion of Zarathustra', p. 23.

26. The philosopher deemed by many to have had the last word on suffering is Schopenhauer. His famous essay 'On the Suffering of the World' (1850) opens with the following rhetorical flourish: 'If the immediate and direct purpose of our life is not suffering then our existence is the most ill-adapted to its purpose in the world.' One can only assume a question-begging playfulness here given Schopenhauer's view of the world as one that is driven by a blind metaphysical will as primordial as it is inexorable and that therefore excludes any purpose or final cause. Rhetoric aside, his argument is abundantly clear: suffering is an immutable law of human nature, the sole constant in the flux of human existence. And while suffering is sporadically alleviated by fleeting moments of pleasure, it is the ephemerality of these bursts of pleasure that generates yet more suffering. What I find most interesting in Schopenhauer's essay is the negligible role it accords to love as a source of human suffering. Between the poles of physical need and boredom to which Schopenhauer reduces the human condition, love is relegated to a mere by-product of carnality. Whereas thought, knowledge, memory and anticipation, together with man's all-consuming preoccupation with ambition and honour, are cited as sources of intense pleasure and pain, 'a more or less passionate love' is described as the occasional intensification of 'a very obstinate selectivity [of sexual gratification]'. Arthur Schopenhauer, *Essays and Aphorisms*, trans. R. J. Hollingdale (London: Penguin, 1970), pp. 41 and 45.

27. 'On the Suffering of the World' in Schopenhauer, *Essays*, p. 42. Cf. 'All that happens, all movement, all becoming as a determining of relations of degree and force, as a *struggle*' (WLN 9[91]:155, KSA 12:385).
28. Cf. 'But sometimes, when I am tired, I envy [the poor in spirit]: because *administering* such wealth [the wealth of one's wisdom] is a weighty business, and its heaviness not seldom crushes all happiness . . . If only one were a miser with one's knowledge!' (D 476, KSA 3:284).

Conclusion

> *Overcoming the affects?* – No, not if it means weakening and annihilating them. *Instead, drawing them into service*, which may include exercising a long tyranny over them.
>
> (WLN 1[122]:63, KSA 12:39)

Chapter 1 of this study opened with three Nietzsche quotations on the subject of truth. Two of these equated truth and honesty with morality, while the third declared Zarathustra's teaching to be the only one to posit truthfulness as the highest good. I shall conclude with three more citations on truth. The first closes out *Gay Science* 110: 'To what extent can truth endure (*vertragen*) incorporation? – that is the question; that is the experiment' (KSA 3:471). A similar question is asked by Nietzsche in his preface to *Ecce Homo*: 'How much truth can one *endure* (*ertragen*), how much truth does a spirit *dare*? More and more that became for me the true measure of value' (EH F 3, KSA 6:259). And in another *Gay Science* passage, Nietzsche speaks of 'a completely new task' for mankind, that of '*incorporating knowledge* and making it instinctive' because 'so far we have incorporated only our *errors*' (GS 11, KSA 3:383). That question, that experiment and that task, I submit, are all synonymous with Zarathustra's doctrine of self-overcoming, the severity of which is red-flagged above by the reiterated verb *endure*. Appearing high up in Nietzsche's table of values, endurance or fortitude serves to separate the wheat from the chaff, which is to say, those who will perish from the experiment of truth-incorporation and those who will prevail, albeit pyrrhically.

Zarathustra's Violent Rhetoric of Truth Incorporation

We learn from Zarathustra's pivotal Part 2 discourse 'On Self-Overcoming' that the three primary truths known to the knower are the Heraclitean truth of becoming, the Nietzschean concept of will to power and that life '*must always overcome itself*' (Z2 'On Self-Overcoming', KSA 4:148). Upon acquiring this knowledge, the knower is required not only to incorporate these truths into his daily life, but to endure the pain of perpetual self-overcoming. In *Zarathustra*, this pain is expressed through a prodigious array of emblems and epithets, the first of which is the sickle-blade. Towards the end of the prologue, Zarathustra speaks of his need for fellow 'harvesters' and 'celebrators' who will join him in cutting down the blighted but tenacious crop of Christianised good and evil deep-rooted in the human psyche. In order to reap effectively, however, these harvesters must first 'know how to whet their scythes'. Zarathustra does not elaborate here, but if the harvester is to be a 'destroyer' (*Vernichter*), a 'despiser' (*Verächter*) – the half-rhyme serves Nietzsche well here – and also a 'celebrator', he will be better able to celebrate self-vivisection as an act of self-re-creation if his sickle is whetted with contempt for Christian values (ZP 9, KSA 4:26). As Zarathustra descants in Part 2 of *Zarathustra*, the spirit which has the courage to cut into its own life (without bleeding to death) will experience the joy of being 'anointed and consecrated with tears as a sacrificial victim' (Z2 'On the Famous Wise Men', KSA 4:134).

In Part 1 of *Zarathustra*, the rhetoric of truth incorporation is relatively anodyne. In the opening discourse, the incorporator of knowledge is depicted as one who wades into the dirty water of truth to do battle with frogs and toads or, somewhat less ludicrously, as a heroic dragon-slayer ('On the Three Metamorphoses', KSA 4:29–30). In 'On the Joyful and Painful Passions', the pain of truth incorporation is similarly muted in the idealised transmutation of wild dogs into singing birds and in the fecund image of planting one's goal or highest aim in the soil of the passions (KSA 4:43). There is more fecundity in 'On Children and Marriage', the titular offspring connoting the 'higher body' qua offspring of the putative marriage between knowledge and nature (KSA 4:90). The same higher body appears two discourses later in 'On the Bestowing Virtue' (KSA 4:97-102). Once again, the focus is on ends rather than means: 'Knowingly (*Wissend*) the body purifies itself; experimenting with knowledge it exalts itself; to the knower all instincts are sanctified.' Airbrushed out of this last image, of the 'knowing' body exalting in its purification, is the altogether messier business of reconfiguring the lower body. A similar rhetorical sleight of hand is at work in another conjugal image, that of 'a golden sun' around which a serpent, symbolising earthbound truths as opposed to transcendent fictions, is intimately coiled (ibid.).

There are two striking exceptions in Part 1 to the idealised images of truth incorporation listed above. The first is 'the pale criminal', wracked with guilt after having presided as judge and high priest over his own propitiatory self-sacrifice on the altar of truth ('On the Pale Criminal', KSA 4:45) – the same ritual, minus the bad conscience, which Zarathustra presumably has in mind when extolling the 'saints of knowledge' ('On War and Warriors', KSA 4:58-9). The second exception is a chilling, metaphor-choked account of the type of suffering the incorporator of truth must endure in his attempt to create a higher body out of the ingrained and inflexible material of the lower body. This type of suffering, confides Zarathustra, is the terror of being 'alone with the judge and avenger of one's own law', engulfed in 'the icy breath of aloneness'. No longer a saint of knowledge, 'To yourself you shall be a heretic and a witch . . . an unholy man and a villain. You must want to burn yourself in your own flame' ('On the Way of the Creator', KSA 4:80-2).

In Part 2 of *Zarathustra*, metaphors of self-inflicted cruelty punctuate the narrative at every turn. We read of the death throes and birth pangs of self-overcoming and how spirit's hammer must 'rage cruelly against its prison' ('On the Blessed Isles', KSA 4:111). But these are as nothing compared to the extremes of deprivation described in Zarathustra's discourse 'On the Famous Wise Men' (KSA 4:132–5). In this discourse, we are told that the knower-creator must go into 'godless deserts' and break his former genuflecting heart. Under the scorching desert sun he must suffer the thirst and hunger of loneliness and plunge the sacrificial knife into his own entrails. To these images are added Gothic graves and strangled songbirds, symbolising the murdered 'visions and consolations' of the knower's youth. Sitting mournfully upon these 'yellowing grave-ruins' of slaughtered illusions, Zarathustra struggles to focus on the 'resurrections' and overcomings rather than on the wanton self-destruction ('The Grave Song', KSA 4:142–5). And so too must the reader struggle to reconcile *Untergang* and *Übergang*, heretic and saint, immolation and consecration.

The inference is clear: despite Nietzsche's avowed intention to put an end to the '*tyranny*' of the 'anaemic Christian ideal' by making way 'for new ideals, *more robust* ideals' (WP 361, KSA 12:10[117], 523), Zarathustra's doctrine of self-overcoming has proven to be more tyrannical and etiolating than the Christian ideal it was designed to overcome. Certainly, both ideals demand self-restraint, self-denial and obedience. Both need their saints and sacrificial victims, although Christ's crucifixion was intended to obviate the need for any further blood sacrifice. Both require foot soldiers to defend the faith; as Zarathustra teaches, 'if you cannot be saints of knowledge, then at least be its warriors' (Z1 'Of War and Warriors', KSA 4:58). And both hold out the prospect of a Second Coming. But whereas the repentant Christian can hope for forgiveness and redemption on the Day of Judgement, the practitioner of self-overcoming, diligently preparing the ground for a far-distant *Übermensch*, can expect no reward for his hard labour. 'I do not even teach that virtue is its own reward', says Zarathustra (Z2 'On the Virtuous', KSA 4:120). On the contrary, at the 'great noontide', when 'the sun of knowledge' is at its height, the knower must be prepared to destroy himself (*untergehen*) in order to overcome (*übergehen*) himself. (Z1 'On the Bestowing Virtue' 3, KSA 4:102).

Zarathustra's Moral Tyranny

In a comic Part 4 vignette (cited in Chapter 1), Zarathustra trips over a personified truth-seeking spirit lying prone on the ground with his arm thrust into the metaphorical swamp of ugly truths. Drawn by Nietzsche as a candid self-parody, the scrupulous truth-seeker dutifully recites before Zarathustra the latter's teaching: 'Where I want to know, I also want to be honest, namely hard, strict, narrow, cruel and inexorable' (Z4 'The Leech', KSA 4:311–12). As discussed in Chapter 2, this unconditional will to truth, this truth at any price, is what Nietzsche in the third essay of his *Genealogy of Morals* refers to as a '*metaphysical faith*' in that it '*affirms another world* than that of life, nature and history' (GM III 24, KSA 5:400). Such unwavering devotion to the value of truth, remarks Nietzsche, can be viewed either indulgently as 'a quixotism', or as 'a destructive principle that is hostile to life' (GS 344, KSA 3:576). On the evidence provided in the previous section, will to truth incorporation qua tenet of faith is egregiously hostile to life and limb. As Nietzsche himself attests, '"truth at any price" ... oh, we understand that all too well, having offered and slaughtered one faith after another on this altar!' (ibid.).

Zarathustra's euphemistic epithet for faith-slaughtering is *Überwindung* (overcoming). But the text's preponderant descriptors for this kind of slaughter are the verbs *zerbrechen* (to shatter) and *untergehn, unterzugehen* or *zu Grunde gehen* (to perish or go under). These verbs jointly underpin the ascetic discipline of self-mastery, self-legislation, self-denial and self-sacrifice, which on my reading of the text comprises Zarathustra's doctrine of self-overcoming. I shall end my critique with a synoptic account of how each of these ascetic practices, the respective foci of the for(e)going chapters, is fundamentally and tyrannically inimical to both life and nature.

Self-mastery. Chapter 1 highlighted selected passages from *Human, All Too Human* and *Daybreak* in which Nietzsche extols the self-mastery of the Jesuit priests as a moral virtue to which one ought to aspire. A cardinal, if not *the* cardinal virtue, in what Nietzsche commends as a 'morality of reason', self-mastery 'demands self-control, severity, obedience' as an effective antidote to the emotional incontinence he identifies with Christian morality (D 215, KSA 3:192). A rational morality, he writes, is 'a continual self-mastery and self-overcoming' (WS 45, KSA 2:574), the primary target of which are those 'pregnant errors' which for two millennia have passed for religious, moral and metaphysical truths (WS 350, KSA 2:702). For Nietzsche personally, the most insidious and emasculating of these errors was 'the whole idealist pack of lies and effeminacy of conscience' that he had discerned in Schopenhauer's Buddhistic will to nothingness and in Wagner's sensually overcharged music. Having spurned the first and denied himself the second, along with every conceivable form of metaphysical comfort, Nietzsche found himself on the brink of suicidal despair. As he confides shortly before writing *Zarathustra*, when the 'overly severe demands' of a relentless and uncompromising honesty had reduced him to a 'virtuous monster and scarecrow', the only this-worldly redemption available to him was the artifice of self-parody and ironic distance (GS 107) – hence the *Doppelgängers*, comic sketches and Part 4 satyr play we encounter in *Zarathustra*.

Self-legislation. Chapter 2 focused on the principal agent of truth incorporation, namely the self-legislating rational will. The chapter revolved around two kindred assertions: the first in *Zarathustra*, the second in *Beyond Good and Evil*. According to the first assertion, 'whoever must be a creator in good and evil . . . must first be a destroyer and shatter values' (Z2 'On Self-Overcoming', KSA 4:149). Note here the imperative command delivered through the reiterated 'must', a command weighted more towards destruction than creation as indicated by the double negative of noun (destroyer) and verb (shatter). These creators in good and evil are the ones who have transposed the universal law of becoming into the practical law of self-overcoming – a law that decrees the wholesale destruction of the old Christian values. In the second assertion, Zarathustra's creator-destroyers reappear in *Beyond Good and Evil* as the 'commanders and legislators' who create the future with a hammer rather than merely systematise the accumulated knowledge of the past. These are the 'real philosophers' whose knowing is creating, whose creating is legislating, and whose 'will to truth is – *will to power*' (BGE 211, KSA 5:145). Here the legislative hammer and the identity of will to truth and will to power reinscribe the qualitative relation that Zarathustra had drawn between the destructive-generative metaphysical will to power qua becoming (i.e., knowing) and the destructive-generative will to truth qua self-overcoming (i.e., creating). The chapter closed with a discussion on Zarathustra's calls for martyrdom, for the 'glowing, pierced . . . annihilating sun-arrows' at the noontide of *Untergang* or self-destruction (Z3 'On Old and New Tablets' 30, KSA 4:269).

Self-negation. Chapter 3 mapped Zarathustra's creator-destroyer onto Hegel's concept of 'determinate negation', thereby disclosing an affinity between the Hegelian spirit labouring towards its own transformation and Zarathustra's doctrine of self-overcoming. In both formulations, the internal dynamic is a dialectical negation entailing the type of destruction referred to above. As expressed by Hegel in his *Phenomenology of Spirit*, 'the life of Spirit is not the life that shrinks from death and keeps itself untouched by devastation, but rather the life that endures it and maintains itself in it' (PhS §32, W 3:36). In much the same vein, Nietzsche depicts the 'hard, involuntary, imperative task' of real philosophers as applying 'a vivisecting knife' to 'the chest of the *virtues of the age*' and, more piercingly (like the 'annihilating sun-arrows'), to their own chest (BGE 212, KSA 5:145-6). In *Zarathustra*, dialectical negation is figuratively represented as a nay-saying lion spirit that frees itself from error and illusion by ripping open the underbelly of long-cherished but erroneous 'truths'. Admittedly, negation/destruction is just one pole of knowledge incorporation; the other is creative and involves the yoking of the recalcitrant passions to a higher, *übermenschlich* ideal of man. Without the combined forces of the rational will and the affective will, or to use Nietzsche's formulation, will to truth and will to power, the ideal remains an abstract idea rather than a lived, or approximately lived, reality. As Hegel states, 'the will is a particular way of thinking – thinking translating itself into existence, thinking as the drive to give itself existence' (PR §4, 35; W 7:46–7). But as the chapters of this study have shown, any such attempt to graft a thought or idea onto the passions is inevitably going to be felt by the grafted subject as 'anti-nature', as 'turning *against* the instincts of life' (TI 'Morality as Anti-Nature' 4, KSA 6: 85).

Self-sacrifice. As noted above, turning against the instincts and desires is made considerably easier if they can be despised in what Nietzsche holds to be their debased, Christianised form. Thus, just as the harvester's task of clearing the ground in readiness for the sowing of post-Christian values is greatly facilitated by having his sickle-blade whetted with contempt for the soon-to-be-razed Christian values, so a re-purposed love that despises what it used to love will be better able to undertake the painful task of labouring towards a higher ideal of man. 'You go the way of the lover (*Liebenden*)', exhorts Zarathustra; 'you love yourself and that is why you despise yourself as only lovers despise' (Z1 'On the Way of the Creator', KSA 4:82). Or again, 'Will to love: that is willing also for death' (Z2 'On Immaculate Perception', KSA 4:157). This type of sacrificial love, I argued in Chapter 4, is exemplified in Zarathustra's all-consuming love for an ideal of human perfection. But as Feuerbach reminds us, the understanding that grasps the innate human perfections of man qua species knows nothing of the suffering and frailties of the human heart. It is precisely this gulf between an ideal of human perfection and the self-sacrifice required to instantiate it which on my reading of the text is laid bare in the *Zarathustra* narrative. Indeed, might it not be the case that Zarathustra's poignant accounts of graveyard vigils, Gothic nightmares, desolate loneliness and failed overcomings is the kind of truth-telling that makes Zarathustra 'more truthful than any other thinker' (EH 'Why I am a Destiny' 3, KSA 6:367)?

Zarathustra's Prologue ends with the words: 'Thus began Zarathustra's destruction (*Untergang*).' And as I have endeavoured to show in the pages of this study, that destruction is intrinsic to Zarathustra's doctrine of self-overcoming, which in turn is articulated in *Zarathustra* as self-slaughter on the altar of an ideal. Like 'all the pale atheists, Antichrists, immoralists, nihilists ... these ultimate idealists of knowledge in whom alone the intellectual conscience lives and is incarnate today' (GM III 24, KSA 5:398-9), Zarathustra is but the latest incarnation of the ascetic ideal. Having dispensed with God and Christian values, he paradoxically resembles the saint more than the heretic and the virtuous scarecrow more than the triumphant immoralist. To return to Max Stirner with whom I began this monograph, when mind or spirit becomes 'your *ideal*, the unattained, the otherworldly; spirit is the name of your – god' (*Ego* 39). In *Zarathustra*, the name of this spirit-god is 'child spirit', emblematising effortless self-re-creation. But after the savage belly-ripping of the lion spirit, the hammering of the instincts to the point of annihilation and the relentless returns of failed overcomings, the forgetting and fresh beginnings of the child spirit obstinately remain an unattained and unattainable otherworldly ideal.

Bibliography

Abbey, Ruth. *Nietzsche's Middle Period* (New York: Oxford University Press, 2000).

Acampora, Christa Davis, ed. *Nietzsche's 'On the Genealogy of Morals': Critical Essays* (Lanham, MD: Rowman & Littlefield, 2006).

Aiken, David Wyatt. 'Nietzsche's Zarathustra: The Misreading of a Hero', *Nietzsche-Studien*, 35:1 (2006), 70–103.

Anderson, R. Lanier. 'What is a Nietzschean Self?', in *Nietzsche, Naturalism, and Normativity*, eds. Janaway and Robertson (2012), 202–35.

Ansell-Pearson, Keith. *Nietzsche's Search for Philosophy: On the Middle Writings* (London: Bloomsbury, 2018).

Babich, Babette E., ed. *Nietzsche, Epistemology, and Philosophy of Science: Nietzsche and the Sciences II* (Dordrecht: Springer Science, 1999).

Bailey, Tom. 'Nietzsche's Kantian Ethics', *International Studies in Philosophy*, 35:3 (2003), 5–27.

— 'Nietzsche the Kantian?', in *The Oxford Handbook of Nietzsche*, eds. Gemes and Richardson (2013), 134–59.

Berger, Douglas L. *The Veil of Maya: Schopenhauer's System and Early Indian Thought* (New York: Global Academic Publishing, 2004).

Berkowitz, Peter. *Nietzsche: The Ethics of an Immoralist* (Cambridge, MA: Harvard University Press, 1995).

Blake, William. *The Complete Writings of William Blake with all the variant readings*, ed. G. Keynes (London: Nonesuch Press, 1957).

Blanchot, Maurice. *The Work of Fire*, trans. Charlotte Mandell (Stanford, CA: Stanford University Press, 1995).
Böhme, Jacob. *Six Theosophic Points and Other Writings*, trans. John Rolleston Earle (New York: Alfred A. Knopf, 1920).
Breazeale, Daniel. 'The Hegel-Nietzsche Problem', *Nietzsche-Studien*, 4 (1975), 146–64.
Brobjer, Thomas H. 'A possible solution to the Stirner-Nietzsche question', *The Journal of Nietzsche Studies*, 25 (2003), 109–14.
— *Nietzsche's Philosophical Context: An Intellectual Biography* (Urbana and Chicago: University of Illinois Press, 2008).
— 'Thus Spoke Zarathustra as Nietzsche's Autobiography', in *Nietzsche's 'Thus Spoke Zarathustra': Before Sunrise*, ed. James Luchte (2008), 29–46.
Brusotti, Marco, Herman Siemens, João Constâncio and Tom Bailey, eds. *Nietzsche's Engagements with Kant and the Kantian Legacy*, 3 vols (London: Bloomsbury, 2017).
Cartwright, David E. 'Kant, Schopenhauer, and Nietzsche on the Morality of Pity', *Journal of the History of Ideas*, 45:1 (1984), 83–98.
Cauchi, Francesca. *Zarathustra contra Zarathustra: The Tragic Buffoon* (Aldershot: Ashgate, 1998; repr. Routledge, 2018).
— 'Nietzsche and Kant: Self-legislation and the rational will in Zarathustra's ethics', *Oxford German Studies*, 42:3 (2013), 280–95.
— 'Blake and Nietzsche on self-slaughter and the moral law: A reading of *Jerusalem*', *Journal of European Studies*, 45:1 (2014), 1–18.
— 'Hegel and Nietzsche on thought, freedom, and "the labour of the negative"', *Journal of European Studies*, 46:2 (2016), 1–16.
Cohen, Jonathan. 'Nietzsche's Fling with Positivism', in *Nietzsche, Epistemology, and Philosophy of Science*, ed. Babette E. Babich (1999), 101–7.
Constâncio, João and Tom Bailey, eds. *Nietzsche and Kantian Ethics*, in *Nietzsche's Engagements with Kant and the Kantian Legacy*, eds. Brusotti et al. (2017).
Conway, Daniel W. 'Nietzsche's Art of This-Worldly Comfort: Self-Reference and Strategic Self-Parody', *History of Philosophy Quarterly*, 9:3 (1992), 343–57.

Damon, S. Foster, *A Blake Dictionary: The Ideas and Symbols of William Blake* (Providence, RI: Brown University Press, 1965).
Del Caro, Adrian. '"Zarathustra Is Dead, Long Live Zarathustra!"', *Journal of Nietzsche Studies*, 41:1 (2011), 83–93.
Deleuze, Gilles. *Nietzsche et la philosophie* (Paris: Presses Universitaires de France, 1962).
— *Nietzsche and Philosophy*, trans. Hugh Tomlinson (London: Continuum, 2002).
Desmond, William, Ernst-Otto Onnasch and Paul Cruysberghs, eds. *Philosophy and Religion in German Idealism* (New York: Kluwer Academic Publishers, 2004).
Dudley, Will. *Hegel, Nietzsche, and Philosophy: Thinking Freedom* (New York: Cambridge University Press, 2002).
Engels, Friedrich. *Ludwig Feuerbach and the End of Classical German Philosophy* (Moscow: Progress Publishers, 1978).
Feuerbach, Ludwig. *The Essence of Christianity*, trans. George Eliot (New York: Prometheus Books, 1989).
— *Gesammelte Werke*, 3rd edn (Berlin-Brandenburgischen Akademie der Wissenschaften durch Werner Schuffenhauer), vol 5, *Das Wesen des Christentums*, eds. Werner Schuffenhauer and Wolfgang Harich (Berlin: Akademie Verlag, 2006).
Franco, Paul. *Nietzsche's Enlightenment: The Free-Spirit Trilogy of the Middle Period* (Chicago and London: The University of Chicago Press, 2011).
Frazer, Michael. 'The Compassion of Zarathustra: Nietzsche on Sympathy and Strength', *The Review of Politics*, 68:1 (2006), 49–78.
Gardner, Sebastian. 'Nietzsche, the Self, and the Disunity of Philosophical Reason', in *Nietzsche on Freedom and Autonomy*, eds. Gemes and May (2009), 1–31.
Gemes, Ken. '"We Remain of Necessity Strangers to Ourselves": The Key Message of Nietzsche's *Genealogy*', in *Nietzsche's 'On the Genealogy of Morals': Critical Essays*, ed. Christa Davis Acampora (2006), 191–208.
— 'Nietzsche on Free Will, Autonomy, and the Sovereign Individual', in *Nietzsche on Freedom and Autonomy*, eds. Gemes and May (2009), 33–49.

— 'Postmodernism's Use and Abuse of Nietzsche', *Philosophy and Phenomenological Research*, 62:2 (2001), 337–60.
Gemes, Ken and Simon May, eds. *Nietzsche on Freedom and Autonomy* (New York: Oxford University Press, 2009).
Gemes, Ken and John Richardson, eds. *The Oxford Handbook of Nietzsche* (Oxford: Oxford University Press, 2013).
Gerhardt, Volker, ed. *Friedrich Nietzsche: Also Sprach Zarathustra* (Berlin: Akademie Verlag, 2012).
Gipps, Richard G. T. and Michael Lacewing, eds. *The Oxford Handbook of Philosophy and Psychoanalysis* (Oxford: Oxford University Press, 2019).
Glassford, John. 'Did Friedrich Nietzsche (1844–1900) Plagiarise from Max Stirner (1806–56)?', *Journal of Nietzsche Studies*, 18 (Fall 1999), 73–9.
Gonzalez-Crussi, Frank. 'Of metaphoric hearts', *Hektoen International*, 5:2 (2013). n.p. <https://hekint.org/2017/01/27/of-metaphoric-hearts/> (last accessed 11 April 2021).
Gooding-Williams, Robert. *Zarathustra's Dionysian Modernism* (Stanford, CA; Stanford University Press, 2001).
Gottschlich, Max. 'The Necessity and Limits of Kant's Transcendental Logic, with Reference to Nietzsche and Hegel', *The Review of Metaphysics*, 69:2 (2015), 287–315.
Green, Michael Steven. *Nietzsche and the Transcendental Tradition* (Urbana and Chicago: University of Illinois Press, 2002).
Gupta, R. K. 'Freud and Schopenhauer', *Journal of the History of Ideas*, 36:4 (1975), 721–8.
Haldane, Elizabeth S. 'Jacob Böhme and his Relation to Hegel', *The Philosophical Review*, 6:2 (1897), 146–61.
Harris, Daniel I. 'Compassion and Affirmation in Nietzsche', *Journal of Nietzsche Studies*, 48:1 (2017), 17–28.
— 'Nietzsche on Honesty and the Will to Truth', *Journal of the British Society for Phenomenology*, 51:3 (2020), 247–58.
Harvey, Van A. *Feuerbach and the Interpretation of Religion* (Cambridge: Cambridge University Press, 1997).
Hatab, Lawrence J. 'Laughter in Nietzsche's Thought: A Philosophical Tragicomedy', *International Studies in Philosophy*, 20:2 (1988), 67–79.

— *Nietzsche's Life Sentence: Coming to Terms with Eternal Recurrence* (New York and London: Routledge, 2005).
Hegel, Georg Wilhelm Friedrich. *G. W. F. Hegel: Werke*, 20 vols, eds. E. Moldenhauer and K. M. Michel (Frankfurt am Main: Suhrkamp, 1989).
— *Die Vernunft in der Geschichte, Einleitung in die Philosophie der Weltgeschichte*, in *Vorlesungen über die Philosophie der Weltgeschichte*, Band 1/5, ed. Georg Lasson (Leipzig: Felix Meiner, 1930), Der Philosophischen Bibliothek, vol 171a.
— *Reason in History: A General Introduction to the Philosophy of History*, trans. Robert S. Hartman (Indianapolis: Bobbs Merrill, 1953).
— *On Christianity: Early Theological Writings*, trans. T. M. Knox (New York: Harper, 1961).
— *Hegel's Phenomenology of Spirit*, trans. A. V. Miller (Oxford: Oxford University Press, 1977).
— *Lectures on the Philosophy of Religion*, vol. 1, 'Introduction and The Concept of Religion', ed. Peter C. Hodgson, trans. R. F. Brown, P. C. Hodgson and J. M. Stewart (Berkeley and Los Angeles: University of California Press, 1984).
— *Elements of the Philosophy of Right*, ed. Allen W. Wood, trans. H. B. Nisbet (Cambridge: Cambridge University Press, 1991).
— *Lectures on Natural Right and Political Science: The First Philosophy of Right: Heidelberg 1817–1818 with Additions from the Lectures of 1818–1819*, trans. J. M. Stewart and P. C. Hodgson (Berkeley: University of California Press, 1995).
— *Encyclopedia of the Philosophical Sciences in Basic Outline Part I: Science of Logic*, trans. and ed. Klaus Brinkmann and Daniel O. Dahlstrom (Cambridge: Cambridge University Press, 2010).
— *The Science of Logic*, trans. George Di Giovanni (New York: Cambridge University Press, 2010).
Heller, Erich. *The Disinherited Mind* (New York: Harcourt Brace Jovanovich, 1975).
Higgins, Kathleen-Marie. *Nietzsche's Zarathustra* (Philadelphia: Temple University Press, 1987).
— *Comic Relief: Nietzsche's 'Gay Science'* (New York: Oxford University Press, 2000).

Hill, R. Kevin. *Nietzsche's Critiques: The Kantian Foundations of his Thought* (Oxford: Oxford University Press, 2003).
Himmelmann, Beatrix, ed. *Kant und Nietzsche im Widerstreit* (Berlin: de Gruyter, 2005).
— 'Kant, Nietzsche und die Aufklärung', in *Kant und Nietzsche im Widerstreit* (2005), 29-46.
Horn, Christoph and Dieter Schönecker, eds. *Groundwork for the Metaphysics of Morals* (Berlin: Walter de Gruyter, 2006).
Houlgate, Stephen. *Hegel, Nietzsche and the Criticism of Metaphysics* (Cambridge: Cambridge University Press, 1986).
— *The Opening of Hegel's Logic: From Being to Infinity* (West Lafayette, IN: Purdue University Press, 2006).
— 'Religion, Morality and Forgiveness in Hegel's Philosophy', in *Philosophy and Religion in German Idealism*, eds. Desmond et al. (2004), 81-110.
Höwing, Thomas, ed. *The Highest Good in Kant's Philosophy* (Berlin and Boston: Walter de Gruyter, 2016).
Hutter, Horst. *Shaping the Future: Nietzsche's New Regime of the Soul and Its Ascetic Practices* (Lanham, MD: Lexington Books, 2006).
Janaway, Christopher. *Beyond Selflessness: Reading Nietzsche's 'Genealogy'* (Oxford: Oxford University Press, 2007).
Janaway, Christopher and Simon Robertson, eds. *Nietzsche, Naturalism, and Normativity* (Oxford: Oxford University Press, 2012).
Jaspers, Karl. *Nietzsche: An Introduction to the Understanding of His Philosophical Activity*, trans. Charles F. Wallraff and Frederick J. Schmitz (South Bend, IN: Regnery/Gateway, Inc., 1979).
Jenkins, Scott. 'Nietzsche's Questions Concerning the Will to Truth', *Journal of the History of Philosophy*, 50:2 (2012), 265-89.
Jenson, Robert W. *Systematic Theology, Volume 1: The Triune God* (New York: Oxford University Press, 1997).
Jüngel, Eberhard. *God as the Mystery of the World: On the Foundation of the Theology of the Crucified One in the Dispute between Theism and Atheism*, trans. Darrell L. Guder (Grand Rapids, MI: Wm. B. Eerdmans Publishing, 1983).

Jurist, Elliot L. *Beyond Hegel and Nietzsche: Philosophy, Culture, and Agency* (Cambridge, MA: The MIT Press, 2000).
Kant, Immanuel. *Akademieausgabe: Gesammelten Werken*, ed. the Royal Prussian (later German, then Berlin-Brandenburg) Academy of Sciences (Berlin: Georg Reimer, later Walter de Gruyter, 1900–).
— *Groundwork of the Metaphysic of Morals*, trans. H. J. Paton (New York: Harper & Row, 1964).
— *The Metaphysics of Morals*, trans. Mary Gregor (Cambridge: Cambridge University Press, 1991) 11–21.
— 'An answer to the question: What is enlightenment?', in *Practical Philosophy*, trans. and ed. Mary J. Gregor (Cambridge: Cambridge University Press, 1999), 11–21.
Katsafanas, Paul. 'The Problem of Normative Authority in Kant, Hegel and Nietzsche', in *Nietzsche and Kantian Ethics*, eds. Constâncio and Bailey (2017), 19–50.
Kaufmann, Walter. *Nietzsche: Philosopher, Psychologist, Antichrist*, 4th edn (Princeton: Princeton University Press, 1974).
Keeping, J. 'The Thousand Goals and the One Goal: Morality and Will to Power in Nietzsche's *Zarathustra*', *European Journal of Philosophy*, 20:1 (2011), 73–85.
Kleingeld, Pauline. 'Kant on "Good", the Good, and the Duty to Promote the Highest Good', in *The Highest Good in Kant's Philosophy*, ed. Thomas Höwing (2016), 33–49.
Koelb, Clayton, ed. *Nietzsche as Postmodernist: Essays Pro and Contra* (Albany, NY: SUNY Press, 1990).
Krell, David Farrell. *Postponements: Woman, Sensuality, and Death in Nietzsche* (Bloomington: Indiana University Press, 1986).
Larmore, Charles. *The Autonomy of Morality* (New York: Cambridge University Press, 2008).
Leiter, Brian. *Nietzsche on Morality* (London: Routledge, 2002).
— 'Nietzsche's Theory of the Will', in *Nietzsche on Freedom and Autonomy*, eds. Gemes and May (2009), 107–26.
— 'Nietzsche's Naturalism Reconsidered', in *The Oxford Handbook of Nietzsche*, eds. Gemes and Richardson (2013), 576–98.
— 'Nietzsche and the Morality Critics', *Ethics*, 107:2 (1997), 250–85.

Loeb, Paul S. *The Death of Nietzsche's Zarathustra* (New York: Cambridge University Press, 2010).
— 'Zarathustra Hermeneutics', *Journal of Nietzsche Studies*, 41:1 (2011), 94–114.
Louden, Robert B. 'Phantom Duty? Nietzsche versus Königsbergian Chinadom', in *Nietzsche and Kantian Ethics*, eds. Constâncio and Bailey (2017), 193–218.
Lowe, Walter. *Theology and Difference: The Wound of Reason* (Bloomington and Indianapolis: Indiana University Press, 1993).
Lubac, Henri de. *The Drama of Atheist Humanism*, trans. Edith M. Riley (Cleveland and New York: Meridian Books, 1967).
Luchte, James, ed. *Nietzsche's 'Thus Spoke Zarathustra': Before Sunrise* (London: Continuum, 2008).
Mann, Thomas. *Last Essays*, trans. Tania and James Stern (New York: Knopf, 1959).
Meier, Heinrich. *What is Nietzsche's Zarathustra?: A Philosophical Confrontation*, trans. Justin Gottschalk (Chicago and London: The University of Chicago Press, 2021).
Mitchell, Jonathan. 'Nietzschean Self-Overcoming', *Journal of Nietzsche Studies*, 47:3 (2016), 323–50.
Moyer, Dean. *The Routledge Companion to Nineteenth Century Philosophy* (Oxford: Routledge, 2010).
Muratori, Cecilia. *The First German Philosopher: The Mysticism of Jakob Böhme as Interpreted by Hegel*, trans. Richard Dixon and Raphaëlle Burns, in *The International Archives of the History of Ideas*, 217 (Heidelberg, New York, London: Springer, 2016).
Nehamas, Alexander. 'For whom the Sun shines. A Reading of *Also sprach Zarathustra*', in *Friedrich Nietzsche: Also Sprach Zarathustra*, ed. Volker Gerhardt (2012), 123–42.
Nietzsche, Friedrich. *Nietzsche's Werke*, vol. XV, *Nachgelassene Werke: Ecce homo; Der Wille zur Macht* (first and second books), (Leipzig: Alfred Kröner Verlag, 1922).
— *The Will to Power*, ed. Walter Kaufmann (New York: Vintage, 1968).

— *Sämtliche Werke: Kritische Studienausgabe in 15 Bänden*, eds. Giorgio Colli and Mazzino Montinari (Berlin: Walter de Gruyter, 1980).

— *Selected Letters of Friedrich Nietzsche*, ed. and trans. Christopher Middleton (Indianapolis: Hackett, 1996).

— *Sämtliche Briefe: Kritische Studienausgabe in 8 Bänden*, eds. G. Colli and M. Montinari (Berlin: Walter de Gruyter, 2003).

— *Writings from the Late Notebooks*, ed. Rüdiger Bittner, trans. Kate Sturge (Cambridge: Cambridge University Press, 2003).

Parkes, Graham. *Nietzsche and Asian Thought* (Chicago and London: University of Chicago Press, 1991).

Pippin, Robert B. *Hegel's Practical Philosophy: Rational Agency as Ethical Life* (New York: Cambridge University Press, 2008).

— 'How to Overcome Oneself: Nietzsche on Freedom', in *Nietzsche on Freedom and Autonomy*, eds. Gemes and May (2009), 69–87.

Poellner, Peter. 'Nietzschean Freedom', in *Nietzsche on Freedom and Autonomy*, eds. Gemes and May (2009), 151–79.

Railton, Peter. 'Nietzsche's Normative Theory? The Art and Skill of Living Well', in *Nietzsche, Naturalism, and Normativity*, eds. Janaway and Robertson (2012), 20–51.

Reginster, Bernard. *The Affirmation of Life: Nietzsche on Overcoming Nihilism* (Cambridge, MA: Harvard University Press, 2006).

Richardson, John. 'Nietzsche's Freedoms', in *Nietzsche on Freedom and Autonomy*, eds. Gemes and May (2009), 127–49.

Robertson, Simon. 'Nietzsche's Ethical Revaluation', *Journal of Nietzsche Studies*, 37 (Spring 2009), 66–90.

— 'The Scope Problem – Nietzsche, the Moral, Ethical, and Quasi-Aesthetic', in *Nietzsche, Naturalism, and Normativity*, eds. Janaway and Robertson (2012), 81–110.

— 'Normativity and Moral Psychology: Nietzsche's Critique of Kantian Universality', in *Nietzsche and Kantian Ethics*, eds. Constâncio and Bailey (2017), 51–89.

Schacht, Richard. 'Nietzsche's Naturalism and Normativity', in *Nietzsche, Naturalism, and Normativity*, eds. Janaway and Robertson (2012), 236–57.

Schopenhauer, Arthur. *On the Basis of Morality*, trans. A. B. Bullock (London: George Allen & Unwin, 1915).
— *The World as Will and Representation*, trans. E. F. J. Payne (New York: Dover, 1969).
— *Essays and Aphorisms*, trans. and ed. R. J. Hollingdale (London: Penguin, 1970).
Sedgwick, Peter R. 'Hyperbolic Naturalism: Nietzsche, Ethics, and Sovereign Power, *Journal of Nietzsche Studies*, 47:1 (2016), 141-66.
Seung. T. K. *Nietzsche's Epic of the Soul: 'Thus Spoke Zarathustra'* (Oxford: Lexington Books, 2005).
Sjöstedt, Peter. 'Metaphysical Doctrine of Nietzsche's Will to Power: Critique of Maudemarie Clark's Position', <www.philosopher.eu/metaphysical-doctrine-of-nietzsches-will-to-power/> (last accessed 8 April 2022).
Stambaugh, Jean. 'Thoughts on Pity and Revenge', *Nietzsche-Studien*, 1 (1971), 27-35.
Stepelevich, Lawrence S. 'Max Stirner and Ludwig Feuerbach', *Journal of the History of Ideas*, 39:3 (1978), 451-63.
Stirner, Max. *Der Einzige und sein Eigentum*, 3rd edn (Leipzig: Otto Wigand, 1901).
— *The Ego and His Own*, trans. Steven T. Byington (New York: Benj. R. Tucker, 1907).
Timmons, Mark. 'The Categorical Imperative and Universalizability', in Immanuel Kant, *Groundwork for the Metaphysics of Morals*, eds. Horn and Schönecker (2006), 158-99.
Ure, Michael. *Nietzsche's Therapy: Self-Cultivation in the Middle Works* (Plymouth: Lexington Books, 2008).
— 'The Irony of Pity: Nietzsche contra Schopenhauer and Rousseau', *Journal of Nietzsche Studies*, 32 (2006), 68-91.
Wartofsky, Marx W. *Feuerbach* (Cambridge: Cambridge University Press, 1977).
Williams, Garrath. 'Nietzsche's Response to Kant's Morality', *The Philosophical Forum*, 30:3 (1999), 201-16.
Williams, Robert R. *Tragedy, Recognition, and the Death of God: Studies in Hegel and Nietzsche* (Oxford: Oxford University Press, 2012).

Winfield, Richard Dien. 'Negation and Truth', *The Review of Metaphysics*, 64:2 (2010), 273–89.
Wood, Allen W. 'The Moral Theory of German Idealism', in *The Routledge Companion to Nineteenth Century Philosophy*, ed. Dean Moyer (2010), 104–30.
Young, Christopher and Andrew Brook, 'Schopenhauer and Freud', *The International Journal of Psycho-Analysis*, 75:1 (1994), 101–18.
Zambrana, Rocío. *Hegel's Theory of Intelligibility* (Chicago: University of Chicago Press, 2015).

Index

Abbey, R., 57 n14
Aiken, D.W., 60-1 n38
Anderson, R. L., 23-4 n16, 24 n18, 65, 93 n7
Ansell-Pearson, K., 55-6 n4
Apollo and Dionysus, 61 n39, 94-5 n20, 103-4, 127 n9
amor fati, 135 n44
amour propre, 140, 141, 143, 152, 153, 154, 155, 156-9
art, 12, 14, 37, 48-9, 51, 52-3, 61 n40, 103-4; *see also* Wagner, R.
asceticism, 1, 3, 19, 29, 31, 39-40, 49, 53, 54, 66, 130 n19, 175
  ascetic ideal, 27 n29, 74-5, 179
  see also will to truth
autonomy, 2-3, 4, 22 n3, 65-9, 92 n4, 114, 130 n24
  see also free will; freedom; Kant; rational will; sovereign individual

Bailey, T., 68, 93 n13
becoming
  in Hegel, 107, 121-2
  in Nietzsche, 7, 20, 26 n27, 61 n39, 69, 71-2, 73, 76, 78-80, 83, 84, 95 n20, 97 n28, 102, 103, 104, 106, 113, 121-2, 127-8 n10, 141, 149, 169 n27, 172, 176, 177
being, 16, 61 n39, 76, 79, 83, 103-4, 127 n10, 129 n16, 131 n25
benevolence
  in Christianity, 11-12, 14, 33, 35-6, 38, 154, 160-1; *see also* pity; self-sacrifice
  in Nietzsche *see* love, bestowing
Bentham, J., 32; *see also* utilitarianism
Berger, D. L., 60 n37
Berkowitz, P., 18, 25 n23, 97 n28
Blake, W., 72, 95 n21, 98 n33, n36, 164-5 n13
Blanchot, M., 134-5 n39

Böhme, J., 128–9 n14, 131 n26
Breazeale, D., 126 n1, 127 n4
Brobjer, T., 23 n12, 97 n27, 134 n36
Buddhism, 37, 176; *see also* Schopenhauer, A.

camel spirit, 80, 90, 110, 112, 131 n26, 141
Cartwright, D., 167 n23, 167–8 n24
child spirit, 113–14, 120, 122, 130 n24, 131 n25, n26, 134 n38, 141–2, 173, 179
children (Zarathustra's), 3–4, 141–2
Christ, 49, 90, 139, 142, 145, 165 n13
  Passion of, 21, 151, 154
Cohen, J., 58 n21
compassion, 14, 21, 32, 33, 35–6, 37, 45–6, 47, 51–2, 54, 56 n9, 57 n12, n15, 120, 142, 143, 152–5, 158–60, 161, 164 n11, 165 n13, 166 n20, 166–7 n21, 167 n22, 167–8 n24, 168 n25
Comte, A., 162 n1; *see also* positivism
contempt, 135 n43, 159; *see also* self-contempt
Conway, D., 61 n40
courage, 10, 21, 44, 50, 51, 80, 86, 87, 98 n33, n38, 120, 122, 125, 131 n26, 157, 172; *see also* lion spirit

Damon, S. F., 165 n13
death of God, 36–7, 41, 59 n31, 101, 137
decadence, 12, 61 n40, 109, 134 n36
Del Caro, A., 3
Deleuze, G., 26 n29, 102–3, 105, 127 n4, n6
Dudley, W., 101
duty, 39, 43, 45, 47, 67, 87–9, 91, 98 n34, 98–9 n39, 109, 111, 130 n22, 167 n23

Eliot, G., xi, 163 n7
Engels, F., 142, 164 n9, n10
Enlightenment, 36–7, 46, 75
eternal return, 121, 122–6, 127 n9, 134–5 n39, 135 n41, n43, 136 n45, 150

Feuerbach, L.,
  and I–thou, 142, 143, 155–6
  and materialism, 5, 140, 142, 151, 162 n1
  and pure love, 143–5, 150, 154, 156; *see also* Christ, Passion of
  and self-love, 140, 141
  and species perfection, 142, 147, 151, 165 n15, 178
  and the divine trinity in man, 17, 137, 139, 143–4, 151, 153, 156; *see also* trinity
  and the indivisible trinity in man, 1; *see also* trinity
  and theology as anthropological projection, 27 n30, 138–40, 151, 165 n15

The Essence of Christianity,
  16, 19, 21, 59 n31, 137–45,
  147, 150, 151, 154–6, 162
  n1, 162–3 n2, 163 n5,
  n7, 164 n12, 165 n13,
  166 n18
Fink, E., 5
Franco, P., 55 n3, 57 n17, 58
  n21, 59 n33
Frazer, M., 154, 164 n11, 167
  n22, 168 n25
free spirit(s), 17, 19, 20, 40, 41,
  47, 49, 50, 58 n21, n25,
  65, 67, 74–5, 88, 106, 119,
  130 n21, 133 n33
free will, 2, 4, 22 n3, n9, 28
  n31, 65, 68
freedom, 4, 52, 64, 68, 92 n4,
  97 n26, n28, 101, 112–14,
  115, 131 n26, 162 n1, 167
  n21; *see also* child spirit;
  Kant, and the freedom of
  internal law-giving; lion
  spirit; sovereign individual
Freud, S., 24 n17, 122, 163 n8

Gardner, S., 4, 8, 24 n18
Gemes, K., 21 n1, 22 n3, 96
  n24
German Idealism, 18, 140, 143,
  151, 164 n9, n10
Glassford, J., 27 n29
goal
  of self-overcoming, 3, 14, 18,
    20, 28 n31, 30, 34, 46, 50,
    71, 83, 86, 89–91, 92 n4,
    102, 117–18, 133 n34, 142,
    146, 149, 173
  universal, 42, 43

Gonzalez-Crussi, F., 166 n19
Gooding-Williams, R., 131 n25,
  134 n38
Gottschlich, M., 129 n16
Green, M. S., 56–7 n10

Haldane, E., 128–9 n14
Harris, D., 95 n20, 96 n24, 166
  n20
Harvey, V. A., 162 n1, 163 n3,
  163–4 n8
Hatab, L., 61 n39, 94–5 n20,
  127 n9, 135 n41
Hegel G. W. F.
  and dialectical negation, 102–5,
    106, 107, 111, 118, 121,
    122, 126, 127 n4, 128 n12,
    n14, 130 n24, 140, 156, 163
    n3, n6, 177
  and the higher universal,
    109, 111, 113, 114, 115,
    117–19, 132 n31
  and immanent freedom of
    spirit, 113, 118, 132 n27
  and practical freedom, 102,
    114, 118, 132 n28, n29
  Encyclopaedia, 111
  Philosophy of History, 107,
    109, 111, 113, 114, 115,
    116, 118, 119, 121, 132
    n27, 133 n35
  Philosophy of Religion, 128 n14
  Philosophy of Right, 114, 116,
    117, 177–8
  Science of Logic, 104
Heller, E., 131 n25
heroism, 40, 57 n17, 60–1 n38,
  74, 155, 172
Higgins, K-M., 58 n24, 163 n4

Hill, R. K., 63–4, 69, 92 n1
Himmelmann, B., 59 n29
Hollingdale, R. J., 58 n23, 59 n30
honesty, 29, 52–4, 57 n17, 58 n21, 66, 75, 81, 102, 121, 135 n43, 171, 176; *see also* intellectual conscience
Houlgate, S., 126 n1, 127 n4, 127–8 n10, 132 n29, n31
Hutter, H., 55 n3

immoralists, 11–12, 18, 74–5, 90, 179
innocence
  of the affects, 49, 78, 143, 157
  of becoming, 78–9, 113, 122
intellectual conscience, 30, 36, 37, 44, 53, 56 n5, 66, 74–5, 88, 106, 108, 110, 179; *see also* ascetic ideal; free spirits; honesty

Janaway, C., 4
Jaspers, K., 99 n41, 134 n37, 134–5 n39
Jenkins, S., 96 n24
Jenson, R., 164 n8
Jesuitism, 31, 49, 175
Jüngel, E., 27 n30
Jurist, E. L., 127 n6

Kant, I.
  and the autocracy of practical reason, 64
  and the free public use of one's reason, 45, 47, 88
  and the freedom of internal law-giving, 13, 34, 64, 67, 70, 76, 91, 97 n26, n28
  and the good will, 20, 70, 81–2, 83, 87, 88–9, 90
  and the highest good, 70, 81–2, 98 n34, 99 n40
  and ordinary practical reason, 97–8 n30
  and universalisability, 9, 68–9, 93 n17
  Critique of Practical Reason, 82
  Groundwork of the Metaphysic of Morals, 20, 70, 76, 81, 82, 83, 84, 87, 88, 89, 91, 97–8 n30
  The Metaphysics of Morals, 13, 34, 64, 67, 70, 76, 80, 98 n35
  'What is Enlightenment?' 44, 45, 80
Katsafanas, P., 56 n8
Kaufmann, W., 103, 126 n2
Keeping, J., 95 n22
Kleingeld, P., 98 n34
knowers, the (*der Erkennenden*), 2, 14, 34, 42, 69, 73–5, 76, 79, 80, 81, 85–6, 88, 90, 110, 147, 162, 172, 173–4; *see also* knowledge
knowledge, 20, 30, 36, 38, 44, 49, 56 n5, 79, 80, 83, 84–5, 86, 104, 125, 130 n19, 132 n28, 134–5 n39, 141, 148, 152, 168 n26, 169 n28, 176–7
  deadly hatred of, 49; *see also* Romantic pessimism
  idealists of, 27 n29, 74–5, 179; *see also* ascetic ideal; honesty; intellectual conscience; will to truth

incorporation of, 2, 4, 8, 14, 30, 50, 51, 54, 90, 105, 110, 132 n32, 171–4, 177; *see also* goal, of self-overcoming
saints of, 173, 174
serpent of, 162
see also self-knowledge
Krell, D. F., 133 n36

La Rochefoucauld, F. de, 135 n43
Lange, F., 5, 23 n12, 63
Larmore, C., 92 n4, 96 n24, 98 n37
last man, 46–7, 59 n26, n31
laughter, 52, 60–1 n38, 61 n39, n40, 121
Leiter, B., 4–5, 7, 21 n2, 23 n13, 24 n17, 25 n25
lion spirit, 19, 49–50, 52, 80, 83, 102, 111–14, 126, 131 n26, 141, 177, 179; *see also* courage; dialectical negation; freedom
Loeb, P., 3, 28 n31
Louden, R. B., 98–9 n39
love
  bestowing love, 35–6, 88, 115, 145–6, 147, 169 n28
  of one's neighbour, 10, 38, 47, 142; *see also* philanthropy
  of species man, 146, 149, 158, 165 n15, 178; *see also* Feuerbach, and species perfection
  sacrificial love, 19, 21, 55, 90, 142, 144–5, 148–50, 151, 178; *see also* Christ, Passion of; martyrdom; self-sacrifice

Lowe, W. J., 82, 97 n26, 99 n40
Lubac, H. de, 162 n1

madman (GS 125), 37, 41, 137
Mann, T., 60 n38
martyrdom, 41, 69–70, 89, 90, 177; *see also* self-sacrifice
Meier, H., 136 n45
Mitchell, J., 22 n7
Montaigne, M. de, 135 n43
morality, 3, 9–15, 21 n2, 25 n25, 29–30, 32, 41, 42–4, 52–3, 80, 82, 84, 85, 89, 171
  Christian morality, 1, 2, 3, 11–12, 14, 19, 30, 33, 36, 38–9, 47, 66, 76–80, 85, 86, 95 n21, 109, 132 n30, 176
  of custom and tradition, 31–2, 56 n7, 65, 76
  higher morality, 9, 18, 29, 68
  of the mature individual, 31, 32
  of reason, 14–15, 33, 38, 39, 65–6, 68, 69, 176; *see also* Kant; rational will; sovereign individual
  of voluntary suffering, 19, 39–40, 52–4, 69; *see also* asceticism
music, 12; *see also* Romanticism; Wagner, R.

naturalism, 2–3, 4–6, 7, 10–11, 12, 14–15, 23 n14, 23–4 n16, 25 n25, 56–7 n10, 66, 67, 81, 85, 95 n20, 132 n31, 133 n32, 164 n9; *see also* Feuerbach, and materialism

Nehamas, A., 3
Nietzsche, F.
  Antichrist, The, 10, 96 n24, 108, 130 n20
  Assorted Opinions and Maxims, 38, 55 n2
  'Attempt at a Self-Criticism', 52, 61 n40
  Beyond Good and Evil, 9, 10, 11, 12-13, 14, 23 n16, 25 n25, 66, 69, 70, 73, 76, 85, 86, 87, 88, 96-7 n25, 99 n39, 108, 110, 130 n21, n22, 153, 176-7
  Birth of Tragedy, The, 37, 39, 40, 48, 58 n22, 61 n40, 92 n1, 94-5 n20, 103-4, 127 n9
  Case of Wagner, The, 48-9
  Daybreak, 19, 25 n26, 30, 36, 38, 39, 40, 41, 42, 43, 44, 45, 46, 47, 54, 56 n7, 58 n22, n25, 61 n39, 65, 66, 80, 98 n31, n38, 99 n39, 112, 130 n18, 152, 166 n20, 167 n23, 169 n28, 176
  Ecce Homo, 3, 6, 11-12, 25 n22, 28 n31, 29, 30, 55 n1, 77, 96 n24, 103, 104, 108, 135 n44, 168 n25, 171, 178
  Gay Science, The, 2, 5, 12, 23 n14, 30, 33, 35, 36, 37, 41, 45-6, 47, 52-3, 56 n6, 57 n15, 66, 74, 75, 76, 101, 103, 104, 105, 110, 122, 137, 163 n4, 165 n14, 166 n20, n21, 171, 175, 176
  Genealogy of Morals, On the, 22 n3, 27 n29, 28 n31, 36, 65, 66, 68, 74-5, 85, 93 n15, 96 n24, 110, 114, 132 n30, 175, 179
  Human, All Too Human, 14, 19, 30, 31-3, 35, 39, 44, 48, 49, 50, 55 n2, 56 n5, 58 n22, 59 n34, 60 n35, 65, 105, 106, 123, 157, 160-1
  Nachlass, 6, 7, 27 n29, 29, 32, 56 n9, n10, 58 n20, 63, 64, 66, 70, 76, 80, 81, 85, 98 n32, 120, 129 n16, 130 n23, 133 n33, 139, 167 n23, 169 n27, 171, 174
  Nietzsche Contra Wagner, 48, 108
  Thus Spoke Zarathustra, passim
  Twilight of the Idols, 10, 11, 14, 15, 27 n29, 68, 101, 109, 127 n10, 178
  Untimely Meditations, 57 n16, 106, 135 n43
  Wanderer and His Shadow, The, 14, 33, 38, 46, 55 n2, 65, 69, 176
  Will to Power, 25 n24, 56-7 n10, 94 n19, 167 n23, 174
nihilism, 19, 28 n31, 74, 102, 124, 125, 179;
  see also Romanticism; Schopenhauer, A.
normativity, 1-3, 4, 6, 9, 15, 19, 20, 22 n7, 25 n19, 56 n8, 65-7, 69, 94 n17, 135 n41, 138, 142

obedience
  in Christian morality, 13-14, 102, 142, 174

in Zarathustra's doctrine of
self-overcoming, 12–14, 19,
30, 39, 66, 91, 102, 142,
174, 176

Pascal, B., 135 n43
passions, 2, 26 n29, 34, 56 n6,
n10, 66, 95 n20, 98 n31,
n35, 114, 116–17, 133
n32, 141, 160
  mistaking of passion and
    reason, 56–7 n10, 66, 67
  reason over passion, 2, 8–9,
    18–19, 20, 26 n27, 30,
    34, 36, 37–8, 39, 50, 56
    n6, 64, 65–6, 68–9, 81–4,
    87, 102, 114, 117–19,
    132 n29, 172–3, 177–8;
    see also Kant; knowledge,
    incorporation of
perspectivism, 6–7, 21 n1, 64, 85
philanthropy, 146, 153, 158;
  see also love of one's
  neighbour
Pippin, R. B., 128 n11, 132
  n28, 135 n43
pity, 57 n14, 111, 123, 130 n20,
  146, 153–4, 167 n23, 167–8
  n24; see also compassion
Plato, 4, 15, 42, 59 n26, 65, 74,
  108
Poellner, P., 22 n9
positivism, 37, 58 n21, 109,
  162 n; see also Comte, A.
postmodernism, 1, 21 n1, 95 n20

Railton, P., 9
rational will, 1, 2, 9, 12–13,
  14–15, 19–20, 21, 33, 34,
  55, 56 n6, 64, 69–70, 71,
  73, 76, 83, 91, 92 n4, 94
  n17, 117, 119, 132 n31,
  138, 147, 149, 176, 177;
  see also Kant; morality, of
  reason; passions, reason
  over passion; sovereign
  individual; will to truth
Reginster, B., 94 n19
ressentiment, 102, 115–16, 132
  n30, 143, 157–8, 161
Richardson, J., 56 n6, 133 n32
Robertson, S., 21 n2, 67, 85,
  93–4 n17
Romanticism, 19, 37, 48–9,
  50–1, 131 n25
  Romantic music, 19, 48
  Romantic pessimism, 51, 125,
    152; see also knowledge,
    deadly hatred of;
    Schopenhauer, A.

Sacred Heart, 166 n19
Schacht, R., 5, 23 n14
Schopenhauer, A., 24 n17,
  36–7, 48, 51, 56 n9, 57
  n16, n17, 58 n19, 63, 103,
  155, 167 n23, 168 n26;
  see also Buddhism;
  nihilism; Romanticism
Sedgwick, P., 5
self-contempt
  pernicious, 119, 157, 158,
    161; see also ressentiment
  productive, 22 n7, 81, 83,
    89, 110, 141, 147, 148–9,
    157, 172, 178
self-knowledge, 33, 35, 120,
  139–41, 147, 156

self-legislation *see* rational will
self-overcoming, *passim*; *see also* goal; rational will
self-sacrifice
  in Christianity, 19, 38
  in Nietzsche, 1, 17–18, 19, 21, 30, 39–40, 47, 50, 52, 55, 67, 69–70, 71, 84, 90–1, 96 n24, 99 n41, 106, 119, 134 n37, 142, 143, 145, 147, 148–50, 152, 155, 172, 173, 174–5, 178; *see also* asceticism; love, bestowing; sacrificial
selfishness (healthy), 20, 77, 78, 86, 115
selfishness (unhealthy), 77, 78, 84, 105, 115, 147, 148, 155
Seung, T. K., 26 n27, 59 n31
shame, 35, 36, 77, 81, 120, 121, 148, 153, 156, 166–7 n21
Sjöstedt, P., 94 n19, 95 n20
solitude, 21, 50, 110, 145, 157–8, 159
sovereign individual, 22 n3, 65, 68; *see also* free spirit(s); free will; freedom
Spinoza, B., 132–3 n32, 167 n23
Stambaugh, J., 167–8 n24
Stepelevich, L., 164 n9
Stirner, M., 15–16, 18, 26 n28, 26–7 n29, 150, 164 n9, 165 n15, 179

Timmons, M., 93 n17
transcendental 'I', 2, 24 n18, 65

trinity
  of love, sacrifice and suffering, 1, 21, 55, 142, 149, 152; *see also* Christ; Feuerbach, and the indivisible trinity in man; self-sacrifice, in Nietzsche
  of reason, will and love, 17, 137, 138, 141, 146, 147, 148, 150, 153, 156, 158; *see also* Feuerbach, and the divine trinity in man

Übermensch, 14, 16–18, 19, 20–1, 26 n27, n29, 28 n31, 43, 46, 59 n31, 79, 81, 88–91, 99 n40, 113, 117, 121, 132 n31, 133–4 n36, 137–8, 147–8, 149–50, 153, 174, 177; *see also* goal, of self-overcoming
Ure, M., 57 n12, 167 n23
utilitarianism, 32; *see also* Bentham, J.

Vogel, M., 165 n15

Wagner, R., 48, 51, 176; *see also* Romanticism
Wartofsky, M. W., 163 n6, 165 n17, 166 n18
will to power, 95 n22
  qua ontological principle, 12, 13, 20, 22 n7, 70–2, 73, 79, 80, 81, 94 n19, 94–5 n20, 103, 108, 116–17, 129 n16,

131 n26, 143, 153, 155, 156, 161, 162, 172, 177
qua rational will, 12, 73, 75, 79, 80, 149, 177
will to truth, 2, 20, 29–30, 35, 36, 73–5, 79, 80, 83, 86, 96 n24, 110, 112, 117, 120–1, 134 n37, 171–2, 175, 177; *see also* ascetic ideal; honesty; intellectual conscience; knowledge, incorporation of

Williams, G., 68
Williams, R., 101
Winfield, R. D., 130 n24
Wood, A.W., 76, 99 n42

Zambrana, R., 128 n12

EU representative:
Easy Access System Europe
Mustamäe tee 50, 10621 Tallinn, Estonia
Gpsr.requests@easproject.com

www.ingramcontent.com/pod-product-compliance
Lightning Source LLC
Chambersburg PA
CBHW070355240426
43671CB00013BA/2504